HUNGER & HOPE

For Jim and Adeline Callery
Without whom these discoveries would not have been possible.

HUNGER & HOPE

The Irish Famine Migration from Strokestown, Roscommon in 1847

Edited by
CHRISTINE KINEALY,
JASON KING
and **MARK G. McGOWAN**

QUINNIPIAC UNIVERSITY PRESS
CORK UNIVERSITY PRESS

Published by:
Quinnipiac University Press
275 Mount Carmel Ave
Hamden, CT 06518–1908
www.quinnipiac.edu
for

Ireland's Great Hunger Institute:
www.qu.edu/institutes-and-centers/irelands-great-hunger-institute/
Cork University Press:
www.corkuniversitypress.com

ISBN: 978–1–7361712–2–6

Cover design by the Office of Integrated Marketing Communications

Interior design and typesetting by Marsha Swan
Printed in Villatuerta, Spain, by GRAPHYCEMS

Contents

ACKNOWLEDGEMENTS

The writing of the history of the Strokestown estate and migration scheme has been a team effort from the beginning. The editors would like to thank the staff and management of Strokestown Park and the National Famine Museum, and more recently the Irish Heritage Trust, for making its facilities and archives open to all of the writers in this volume. We are particularly indebted to the support given us by John O' Driscoll and Martin Fagan. The many participants at the annual Famine Summer Schools, hosted in alternate years at the National Famine Museum, Strokestown Park and Ireland's Great Hunger Institute at Quinnipiac University, in Hamden Connecticut, inspired the authors to dig deeper in their research and bring their findings forward in a formal scholarly way.

We are very grateful for the maps provided by Michael Murphy of University College Cork. Michael created specific maps of the townlands of the Roscommon estate for this volume. The Canadian Catholic Historical Association permitted the use of the map of Ontario, and the early settlement map of Canada was generously offered by Professor David Bercuson of the University of Calgary, Canada. The cover image of Frances Hyne's *The Leaving* (1995), is part of Ireland's Great Hunger Museum Collection and was designed by Tad Sterling of Quinnipiac University.

Chapters 4 and 5 could not have been completed without the valiant research assistance of two teams of senior undergraduates from the University of Toronto, who, for university credit, in 2015 and 2016, helped to build profiles of the 271 families who participated in the Mahon migration scheme. Many thanks to Keira O'Sullivan,

Elizabeth McDermott, Julia Maher, Pamela Smofsky, Jessica Bush, and Chiara Fallone, who learned the trials, tribulations, and joys of combing through mountains of routinely generated records. Our thanks are also extended to St. Michael's College (UofT) and the Centre for International Experience (UofT) who provided financial assistance to both teams to attend two international famine conferences in Ireland to assist Mark in presenting their preliminary findings. Kathleen McGowan generously managed the teams' needs while in Ireland.

This book would not have seen the light of day without the financial assistance offered by Ireland's Great Hunger Institute, Quinnipiac University and the Westward Group, Ireland.

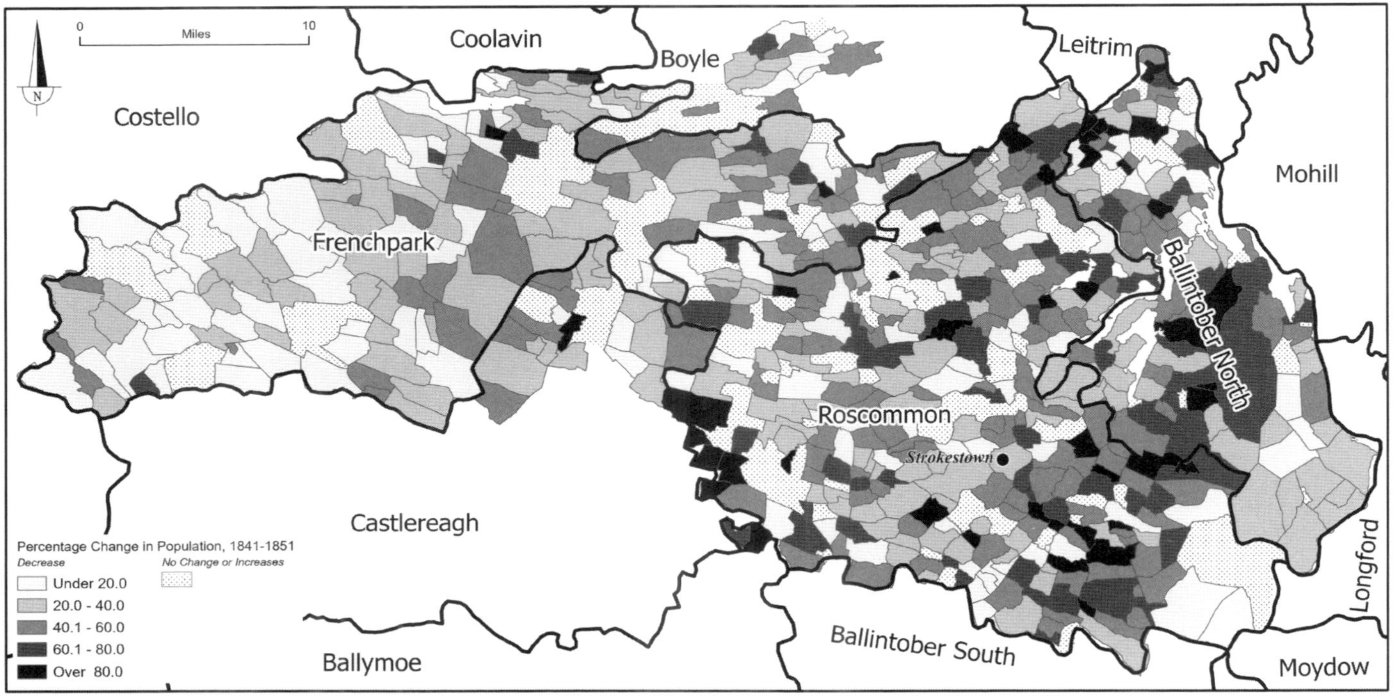

Strokestown Area Townland Population Change. 1841–1951 (Credit: M. Murphy)

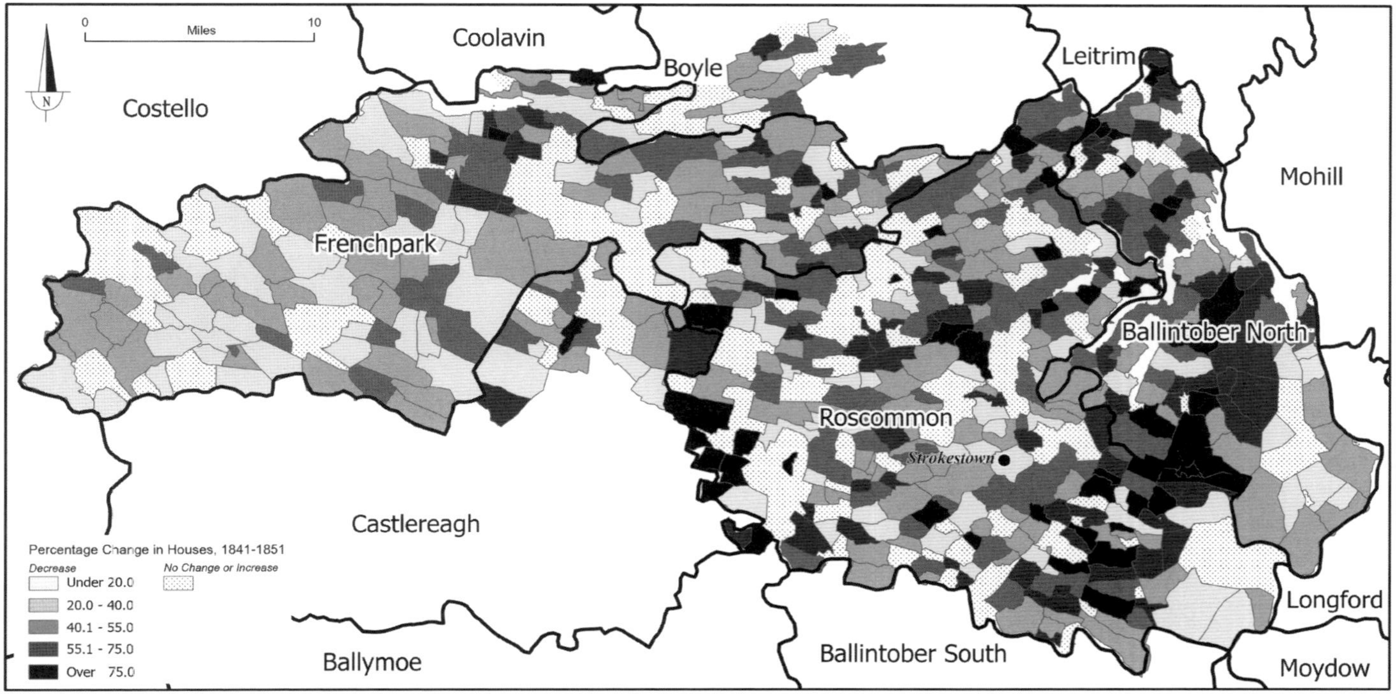

Strokestown Area Townland Housing Change, 1841–1851 (Credit: M. Murphy)

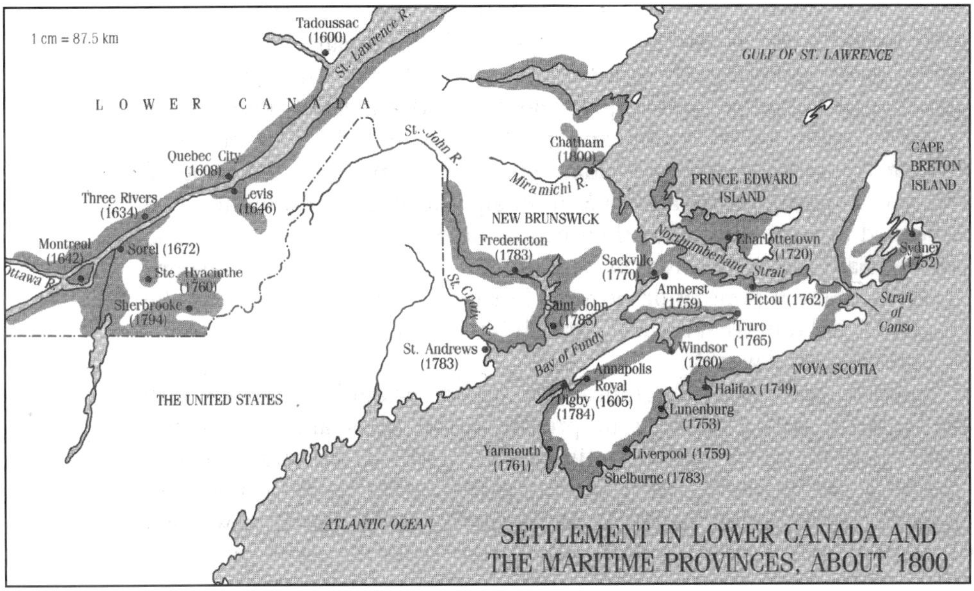

Lower Canada and Maritime Colonies Settlement, 1800 (Credit: D. Bercuson)

Catholic Dioceses of Upper Canada (Canada West), 1851 (Credit: CCHA)

INTRODUCTION

Re-reading History

It seemed like an ordinary early autumn evening on All Souls' Day, in County Roscommon, 2 November 1847. The meeting of the Poor Law's Board of Guardians had just ended. It was early in the evening and the carriage ride from Roscommon Town to Strokestown would take just over an hour. As the evening grew darker, local farmers would be lighting the familiar bonfires that marked the passing of *Samhain,* the feast of the dead, and in Irish lore a time when the veil between this life and the next was at its thinnest. Any passerby would have noted a carriage bumping along the road from Roscommon Town to Strokestown, although the two men in the open buggy would be blurred as the darkness increased along the road. The two prominent figures in the carriage, Major Denis Mahon, the landlord at Strokestown Park House, and his colleague Dr. Terence Shanley, had just finished another meeting of the local Poor Law Union, in which Mahon had been active in his support for continued relief in the region. Both would be hungry and anticipating their supper—Shanley when he would be dropped near his surgery in town, and Mahon when he arrived at his estate home, which dominated the Strokestown area. Mahon held over 11,000 acres of estate lands, but with the recent marriage of his only daughter Grace to Henry Pakenham, the combined Pakenham-Mahon holdings were now tripled in size. Perhaps weighing on the Major's mind was the current crisis facing nearly 10,000 of his tenants, and the miserable fate of 1,490 tenants he had assisted off the estate in the spring of that year.

As the carriage approached the Doorty Bridge, a shadowy figure appeared at the side of the road, and the carriage reared to a halt. It was not reported that this ominous figure said anything to the two men as the carriage stopped, but words were not his intent. The man, hardly recognizable in the darkness, flashed two pistols. The first pistol misfired, but the second found its mark. The shot hit Denis Mahon in the chest, and he slumped in the carriage. The man disappeared into the brush, and Shanley moved immediately to assist the Major, but it was too late. Denis Mahon had become the first landlord murdered during the Great Irish Famine.

The murder of Denis Mahon became headline news throughout the United Kingdom, was debated in Parliament, and commented upon by Queen Victoria herself. In the eyes of the British, the so-called "Irish problem", had taken a new and more serious turn. County Roscommon had long been recognized as an area of extreme rural violence leading up the potato crop failures and the famine conditions that ensued thereafter.[1] Now, one the leading members of the local gentry had been murdered and further attention was to be given to the problems on his estate, which seemed to mirror other estates across Ireland. It is unfortunate that the murder of Denis Mahon became the attention-grabbing moment that it was in 1847–1848, years when the effects of hunger and disease had already killed thousands across Ireland. Government programmes had proven ineffective in relieving the destitution and starvation, largely because the parliamentarians at Westminster had become too closely wed to the dogmas of laissez-faire capitalism and the strong belief that if spared government interference, the market would correct itself. Mahon's death, in the eyes of the ruling class, was a testament less to colonial mismanagement than to the treachery of the Irish people, and the complicity of the Catholic Church in the violence.

To read the Famine through the lenses of the murder of Denis Mahon, is as problematic for historians today, as it was for observers in the 1840s. Of course, a murder amid social chaos makes for an interesting, if not a salacious story. There have been several writers who have managed to focus on the murder itself, and unfortunately read the history backwards from it, as if the developments on the Strokestown estate naturally led to the Molly Maguires' cabal that "executed" the local landlord.[2] The murder has become a centrepiece of historical writing on the Famine, assuming Denis Mahon as having been so notorious, that his assassination was inevitable, or at least understandable.[3] Unfortunately, much of what has been written on the Strokestown estate has been an exercise in retrospective history, reading backwards from a specific event as if the developments that came before it lead naturally to it—in this case the murder. Instead, it is the task of the historical detective to look at the events of what took place on the Mahon estate, less as that of a crime scene than a canvass to be explored by not anticipating what transpired on the estate on All Souls' Day, 1847.

No less important is to consider the estate's wider social context beyond the tragic fate of its landlord. A diverse range of voices from not only the upper but also lower classes can be recovered from records in the Strokestown Park Archive and National Library of Ireland. The extensive correspondence between Denis Mahon and his agent John Ross Mahon that gave rise to the 1847 assisted emigration scheme is examined in rich detail in this volume.[4] Much more fleeting and often poignant are the voices of vulnerable tenants, subtenants, and cottiers found in petitions addressed to their social superiors who otherwise left little trace of their existence. Those most afflicted expressed their deep, generational sense of attachment to the land while often pleading to retain their place on it. Thomas Grace of Cordrumman wrote to John Ross Mahon attesting that his poor family had rented from the Mahons for 200 years.[5] Similarly, Peter Noonan sought to be reinstated to his holding and "end his latter days where generations before me for nearly a century and a half has [dwelled]."[6] The highly constrained imagined geography of the tenantry during the Great Hunger is also reflected in the petitions. For example, Anne Owen of Dromooden [Drumamoodan] protested on 14 April 1846 that Patrick Berne was attempting to deprive her of her small plot of land which she used as a cabbage garden to feed her family after her husband had abandoned them twelve years previously when he emigrated to America.[7] On 16 November 1847, Michael Bohannon of North Yard pleaded with John Ross Mahon for "compensation to carry off himself and family to England or Scotland."[8] The Widow Neary of Graffogue noted that she was a tenant and seeking "a few shillings" to enable her to go to England; the Widow Margaret O'Brien of Cregga likewise requested some compensation for her holding having surrendered it, noting that her son has emigrated to America; John Rush, from Scramogue, acknowledged that his rent was overdue and pleaded for assistance for his daughter and son to emigrate to America; Thomas Williams of Graffogue intended to emigrate himself to follow his son to America.[9] On 15 February 1848, Kilbeg tenants Thomas McDermott, John McCormick, Widow McCormick and Stephen Carton sent a petition asking whether the estate "will Emigrate us to America or encourage us to make a crop."[10] "America," "England," "Scotland," represented the petitioners' highly circumscribed, generic rather than specific conceptions of destinations abroad, an only rudimentary knowledge of the world beyond the parish. Ultimately, they attested to a highly localized sense of place that was irrevocably sundered for those who emigrated at the height of the Great Famine.

This multi-authored volume provides a critical overview of the developments on the Mahon estate at Strokestown in the years leading up to the Famine, the discussions that gave birth to the emigration scheme of 1847, and the aftermath of the migration and further evictions on the estate. Each author brings a specific expertise to each phase of this story and, although there is some overlap in chapters, the volume can be read as an uninterrupted history of the Strokestown estate from the time Denis Mahon took possession of it in 1845, to the events arising from Jim Callery's purchase of it in 1979. Ciarán Reilly's introductory chapter offers helpful background to the economic problems characterizing the Strokestown estate on the eve of the Great Famine. His essay draws from his considerable research in the Strokestown Park Archive and the National Library of Ireland,[11] and uncovers the challenges facing the new landlord: poverty, rural violence, overpopulation, rents in arrears, and a massive, accumulated debt from previous generations of the Mahon family. In 1845, Denis Mahon faced an estate wherein the tenants' dependence on the potato monoculture, and the beginning of the potato blight, would create a new layer of crisis, in an already challenging set of circumstances.

The coming of the Famine and the strategies employed by Mahon, and his new estate agent John Ross Mahon, form the corpus of the second chapter, authored by Mark G. McGowan. Based on the extensive correspondence between the landlord and agent, in 1846–1847, while the landlord was wintering in England, one discovers Denis Mahon's desperate attempts to raise money to build a soup kitchen, distribute American maize to the poorest of his tenants, and provide seed to tenants with the hope of planting and diversifying their crops for the coming year. Here, one sees Major Mahon trying to parse out who are the "deserving poor" and who are in "combination" to resist paying rents that they can afford to remit. The repeated potato crop failure in the fall of 1846, followed by one of the worst winters in Irish history, prompted new strategies to deal with the grinding poverty and misery on the Strokestown estate. After considerable disagreement between Mahon and his agent, Denis Mahon raises money to assist at least 271 families off the estate, with the intention of them beginning new lives in Upper Canada. McGowan chronicles the emigration scheme from its inception through to the steamers in Dublin, after 1,490 persons have walked 160 kilometers (100 miles) along the Royal Canal, through the heart of Ireland.

In Chapter Three Christine Kinealy continues to analyse the journey of the 1,490 as they board steamers in Dublin and then navigate the turbulent Irish Sea to Liverpool. Hers is one of the first detailed examinations of what Irish migrants faced as they disembarked in this most important of British port cities for emigrants.

Here the 1,490 faced substandard living conditions as they waited for their ships to board passengers, a time in which gangsters, cheats, and flim-flam artists would do everything in their power to relieve the emigrants of whatever money they had. The presence of Strokestown bailiff John Robinson was a small assurance that each family would receive the tickets paid for by Mahon and promised to them. Mahon would also provide extra provisions for the four ships that John Ross Mahon had chartered from the Robinson Brothers, a less than reputable shipping firm in Liverpool. Kinealy also demonstrates that infectious disease might also incapacitate migrants as they lived and moved in close quarters with fellow emigrants who may have been suffering from the early stages of typhus, smallpox, cholera, and other infectious diseases. It is to be noted that the conditions faced by the Strokestown 1,490 in Liverpool may have had significant impact on life aboard the ships bound for Quebec.

Mark G. McGowan once again takes up the narrative as the Strokestown 1,490 embark on four ships: the *Virginius*, *Erin's Queen*, *Naomi*, and *John Munn*. Chapter Four examines the problems inherent to emigrants crossing the Atlantic Ocean in ships that were not designed for the passenger trade. While each of the ships in question had traversed the Atlantic many times, they had done so with cargo from the Americas—timber, grain, foodstuffs, and chattels. Instead of returning to America with stones for ballast, these ships were refitted in Liverpool, and other ports, to carry human ballast. This chapter chronicles what happens to these hundreds of emigrants, living below decks on an often stormy and rough Atlantic, for six to eight weeks at a time. With the possibility of inadequate food, cramped living conditions, poor sanitation, and spread of infectious diseases brought on board in Liverpool, the lives of these passengers were in peril. By the time these four ships arrive in Quebec's quarantine station of Grosse Île, hundreds had died during the crossing, and many more would expire in the fever sheds and tents on this rocky island in the St. Lawrence River. While the "coffin ship" has become a much-overstated motif in the writing about migration and "Black '47", the Mahon-chartered ships, despite their extra provisions, certainly lived up to this stereotype.

In Chapter Five McGowan continues the narrative of the journey by trying to account for what happened to the survivors of the migration scheme. By means of routinely generated records, and with the assistance of several research teams based at the University of Toronto, McGowan has been able to reconstruct a few of the lives of the Mahon migrants after they departed Grosse Île. Notable among the survivors were at least 40 orphan children, the largest number from any Irish county to arrive at Quebec in 1847–1848. What at first appears to be the benevolent patronage offered by Irish- and French-Canadian families, by taking these children to their homes was, in reality, a means of securing cheap domestic labour from the Irish girls and work as farmhands and labourers from the boys. While a few of these children managed to integrate into Canadian society, most were not treated as family members and fled to other Canadian towns or to relatives and friends in the United States. Other survivors among the 1,490 push further into the Canadian interior, seeking work on farms in Upper Canada (then called Canada West, now Ontario), general labouring jobs in the cities, or canal work on the Niagara peninsula. It is at Niagara, not far from the falls that have made the region famous, where many of the Strokestown migrants found work, rekindled familiar patterns of their old lives, and, in some cases, rehashed old conflicts which led to tragedy. Within a few years, however, McGowan points out that many of these families would move to the United States, with promises of greater economic opportunity.[12]

The lives of several of the Strokestown orphans is the focus of Chapter Six. Jason King explores the life histories of Daniel and Catherine Tighe and the brothers Patrick and Thomas Quinn. While the stories of most of the other Strokestown orphans were tales of indenture and transience, the Quinns and the Tighes represent exceptions to what became of their fellow orphans from the estate. Both sets of siblings were orphaned as a result of the horrific conditions aboard the *Naomi*, the third of Mahon's chartered ships to leave Liverpool. Disease claimed the lives of their parents and siblings either at sea or at Grosse Île. Upon their arrival at Quebec, the Catholic Ladies of Charity received them in their orphanage, and Catholic clergy from the Archdiocese of Quebec managed their subsequent placement in Catholic homes. The Tighe children were relocated to a farm in Lotbinière, southwest of Quebec, where Daniel was eventually willed the property by the childless couple, the Coulombes, who had taken them in. The Quinn brothers were placed with Georges Bourque, who worked for the Seminary in Nicolet. Both Thomas and Patrick studied for the priesthood and served their entire lives in the Eastern Townships region of Quebec. Thomas Quinn became renowned as a defender of the liberties of his French-Canadian parishioners and the most prominent member of the 1,490 cohort. Indeed, he was the only survivor to leave an eyewitness account of his experience. The fact that Daniel Tighe (Tye) owned land, and the Quinn brothers were distinguished Catholic priests, make them much easier to study, but also suggest that the stories of the Strokestown 1,490 sometimes had remarkable North American chapters.

While the survivors of the *Naomi* made new lives in Canada, the fate of the other ships brought unwelcome news back in Ireland. The horrendous loss of life on the *Virginius*, for example, created a major stir in Roscommon by late summer, in 1847. In Chapter Seven, Christine Kinealy examines the fallout on the estate, after the departure of the 1,490, particularly the evictions that transpired under John Ross Mahon's management of the Major's properties during the spring and summer of Black '47. It is in the wake of these evictions, struggles to feed the local population, conflicts between Major Mahon and the local Catholic pastor, and the deaths of so many of the Mahon migrants that local vigilantes take matters into their own hands. Kinealy recounts the immediate series of events leading up to that fateful night, 2 November 1847, the murder of Denis Mahon, and the way in which events unfold on the estate and elsewhere in the aftermath of the assassination. What becomes increasingly clear is that reading the story of the estate exclusively through the lenses of the murder, or backwards from the event itself, obscures many of the realities of life on the estate and the intentions of the local administrators to manage starvation and disease during the worst years of the Irish Famine.

While the murder of Denis Mahon certainly brought attention, if not notoriety to the Strokestown estate, the events of recent history have placed it at the centre of new initiatives to study and remember the events of *An Gorta Mor*. Caroilin Callery's Chapter Eight chronicles the declining years of the Pakenham-Mahon ownership of Strokestown Park House, and its ever-diminishing real estate. The purchase of the property by Jim Callery and the Westward Group in 1979 was a major turning point in the estate's history, with serious repercussions for the commemoration and research of the Famine period in Ireland. This chapter outlines how the creation of the National Famine Museum, at Strokestown Park House, initiated a chain of events and programs that have encouraged Irish and international researchers of the Famine to deepen their work, while making Famine history more public facing, or making Famine history come alive in a profoundly public way. The creation of the National Famine Museum has drawn hundreds of thousands of tourists since its opening in the 1990s. The Strokestown Park Archive, which contains an impressive collection of the Pakenham-Mahon Papers,[13] has attracted numerous researchers from Ireland, Canada, the United States, and Australia. It was the discovery of the lists of Mahon's assisted tenants in 2013 that prompted intensified research on two continents to uncover what happened to the "Strokestown 1,490." The House has become the foci of the Great Famine Voices oral history project (funded by the Government of Ireland Emigrant Support Programme),[14] a biennial summer school,[15] Famine-based drama and music, and other special events. It was from the public presentations at the House and Museum, and the new management of the Irish Heritage Trust, that projects like the historic 160-kilometre walk, "The National Famine Way"[16] and "Treasures of the Strokestown Famine Archive"[17] virtual exhibit were born. Callery's chapter helps to uncover the public history that can arise out of the work of scholars in collaboration with affected families, businesses, public servants, and members of civil society.

This book is by no means the last word on the history of Denis Mahon and the Strokestown migration scheme. Claiming that a work is definitive is not only an exercise in hubris, but also a demonstration of foolishness, when one knows full well that there are more documents and artifacts on the subject to be uncovered. New archival discoveries are being made that will sharpen and perhaps revise the history in the near future. Queries from possible descendants from the 1,490 are often sent to the National Famine Museum, Strokestown Park. This volume comprises the most honest and rigorous research available to date and hopefully will entice scholars, families, and those simply interested in the Famine times to ask more questions and probe more deeply into what happened in Ireland between 1845 and 1852.

NOTES

1. Anne Coleman, *Riotous Roscommon: Social Unrest in the 1840s* (Dublin: Irish Academic Press, Maynooth Studies in Local History, no. 27, 1999) and Michael Huggins, *Social Conflict in Pre-Famine Ireland: The Case of County Roscommon* (Dublin: Four Courts, 2007).
2. Padraig Vesey, *The Murder of Major Mahon, Strokestown, County Roscommon, 1847* (Dublin: Four Courts, Maynooth Studies in Local History, no. 80, 2008) and Peter Duffy, *The Killing of Major Denis Mahon: A Mystery of Old Ireland* (NY: Harper, 2007).
3. John Kelly, *The Graves are Walking: A History of the Great Irish Famine* (New York: Henry Holt and Co., 2012), pp.284–5 and James S. Donnelly, jr., "Mass Evictions and the Great Irish Famine: The Clearances Revisited," in Cathal *Póirtéir*, ed., *The Great Irish Famine* (Dublin: RTE/Mercier, 1995), p. 169; Enda Delaney, *The Great Irish Famine: A History in Four Lives* (Dublin: Gill & Macmillan, 2014), pp.195–6; Stephen J. Campbell, *The Great Irish Famine: Words and Images from the Famine Museum, Strokestown Park, County Roscommon* (Strokestown: The Famine Museum, 1994), pp. 47–8; Cian McMahon, *The Coffin Ship: Life and Death at Sea during the Great Irish Famine* (New York: New York University Press, 2021), pp. 156–7. See also Gillian O'Brien, *The Darkness Echoing: Exploring Ireland's Places of Famine, Death and Rebellion* (London: Penguin, 2020), pp. 146–8.
4. This correspondence between Major Denis Mahon and John Ross Mahon can be found in the National Library of Ireland (MS 10,102) and has been digitized in the "Treasures of the Strokestown Famine Archive" virtual exhibit https://catalogue.nli.ie/Record/vtls000863828. A transcript of their correspondence can be found at https://strokestown-park.ie/wp-content/uploads/sites/2/2022/11/Transcript-of-Correspondence-of-Major-Denis-Mahon-with-John-Ross-Mahon–1846–1847.pdf
5. Strokestown Park Archive [hereafter SPA]. STR/1A/144. "File of letters and petitions to John Ross Mahon, from various correspondents, mainly tenants, with surnames between A and H," 1847–1849.

6. SPA, STR/1A/145. "File of letters and petitions to John Ross Mahon, from various correspondents, mainly tenants, with surnames between K and W," 1847–1849.
7. SPA, STR/1A/118. "File of letters and petitions mainly addressed to Major Denis Mahon, mainly from tenants and labourers between 1846 and 1848."
8. SPA, STR/1A/133. "Petition of Michael Bohannon, Northyard, to John Ross Mahon, seeking compensation to allow him to emigrate; includes annotation 'To get £2 0 0 JRM Nov 16/47,'" 16 Nov. 1847.
9. SPA, STR/1A/145.
10. SPA, STR/1A/167. "Petition from Kilbeg tenants, to Messrs Guinness Mahon, seeking assistance either to emigrate or to remain on their lands," 15 February 1848.
11. Ciarán Reilly, *Strokestown and the Great Irish Famine* (Dublin: Four Courts, 2014).
12. Mark G. McGowan, "Old Sources, new discoveries: in search of the 1,490 assisted immigrants from Strokestown to Canada, 1847," *Archivium Hibernicum* LXXI (2019): 374–96.
13. Susan Hood, "The Strokestown Park House Archive," *History Ireland* 3, no. 4 (Winter 1995). There is also a portion of the collection in the National Library of Ireland in Dublin.
14. See https://greatfaminevoices.ie/
15. See https://strokestownpark.ie/famine-summer-school/
16. See https://nationalfamineway.ie/
17. See https://strokestownpark.ie/treasures-of-the-strokestown-famine-archive/

CHAPTER ONE

PRE-FAMINE STROKESTOWN AND THE SOCIAL BACKGROUND OF THE "1,490"

Ciarán Reilly

In the spring of 1847, the selection process began for the emigration of tenants from the Mahon estate centred on the town of Strokestown, County Roscommon. Tenants were selected from 32 townlands and in most cases offered some enticement to go, although for a few, like John Egan and James Duffy of the townland of Cregga, located between Strokestown and Elphin, no inducement could persuade them. They were not alone in their refusal to emigrate as many were reluctant to undertake the voyage to Canada and embark on a new life.[1] For those that did emigrate, inducements included granting compensation for seed potatoes, for throwing down their houses and for giving up their crop. As will be shown below, many probably revelled in the chance to go as most of the social ills which beset Ireland after the Napoleonic Wars were in evidence at Strokestown.

These social ills were prevalent for some time prior to the Famine but not always documented. Making observations with their patrons in mind, nineteenth-century travel writers were often guilty of embellishing descriptions of Irish towns and villages, or at the very least avoiding the endemic poverty which prevailed on the eve of the Great Famine. This was true of Strokestown where writers such as Skeffington Gibbons claimed that the town was "delightfully situated in a charming glen under Slievebane [sic] mountain ...This is a good market and post town, watered by a beautiful river, situated in a sporting and eligible country, and which produces the best tillage in this county."[2] Likewise, in 1824, the contributor to *Pigot's Directory* noted that Strokestown "with its white houses has a very cheerful appearance at a distance; nor is the stranger disappointed when he enters the place as the streets are clean and spacious."[3] However, nowhere was the dichotomy between rich and poor more evident than at Strokestown. As early as 1809, the Mahon tenants were in such a state of poverty that the British politician, Edward Wakefield, denounced the local agent for the condition of the people:

> I found everywhere, cabins of the most wretched aspect, infamous stone roads, very minute divisions of lands and, what usually follows it, a superabundant but miserable people. I do not recollect to have traveled so many miles through any estate in Ireland which presented such a scene of desolation, and nothing astonished me so much as the multitude of poverty-struck inhabitants, from whom I could learn very little other than that the estate belonged to "My Lord", whom they loathed with imprecations.[4]

Nothing, it seems, had improved for the lower classes since Arthur Young visited 30 years previous when he noted that, although the house of Mahon was very much in the ascent, the conditions of tenants on the estate were wretched. According to Young: "They live on potatoes, milk and butter. Scarce any but what keeps a cow or two. They are not allowed to keep pigs in general, but many will a tolerable quantity of poultry... The men dig turf and plant potatoes, and work for their landlord and the women pay the rent by spinning."[5]

This chapter examines the fortunes of the people of Strokestown on the eve of the Famine. In particular, it provides an overview of the world which the "1,490" assisted emigrants inhabited prior to their departure in 1847, a year of exodus from the Mahon estate. From the 1790s onwards, eviction was a constant threat for tenants on the Mahon estate as the family sought to increase their rentals, carry out improvements, and introduce new agricultural methods. In 1831, for example, the expiration of a middleman's lease resulted in the eviction of 28 families, prompting the land agent, Thomas Conry, to lament: "In all my life I never performed so disagreeable a duty, the poor creatures quit it with extreme reluctance, still they were perfectly obedient to the law. It will remain tenantless for the year as no person would venture to take it."[6] The fact that tenants did not need to be in arrears to be evicted added to the sense of injustice as the creation of larger holdings was targeted. That this was occurring during a period of intense pressure for land naturally fuelled agrarian tensions. From the 1780s onwards, the Irish population grew rapidly, largely due to the availability of a cheap food source—the potato. Families grew larger, people married younger and, perhaps most importantly of all, land was subdivided. When the potato crop failed, as it often did in the lead up to the Great Famine, thousands were left on the brink of starvation and with little prospect of improving their situation. Strokestown provides a perfect example of the pre-Famine problem of subdivision and the intense social tensions that it generated.

Exacerbating the problem of subdivision was the landholding system in Ireland in the pre-Famine decades. Understanding this is essential when considering the social background of the group who would come to be known as the "1,490." At the top of the social pyramid were the landlords, the Mahons and, by at least 1838, Major Denis Mahon. Facilitating the renting of land were the many middlemen on the estate who included Browne, Walpole and Knox, amongst others. Leasing large tracts of land from the Mahons, middlemen in turn sublet land to large farmers, usually in holdings of between 50 to 200 acres. This group sublet land to a class of smaller farmers. These small farmers furthermore kept a group of tenants under them, known as cottiers and landless labourers. These people, who numbered some three million on the eve of the Famine, were provided with a small patch of potato ground in return for labour, usually about 200 days in the year. It was a precarious existence, and their unwritten contracts could be terminated without notice and the people removed. It is noteworthy that when Famine struck in 1845, the Mahons were far removed from the thousands of people living on their land. Indeed, the estate census overseen by the land agent, John Ross Mahon, prior to the 1847 emigration scheme reflected this, with over half of those resident on the estate having no direct link to the estate rental.[7]

According to the estate rental, there were only 745 leaseholders or those paying directly to the Mahons. However, subdivision had occurred on such a scale that almost 12,000 people were living on the estate prior to the emigration scheme, fuelling further competition for land and increasing poverty.[8] Across the 60 plus townlands which comprised the Mahon estate, so overcrowded were the holdings that several generations lived side by side trying to eke out a living from the land. The townland of Gortoose was a case in point, where 40 families had erected houses, although, according to the 1843 rental, only four families held a lease.[9] Indeed, so great was the overcrowding that even the removal of 139 people from one townland did not create the necessary "breathing space" for tenants, as outlined by the Widow Holmes in 1849.[10]

The most obvious manifestation of this intense pressure for land and access to it can be seen in the spiralling crime and disorder at Strokestown on the eve of the Famine. The aforementioned problems pitted all sections of community against each other. There were sectarian tensions too and for over three decades religious animosity had created division within society at Strokestown, and there were regular boycotts of shopkeepers and merchants as a result.[11] The world of the Strokestown emigrants in the period immediate to their departure was also one of extreme danger, where people lived in daily fear of the wrath of the various secret societies which were operating in Roscommon, including the notorious Molly Maguires, "Rockites," and "Ribbonmen." Strokestown and County Roscommon in general were one of the worst affected areas in Ireland, and only counties Tipperary, Clare, Limerick, and Leitrim were considered to be worse off.[12] In many ways, it was a population on the brink of collapse. Amid such circumstances it was hardly surprising that when the Famine commenced in 1845 thousands would clamour to emigrate as a multitude of crimes were committed.

These crimes included the attempted assassination of Richard Irwin, a justice of the peace, in October 1843, which was followed by the shooting of his brother, and land agent, Valentine. He had been on his way to "drive" for rent on lands at Fairymount, near Strokestown, where a man named Brooks was murdered over the taking of land in 1842.[13] Intimidation and violence took on other forms, with house burnings, the favoured tactic of agrarian conspirators.[14] In June 1844, Patrick Hughes, a pensioner, was murdered at Strokestown by four men who stabbed and cracked his skull.[15] The murder prompted one commentator to admit that "the state of society is such in the county of Roscommon that no man can reckon his life for one moment with safety"; while another believed that although the people appeared friendly, they were in fact "deep and distant."[16] This catalogue of crime and intimidation spelled impending trouble in relations between landlord and tenant, and amongst the community at large. When Patrick Sheil was murdered in January 1845, when he tried to raise the price of oats at the local market, it showed how fickle life had become at Strokestown.[17]

There were other factors too which influenced the world the "1,490" inhabited prior to their departure, not least a series of climatic events which had devastating consequences. In January 1839, an event known as the "Night of the Big Wind" significantly affected the resources of the cottier class at Strokestown. Known in Irish as *Oíche na Gaoithe Móire*, the storm which occurred on 6–7 January was a significant moment in pre-Famine Ireland, wreaking havoc on the lower levels of society. Indeed, such was the ferocity of the storm that at Strokestown House trees and plants were uprooted, while the walled garden and outbuildings were severely damaged. Mahon's tenants were greatly affected by the "Big Wind." As late as 1847, Michael Farrell claimed that his house had been damaged on "the windy night."[18] Further exacerbating the plight of the lower orders as the 1840s dawned were the three disastrous wet summers during which time the harvest was rarely saved. Coupled to this was the frequent failure of the potato crop and thus it was hardly surprising that a large arrear amassed on the Strokestown rental.

In order to survive, many families on the Mahon estate, as they did in the west of Ireland, undertook seasonal migration to Britain. This helped establish networks in England, Scotland and Wales that provided the basis for the Famine exodus.[19] Despite this, by the early 1840s tenants on the Mahon estate lived in abject poverty. As Dr Terence Shanley, the medical attendant for the Tarmonbarry and Kilglass dispensary, highlighted, the Mahon tenants lived in habitual disease and many simply lingered from day to day in fear of dying. According to Shanley, in just three years in the early 1830s he had attended over 10,000 people who suffered from "fevers of almost every type, affections of the chest, rheumatism, small-pox, measles, whooping cough, croup, dysentery, diarrhoea, cholera."[20]

The situation was also criticised by William P. Barrett, who carried out a report on the dispensaries of Ireland. He highlighted the "entire neglect" of the Strokestown area during the cholera outbreak of 1832 had had disastrous consequences. In the town's dispensary as many as 60 people had died and no one would remove the dead. In most cases, the poor and dying huddled together unable to move. Those who were well off had fled on the first report of the return of the disease and, for several weeks, the place was deserted; there were no fairs or markets and no business transacted. There was no subscription raised on the part of the inhabitants. Such apathy, according to Barrett, resulted from the fact that "the town was owned by a nobleman absentee for ten months of the year and no information could be gathered from the agent."[21] These challenges naturally affected the ability to pay and to collect rents, something that filtered its way along the landholding pyramid discussed previously. By 1843, the last year for which a rental survives for the estate prior to the Famine, many tenants owed over four years rent and were spiralling towards ruin.

So, who were the people that made up the "1,490" and what was their social background? On 21 March 1847, an estate census was completed and delivered to Major Denis Mahon, then in London attending his daughter's wedding. Recording the townland, parish, and the number of persons living on the estate, the census provided the genesis for the assisted emigration scheme which, in time, would make both Strokestown and Major Mahon notorious.[22] The census was also revealing for landlord and agent alike. Although the 1843 estate rental included the names of 745 lessees, or direct rent payers, John Ross Mahon found a mostly impoverished population of 11,958 people. On closer examination of the tenants, it was also found that several were taking advantage of the potato failure "in order to allow them carry out their combination not to pay any rent."[23] Thus the decision was taken that those who were in arrears prior to 1845 were not to be given any lenience, as 1846 had been the only "bad year." Having conducted the census and appalled by his findings, John

Ross Mahon reported to his employer that: "I think the facts are sufficient without any further remarks of mine to show the impossibility of collecting poor rates or of effecting any change in the condition of the people while the land remains in such small divisions in the hands of paupers unable to support themselves much less to till it to advantage."[24] He further warned: "I am convinced unless the greater part of the population are removed from your estate, the poor rates of this electoral division will exceed the receipts of rent, and the division being almost entirely your property, the greater part of the poor rate must fall upon you."[25]

His rationale was simple. Overpopulation and overcrowding were too great and the estate could not afford either to keep its inhabitants in the workhouse or, indeed, to compensate them for eviction. In one area of the estate, he found 475 families, consisting of 2,444 people, living on 2,105 acres, or an average of 4.4 acres per family. The population of these townlands he estimated held two-thirds more than what the land was capable of producing and so the people were never likely to improve their condition. His belief was that tenants were an "unsustainable burden" for the estate going forward. Whereas to provide for tenants in Roscommon workhouse would cost the estate £11,000 annually, a once off payment of about £6,000 would send, it was hoped, 3,000 people to Canada.

Although there was some initial hesitation, Major Mahon consented, and the plan (as detailed in Chapter 2) was put in place to assist in the emigration of a large body of tenants which would kick-start the clearing of the estate. The process would cause considerable rancour as Mahon looked to attract the "poorer class of tenants." In April, happy that the emigration scheme was underway, Mahon wrote that: "The first class for us to send is those of the poorest and worst description who would be a charge on us for the poor house or for outdoor relief and that would relieve the industrious tenants."[26] Denis Mahon, it seems, was anxious not to lose any "industrious" tenants, many of whom were by now contemplating emigration. On the other hand, John Ross Mahon's attention was directed towards land that would make for profitable grazing in the future. Thus, within the emigrant cohort we can identify certain categories of tenants.

The 1847 emigrants were chosen from 32 of the 68 townlands on the estate, meaning that almost half of the townlands were included in the scheme. Of those that were selected some townlands were more affected than others. For example, five people were chosen from the townland of Farnbeg, while 249 were chosen in Kilmackenny, which amounted for 17 per cent of all emigrants. An examination of these people is revealing about the make-up of Famine emigrants: notably for the fact that departing households had an average of 5.4 people emigrating, although on individual townlands, such as Dooherty, the figure was closer to seven people. This suggests that in a number of instances family members were left behind, or were unwilling to go. This, in turn, suited the landlord and his agent, who hoped that remittances from Canada would be used to pay the rent in future years. Eight families had more than 10 people in their travelling party. These figures of course are likely to have been higher, for, as we know, some of the families had experienced death before departure. This fact is reflected in the number of widows present on the ships—some 13 per cent of the families (36 families) had women as heads. These, it seems, were the lucky ones, as they availed of the passage to Canada and travelled with their neighbours and friends.

However, not everyone was so lucky. Take, for example, the townland of Culliagh that saw 13 families, or 62 people, left behind. Culliagh again exemplified the rapid growth in population that had risen exponentially from the compilation of the Tithe Allotment List in 1825, with only three families listed—namely Wallace, Cox and Lyons. By the time of the 1901 census, only 6 families, or 34 people, remained. Two Lyons' families were part of the 1847 scheme yet, in 1901, four families out of six remaining were Lyons, indicating, more than likely, that some of this branch was left behind. Culliagh, like other parts of the Mahon estate, would be hugely impacted by the Famine and the emigration scheme. By the early 1850s, there were 30 fewer houses in this particular townland.

The pre-Famine problem of subdivision was evident amongst those selected for the scheme. The average holding of the emigrants ranged from 1.7 and 2.5 acres, whereas in other parts of the country, such as on the Fitzwilliam estate in County Wicklow (where tenants also emigrated to Canada and New Brunswick), holdings averaged ten acres. These figures reflect the census findings about the prevalence of smallholders and the dangers associated with carving up land holdings. The assisted emigration scheme, whether intended or not, would check this process of subdivision going forward. For example, at Aughadangan, which was leased by Edward Connor, and was £72 in arrears in 1843, nine families (or 53 people) were selected for emigration. It was a similar situation in Cloonrain where 14 families (amounting to 66 people) were included in the scheme. This population surge and subdivision of the land was also evident in the numbers who were included in emigration. Further examples are instructive. At the townland of Gortoose "Holmes", the land had been subdivided to such an extent that three more families had been added to the townland within a 10-year period.

The selection process also suggested a very youthful population on the estate. At Cornashina, for example, 54 per cent of the emigrants were under 14 years of age, including families such as the Nallys who had six children under that age. The obvious emphasis here was to remove as many children as possible for the long-term benefit of the estate, while it also made financial sense, as children under 14 went half price. Sadly, as will be highlighted elsewhere in this volume, some of the more startling statistics and stories upon arrival in Canada referred to children: both the death rate and the number who were left orphaned. However, as the names for emigration were collated simply by listing the number over 14 and under 14, it is difficult in some circumstances to ascertain the actual make-up of the family unit.

The financial circumstances of the emigrants are also interesting and lends weight to the various motives at play in the selection process. Some tenants, like Bryan Sheeran of Graffogue, owed only five shillings in arrears, yet was still selected because his removal would create more access to land. Likewise, the evidence would also suggest that there was a certain geography concerned in relation to who was chosen for emigration. Mapping the scheme reveals that the majority of tenants were selected to the east of the town along the route to Longford. It is interesting that the proposed railway line linking Strokestown with Longford, of which the Mahons were investors, would have come in this direction. Moreover, many of the townlands included in the scheme ran close to the main Longford to Strokestown road. Was the selection process therefore intended to remove poverty? Mapping the scheme also suggests that the agent was endeavouring to create a ring of strong farmers around the "Big House" at Strokestown, a trait mirrored at other landed estates both during and after the Famine. Grievances and animosity towards tenants may also have played a part in the selection process. Phelim Hanly of Cregga, for example, had fallen foul of Mahon in 1843 for the burning and "pairing" land which might suggest why he was selected.[27]

While some of this is conjecture, what is certain is that most of the "1,490" and their families had lived in perpetual poverty prior to the Famine. Indeed, without the Famine it is unlikely that any of the families would have been able to remove themselves from the circle of debt that they found themselves in. This debt centred mainly on money borrowed from lenders, known as "Gombeen" men, and from the Strokestown Loan Fund, set up in 1839 following the devastation caused by the "Night of the Big Wind." The distress, as witnessed in the upsurge of applicants for relief from the Strokestown Loan Fund, operated by Denis Mahon, gives an indication of the effect that the storm had locally.[28] As a result of the destitution caused by the storm, Mahon initiated a loan scheme, the terms of which were strict.[29] For example, tenants were forbidden to spend money in public houses (for which several were admonished), and no money was loaned until previous instalments had been repaid in full.[30] Ironically, in the majority of cases, Mahon was the ultimate recipient as many used these funds to pay their rent. Not surprisingly, contemporary commentators condemned the practice of loan funds.[31]

In many ways loan fund records provide us with most of the information about the social background and the plight of emigrants prior to departure, while it also raises questions about their mind-set. Did, for example, the Duffys of Laughboy (or Lugboy), who were entirely dependent on the Strokestown Loan Fund, jump at the chance of inclusion in the emigration scheme? This chapter does not allow for a systematic survey of the loan fund records, but it would make an interesting study to examine exactly how many of the "1,490" availed of it. Mahon tenants also used what was known as the Irish Reproductive Loan Fund, distributed through the Clonfinlough and Elphin Charitable Loan Funds.[32] Within these records, we see individuals such as Bridget O'Hara of Kilgraffy, who intermittingly used the loan fund in the early 1840s; while at Farnbeg, the Holdens were also using the loan fund scheme, as early as 1839. And there were those like Thady Hanly of Kilgraffy, who acted as a guarantor for a number of loans throughout the early 1840s, but who was forced to emigrate in 1847. There were those who left for Canada and America owing arrears to the loan fund and, despite the involvement of Major Mahon, these loans went unpaid.

It was a similar pattern for those from the Mahon estate who emigrated to America at the same time as the "1,490" left for Quebec. This group perhaps numbered as many as 100 and await an in-depth study of their own. In September 1847, the Loan Fund issued a warrant for the arrest of John Lyons of Ardkillen for arrears of £12. Lyons had surrendered two houses and plots on the Strokestown estate and was compensated for with a passage to America. Ironically, the warrant was signed by Major Denis Mahon as a Justice of the Peace for Strokestown Petty Sessions, suggesting that the landlord was not aware that he had emigrated that summer. Terence McDermott of Tully, listed in the Poverty Loan Funds in February 1842, later emigrated to America in 1847, as did Peter Sweeney, a tailor from Farnbeg, who received money from the Loan Fund in 1846 and the following year was compensated by Major Mahon and given money to go to America.[33] The personal circumstances of the "1,490" and other 1847 emigrants are also evident in the relief lists which survive in the Strokestown archive highlighting those who received relief on a daily and weekly basis throughout 1846. These included James Carroll, Elia Salts, Pat Tighe and Michael Donnelly of Dooherty, and Martin Kelly of Cornashina, for example, who all received Indian corn, or meal, gratuitously in June 1846.[34] Further examination of these voluminous lists will, undoubtedly, reveal others in a similar circumstance.

While we cannot be sure of the occupations of the "1,490" emigrants, a sample of 2,015 occupations listed in the Strokestown area on the eve of the Famine exemplified the pre-Famine importance of cottage industries to the rural economy and the survival of families. These included the following occupations and trades: dealers; shoe and brogue makers; tailors; weavers; smiths; nailors; hatters; masons; carpenters; sawyers; wheel wrights; turners; coopers; butchers and labourers.[35] While the figure of 1,292 listed as "landholders" might appear misleading, it probably reflected the number who were solely engaged in farming as a means of livelihood. Perhaps the most important skill that the families of the "1,490" had was that of survival. After three failed harvests from 1840 to 1842, they had adopted skills that would be crucial in their voyage to the "New World."

For some of the "1,490" we can piece together their final weeks and months in Ireland, gaining an insight into occupation and circumstance. Some information on individual tenants survives in the form of petitions, and further investigation of the Strokestown Park Archive will reveal more about the lives of these people. For example, Thomas Boland of Tully worked as a "reaper," precariously employed at various farms on the Strokestown estate. In the months prior to departure, Boland looked to estate officials to help recover bills which he was owed as, in his own words, "destitution prevails."[36] Within a few months he was Quebec bound. Undoubtedly, the removal of such a large body of people left scars on the landscape. Townlands such as Aughadangan were utterly decimated with some 61 per cent of its population emigrating in the spring and early summer of 1847.

Another notable feature of the "1,490" cohort was the 22 "widows" who took part in the emigration scheme with their children. Perhaps these women inspired others to undertake emigration even at an advanced age, such as Bridget Hanly, who, aged 60, made her own way to America in 1848. By this stage, those who had striven to survive with their families finally gave in to emigration.[37] The Widow Brett, who, with five orphans, had managed to pay the rent from 1843, but who now looked to emigration, was given the passage money.[38] Others such as the Widow Neary looked for assisted emigration to England and promised to be "no further trouble."[39] In the months that followed the departure of the "1,490", a number of tenants, perhaps as many as 100, were given individual incentives to emigrate. These were largely from the cottier and landless labourer class. James Feeney, for example, described as a turf cutter, was given money to buy clothes to go to America, while Eleanor Cline, described as being blind, was helped likewise.[40] Michael McGlynn of Kilgraffy was compensated for a cow and a calf on account going to America, while Pat Forde at North Yard was compensated for "throwing down" his house, as was Pat Rush in Killinordamore.[41] Some of these emigrants were also Canada-bound in 1847, including the Widow Kennedy of Cloonrain.[42] One wonders did she make it there and, if so, did she ever encounter any of the other 66 inhabitants of her townland who were part of the "1,490" exodus? Likewise, Margaret Giblin, who was compensated for her troubles, was also listed as emigrating to Quebec.[43] The whereabouts of other Strokestown emigrants requires further investigation. In November 1847 Mick Dunne, for example, enquired as to erecting a house on the site of one lately pulled down by James Long who had gone to Quebec as an emigrant.[44]

However, perhaps the most startling statistic about the "1,490" and the other 1847 emigrants was that almost 70 per cent of them were not direct tenants of Major Denis Mahon; that is, their names did not appear on the rent roll. This, of course, raises the question as to whether Mahon should have been directly responsible for these people in the first place? The middlemen, strong and small farmers who had facilitated their existence had little to offer them when the potato blight struck. As the owner of the estate realised, large-scale emigration was necessary in order to alleviate the plight of tenants and also to save the estate going forward. With this in mind, he set in motion an emigration scheme as outlined in detail elsewhere in this book.

NOTES

1. Strokestown Park Archives (SPA), STR/1A/148, Original Lists of Tenants Assisted, 1847. Draft copies show disparities between those initially approached and those finally agreeing to accept the scheme.
2. Skeffington Gibbon, *The Recollections of Skeffington Gibbon from 1796 to the present year, 1829; being an epitome of the lives and characters of the nobility and gentry of Roscommon; the genealogy of those who are descended from the kings of Connaught; and a memoir of the late Madame O'Connor Don* (Dublin, 1829), p. 153.
3. *Pigot & Co's Provincial Directory of Ireland 1824, "Connaught,"* p. 217.
4. Edward Wakefield, *An account of Ireland, statistical and political,* ii (London, 1812), p. 128.
5. Arthur Young, *A Tour in Ireland: with general observations on the present state of the kingdom made in the years 1776, 1777 and 1778, and brought down to the end of 1779* (Dublin: George Bonham, 1780), p. 302.
6. National Library of Ireland (NLI), Pakenham-Mahon (PM) Papers MS10,099 (2), Tom Conry to Baron Hartland, 10 December 1831.
7. SPA, STR/1A/127, "Census recorded on Major Mahon's estate by the Strokestown Rental Office, recording townlands, parish, families, and number of persons or individuals, 21 March 1847."
8. *Freeman's Journal*, 8 November 1845.
9. NLI, MS 16 M 15, Pakenham Mahon map books.

10. See, for example, SPA, STR/1A/144, the petition of Widow Holmes, 27 November 1849, p.4.
11. See, for example, National Archives of Ireland (NAI), SOCP, 1538/20, Bishop of Elphin, Power Le Poer Trench to Mr Gregory, 5 August 1813.
12. House of Commons, *Abstract of the police reports of some of the principal outrages in the counties Tipperary, Clare, Limerick, Leitrim and Roscommon in the year 1845, HC, 1846,* p. 710.
13. *Derby Mercury*, 4 October 1843.
14. *London Standard*, 10 April 1844.
15. *Bath Chronicle and Weekly Gazette*, 27 June 1844.
16. Ibid.
17. *Carlisle Journal*, 11 January 1845.
18. SPA, STR/1A/144, Michael Farrell to John Ross Mahon, 12 December 1847, p. 6.
19. At Strokestown, it was estimated that about 150 people sought seasonal work elsewhere of whom about 50 went to England. See *First Report from His Majesty's commissioners for inquiring into the condition of the poorer classes in Ireland,* with appendix (A.) and supplement, 1835 (369), p. 39.
20. Ibid.
21. Ibid.
22. SPA, STR/1A/127, "Census recorded on Major Mahon's estate by the Strokestown Rental Office, recording townlands, parish, families, and number of persons or individuals, 21 March 1847."
23. NLI, PM Papers, MS 10,102 (1), Major Denis Mahon to John Ross Mahon, 21 November 1846.
24. Ibid., MS 10,102 (2). John Ross Mahon to Denis Mahon, 28 February 1847.
25. Ibid.
26. NLI, PM Papers, MS 10,102 (1), Major Denis Mahon to John Ross Mahon, 14 April 1847.
27. SPA, STR/1A/37, STR/1A/44, Correspondence of the Strokestown Loan Fund, May 1839.
28. Ibid., "Notice of the Strokestown Loan Fund, 1839." Those acquiring assistance from the Loan Fund included landholders, dealers, shoemakers, tailors, weavers, smiths, nailors, hatters, carpenters, sawyers, wheelwrights, turners, coopers, masons and butchers.
29. SPA, STR/1A/144, See, for example, the petition of Michael Farrell to John Ross Mahon, 12 November 1847, that refers to the damage caused in 1839, p.12.
30. SPA, STR/1A/37, Correspondence of the Strokestown Loan Fund, May 1839.
31. House of Commons, *Report from Her Majesty's commission of inquiry into the state of law and practice to the occupation of land in Ireland*, 1845 [605] [606], p. 605.
32. See, for example, English National Archives, Kew, T 91/20, "Clonfinlough Loan Fund ledger, 1846–47."
33. NLI, MS 10, 159, "Note on tenants who received compensation, 1847."
34. SPA, STR/1A/122, A list of those tenants from Leitrim, Dooherty and Curnashina to whom Major Mahon sold meal to at 1/2 price dated 2 July 1846.
35. Whereas in the past, particularly during the mid-eighteenth century, the Mahons had granted long leases to tenants (usually for three lives) to encourage building and investment, by the early nineteenth century leases were generally set for one life or 21 years.

36. SPA, STR/1A/144, Petition of Thomas Boland, Tully, p. 15.
37. NLI, MS 10, 159, "Note on tenants who received compensation, 1847."
38. Ibid.
39. SPA, STR/1A/145, Petition of Widow Neary, p. 15.
40. Ibid.
41. NLI, MS 10, 159, "Note on tenants who received compensation, 1847."
42. SPA, Petition of Widow Kennedy to Henry Sandford Pakenham Mahon, 15 January 1848.
43. NLI, MS 10, 159, "Note on tenants who received compensation, 1847."
44. SPA, STR/1A/144, Mick Dunne to John Ross Mahon, 12 November 1847.

CHAPTER TWO

MAJOR DENIS MAHON AND THE EMIGRATION SCHEME

Mark G. McGowan

Denis Mahon did not enjoy the cold damp winters in Ireland. Despite the calamities of crop failure, debt, and tenant violence swirling about his estate, Mahon decamped Strokestown in the autumn of 1846 and did not return until July the following year. Mahon, like many of his landed class in Ireland, felt it necessary to attend to business, family, entertainments, and estate matters in England. In fact, when not visiting with extended family members and his in-laws, he spent much of his time at the United Service Club,[1] on Pall Mall, in London. He was confident that the new agent on the Strokestown estate, John Ross Mahon, would manage the property, collect rents, and handle any extraordinary matters that might arise during one of the worst winters in modern Irish history. It might be far too easy to pillory Mahon as a "typical Irish landlord" often stereotyped as a rather indolent bunch, self-absorbed, wealth-seeking, and without much regard or sense of responsibility for the mass starvation taking place on their estates.[2] While Mahon possessed many of the social expectations of his class, he actually spent much of his time in England, managing and fretting about his Irish estate from afar. His top priority was how to ensure that his tenants were fed while they paid a just and reasonable rent for their tenancies. Mahon's time in England, from November 1846 to July 1847, generated a substantial correspondence with his agent and, when not writing and planning, he was engaged in securing funds for an emigration venture that he had not initially supported.[3] By early 1847, his agent had convinced him that a scheme of assisted migration of hundreds of his tenants would salvage the finances of his estate, preserve the dignity of his class, and relieve the distress experienced by his poorest tenants.

The decisions made by Denis Mahon and the immediate results of the assisted migration have made him a controversial figure among historians of the Great Famine. The fact that Mahon would be the first landlord murdered in Ireland during the Famine gives his story that much more poignancy. The events leading up to his migration scheme have coloured what happened to him later; the fact that so many tenants died on route to Canada, has led to some speculation that this was a contributing factor to his death on the evening of All Souls' Day, 1847.[4] For some writers, the murder was an expression of general unrest on the estate, created by the mass migration and further evictions approved by Mahon and executed by his agent, John Ross Mahon.[5] Padraig Vesey has been more pointed in the allocation of responsibility: "Mahon's assassination was a protest not against landlordism as such but against his land agent's management process" of which the migration schemes were a part.[6] Other writers take a less harsh view of Mahon, seeing him as being overwhelmed by circumstances beyond his control: he inherited an estate in 1845 that was deep in debt.[7] His tenants then faced the devastation of the potato crop, upon which they depended, and which allowed them some modicum of income to remain on the land. The resultant inability of these same tenants to pay rents, while others joined rent strikes that had become common around Strokestown, cut deeply into the estate revenues and made Mahon's already failing financial standing even more precarious.[8] For some writers, Mahon's failure to manage the crisis effectively enraged many of his tenants, and created the opportunity for a small group of them, supported by the local Molly Maguires, to kill him as an example to other members of his class.[9] Even the Catholic Church vilified Mahon when the local parish priest was reported to have denounced the landlord from the pulpit, claiming that "so many died while he lives."[10] As is clear from the contested historiography, this revisiting of Denis Mahon and the migration scheme attempts to navigate stormy historical waters.

When situated within his historical context, Denis Mahon appears little different from many of his contemporaries who constituted the nearly 10,000 landlords that held as much as 95 per cent of Ireland's arable land.[11] As was examined in the previous chapter , he inherited his 11,000-acre estate from his cousin, Maurice Mahon, the 3rd Baron Hartland, who died in 1845, after years of acute mental illness and without an heir. Although Mahon had managed the estate for several years before "mad Maurice's" demise, he was immediately aware that the £30,000 debt that encumbered the estate was now his responsibility.[12] His situation was similar to at least ten per cent of Irish landlords, who were bankrupt, and many more who were severely indebted.[13] On that same point, historian Terence Dooley has stated that: "Country house owners were wealthy but very often in terms of assets and not in real cash."[14] Mahon's financial woes did not prohibit him from keeping up appearances in managing new works on the estate or taking a London "season" as many of his class did. The landlord class has been generalized as possessing "attitudes towards the people derived from assumptions of social, ethnic, and religious superiority, generally despising those among whom they lived."[15] No doubt, Denis Mahon shared some of these assumptions. His correspondence in 1846–1847, particularly regarding the emigration scheme, however, suggests that such social attitudes did not limit him; his actions during the Famine crisis itself revealed an attitude of concern not only for his assets, but for the tenants on his estate.

As the potato blight struck Ireland in 1845, and as deprivation, starvation, and disease took hold of thousands of Ireland's peasant classes, the Mahon estate was in dire financial trouble. Mahon's realm, which exceeded 11,000 acres and included 11,958 people crammed into 68 townlands, was severely in debt.[16] Many tenants had been truant in the paying of their annual rents. Some tenants simply could not afford the rents given their limited yields on their tiny plots of often less than five acres.[17] Other tenants, perhaps inspired by the longstanding rent strike by tenants in the townland of Ballykilcline, nearby, or fed-up with their grinding poverty, simply refused to pay rent in defiance of Mahon, or engaged in episodes of violence which had occurred with greater frequency in Roscommon.[18] By 1846, facing economic and social disaster on the estate, Mahon retained the services of John Ross Mahon, a distant relative and a partner in the Dublin firm of Guinness and Mahon. Historian Padraig Vesey described John Ross Mahon as a "new" type of agent, with a business-like attitude and a management style that left little room for emotional attachment to the tenants at Strokestown.[19] John Ross Mahon's services would come at a price; in September 1846, Mahon agreed to pay the Dublin-based agent £500 annually, with an additional outlay of £65 to set up an agency office in Strokestown.[20] It was within the context of these dire circumstances on the estate and in the county, and their differing approaches to the Famine challenges, that would shape this important correspondence between the Major and his agent.

Throughout 1846, Denis Mahon was aware of the conditions on his estate and was prepared to swing into action to help the most destitute of his tenants. Mahon had been active in the public work schemes surrounding the estate and advocated for the building of roads that would better link townlands to one another. He even chastised some of his wealthier tenants for not doing enough to support the families who sublet property from their tenancies. In June 1846, Denis Mahon was blunt with Thomas Conry, one of his leading middlemen in Kiltrustan Parish, for withholding the £30 that he had pledged for public works. "I say you ought to pay the money," chided Mahon, "the works will take your people in employment, there are hills to be cut down & some new roads to be made."[21] Conry did eventually pay. In fairness to Conry, he and other large tenants were in debt to the Major, including Dr. Terence Shanley, Robert Warnock, and Michael Egan.[22]

Mahon also chaired the Strokestown Relief Committee and was energetic in his acquisition of the American maize provided by the Peel government for hunger relief.[23] In July 1846, he assured Conry that "I shall take care that your poor are attended to."[24] In July 1846, he secured five tons of meal to be distributed in Strokestown and area claiming, "We can do some useful works when work is required & wanting to relieve distress."[25] While he may have overestimated the Irish people's love for the maize, which was completely unfamiliar to them in terms of preparation and sometimes harmful in the process of digestion, Mahon was noted as having served out maize meal, himself, to the people in need.[26] He was not without some moral swagger in criticizing local Catholic clergy for indulging themselves in food and drink at a meeting in Strokestown, while the peasants around them starved.[27]

In late August 1846, Mahon was still living on the estate when he received a petition from the tenants on the Townland of Cloonahee, near Elphin, in which they begged him for relief, when 100 men were laid off from the public works. Perhaps it was their veiled threat at the end of the petition that spawned further action from him: "Gentlemen, we fear that the peace of the country will be much disturbed if relief not be immediately more extensively afforded to the suffering peasantry," they warned.[28] Within a month of the petition, Mahon had retained the services of John Ross Mahon to manage the estate. Perhaps with a little naïveté, Mahon wrote to his agent, in December, "if you see that there is benefit to my tenants that ought to be applied for I hope you will do so as I depend on your judgement not being on the spot myself to make the necessary enquiries."[29]

The ensuing relationship between the landlord and the agent, ironically men who bore the same surname, was uneasy and potentially fractious. Despite a growing literature on the Mahon migration scheme,[30] there still are sweeping generalizations made by some historians that the tenants did not choose to go or were evicted.[31] What is obvious from the outset is that Denis Mahon was away from his estate from November 1846 to July 1847, the entire time the voluntary migration scheme was planned, approved, and set into motion. He never dealt with his large tenants or small holders directly, nor did he witness the actual gathering of the 271 families across the 32 townlands who consented to leave for Canada. John Ross Mahon was clearly "on the spot" and was actively engaged, for good or for ill, with the tenants, as the Major had observed earlier, but Denis Mahon, himself, was hardly a passive player in the operation. Using the United Service Club as his base of operations, he sojourned in several hotels in London and environs, keeping track of the events being directed by John Ross Mahon on the estate, while he desperately sought financing to underwrite the scheme itself. Denis Mahon appeared involved in a flurry of activities, which even brought him to Liverpool, to rendezvous with his agent as the first wave of migrants were despatched to Quebec.[32]

Key to understanding Mahon's overall thinking about Famine relief was both his knowledge of his shrinking revenues for his estate and his personal categorization of the types of tenants who inhabited his townlands. First, his desire to bring relief to the poorest of his tenants was often compromised by the drain on his revenues by members of his own family, milking him by means of agreements for subsidies and annuities that redirected money away from direct relief of the poor. In November 1846, John Ross Mahon reported to his partners at Guinness and Mahon that he had made payments to the Major's relatives, who received an annuity from the estate, in perpetuity.[33] Such payments became a dangerous drain on Denis Mahon's finances; the indebtedness of his estate had been attributed to irresponsible spending by his predecessors and his obligation to continue these family endowments, promised long before he assumed control at Strokestown.[34] Such debt naturally forced the Major and his agent to think of enhancing the estate's revenue streams and targeting those who still owed him rent. He could neither right the sinking ship of his estate, nor help the poor people who lived on it if the revenue streams were drying up.

Clear in Denis Mahon's mind was that there were several classes of tenants who complicated the execution of his relief policies. He explained to his agent that there were those poor tenants, living on smallholdings, who had simply not been able to pay and had not done so for several years. Denis Mahon was sympathetic and supportive of these "deserving poor," although he never used this common description for the truly needy in the nineteenth century. He worried about these tenants and he reminded his agent that he had already reduced the rent burden of those who were in arrears, and he ordered his agent to continue to do so as an "act of justice."[35] In his own words, he would not cast them out: "I should not like to put such a number of starving creatures loose on the world without any means whatever of feeding them."[36] This revelation comes as no surprise, as acknowledged in the ledgers and bills of his estate papers in the Strokestown Park Archive, that Denis Mahon operated a Charitable Loan Fund for his tenants prior to the potato blight.[37] Moreover, when the food crisis became acute during and after the blight, he was determined that American maize, purchased from the Government, might be distributed *gratis* to those tenants in need, and on alternate days be sold at a modest price to those tenants who had the means to pay.[38] Denis Mahon also wanted to distribute seed to his most needy tenants. He was clear that if the seed was given to them, they could repay him once the crop was harvested in the autumn of 1847.[39] By January of that year, Mahon had a plan to feed the needy of his estate, make those who could pay their rent do so, and make certain that there was a local soup kitchen in place to attend to the immediate needs of the hungry. His letter of 26 February revealed his vexation when he learned that the soup kitchen in Strokestown was not up and running and he demanded that the local head of the committee responsible, George Knox, should be reprimanded for this inaction.[40] His vexation turned to anger when, a month later, the "Soup Shop" in Strokestown had still not opened.[41]

In his thinking, there were also "industriously inclined" tenants who formed a second group, who worked the land and honoured the terms of their leases. These were types of tenants that he elevated above all others because they worked hard and lived by the obligations of their leases. When he learned that, within the context of the emigration scheme, these "industrious" farmers were the most numerous applicants to leave the estate, he was perplexed; "it strikes me that many of those applying are the better sort of tenant and if possible should be kept at home."[42] This "better sort" appeared neither a drain on his revenue because they were not prone to depend on the local Poor Law Union, nor were they remiss in paying to him what he was owed. None of these tenants appear on the lists of those tenants who had sought the free distribution of American maize.[43]

He differentiated these classes of "the poorest" and "the industrious" tenants from two other groups of tenants who raised his ire: the first consisted of several of his larger landholding tenants, whom he felt could pay, but somehow did not.[44] In a number of letters, he is clear that there should be no "hanging gale" insofar as these middlemen and large holders are concerned and that the agent should force the issue with them immediately.[45] The second group of miscreants were identified as those who were "in combination" or could pay their rent but instead withheld it in protest. These were the tenants that he wanted rid of for their conspiracy, and he described clearing them as an act of justice.[46] The implication in the letters is clear—Denis Mahon targeted those tenants who he thought were part of a rent strike conspiracy, a combination, as the ones responsible for imperilling his efforts to right his sinking ship at Strokestown. These delinquent tenants would receive no assistance from him, but he would exercise all in his power to make them pay what he thought he was owed, or they would be evicted from his estate. It is important to see the nuance in Mahon's attitudes towards his tenants instead of seeing his relationship to them as monochromatic, a judgement that would certainly skew the manner in which the emigration scheme might be interpreted and, for that matter, has been interpreted.

There was no nuance in the relationship between Mahon and his agent over what should be done with the indebted tenants on the Strokestown estate. In late February and early March 1847, the correspondence between the Major Mahon and John Ross Mahon became more heated as each seemed to be scheming in a different direction. In a letter written on 27 February, John Ross Mahon was unequivocal in his judgement that the Major's plans to alleviate distress among his poorest tenants was doomed for failure. The agent then laid his cards on the table: unless the estate was cleared of two-thirds of its population (an estimated 8,000 people), it would not be able to survive. He wrote:

> Nothing whatever can be done in the way of improvement until the land is cleared of at least two thirds of its population. I am told that proportion of the tenantry not having any means ... of paying rent. If you do not put out these there is no prospect in my mind of you getting any rent for years if ever again.[47]

John Ross Mahon added that if the Major pursued his current course of action, he would resign his post and another agent would have to replace him. The agent had estimated that the cost of keeping a tenant in the Poor House at Roscommon would cost £7–3*s* per year, whereas the cost of migration would be about half of this.[48]

Within the week, on 7 March, Denis Mahon answered the salvo from his agent with his regrets that John Ross thought he must resign. The Major then explained that he did not intend that the "haberes," the legal notices of eviction, should apply to all, adding that only those who were able to pay should be forced to do so, or be forced off the estate.[49] In fact, Denis Mahon still proposed rent reduction for the poorest of his tenants. These two letters clearly staked out opposing views of what must be done on the estate, and it was in March when the decision for the migration scheme came to the fore as the proposed alternative to Denis Mahon's on-site relief program.[50]

In mid-March, there was almost no back-and-forth between landlord and agent, perhaps indicating that Denis Mahon was taking his time to rethink his position on a possible migration project. Perhaps the severity of Ireland's worst winter in memory, and the further destitution that became evident in all reports out of Ireland, forced him to concede that a more dramatic solution be undertaken. The Major never records why he conceded to the plan hatched by his agent. On 28 March, he appeared to be reconciled to his agent's proposal that tenants should be assisted off the estate and given passage to America, although he was still prepared to provide seed to those tenants who remained on the estate.[51] Two days later, however, he was much more emphatic in the acceptance of a migration scheme, and less committed to the provision of seed, directing his agent:

> I am aware that you have from the commencement recommended Emigration to a great extent. I have no doubt it would be attended with the best results. I am therefore willing if you will but undertake to carry out the plan of Emigration to provide funds to be at your command and I should also willingly try Mr. Samuel Gale's plan on one or two townlands, if I can get a sufficient sum of money to do both—but if I undertake this it must be with your assistance to carry it out[52]

Denis Mahon even suggested that the first "batch" of tenants ought to be sent through the port of Sligo, which was closest to the estate, offering very cheap trans-Atlantic fares, and where its local landlord, Lord Palmerston, had already prepared similar schemes to assist his own tenants to America.[53]

Denis Mahon, however, was clear that not all tenants were eligible for the scheme. He was insistent that some tenants deserved "no indulgence" and by this phrase, he targeted those whom he believed to have been in "combination" to withhold their rents, even though they had been able to pay. Even in the early stages of the migration scheme, it appeared that Mahon was most interested in assisting the poorest tenants off—ones for which the "once off" cost of a ticket to Quebec and their provisions would be less than the Poor Law tax, which might have to be paid annually if the agricultural economy continued in its slump and the hunger persisted. Mahon began looking for the cheapest tickets to the Americas, questioning the rates, baggage fees, and food allocations on trans-Atlantic passages to New York, Boston, Philadelphia, New Orleans, and Quebec. In an unsigned question-and-answer sheet to a surveyor, Samuel Gale, Mahon secured a list of the various rates of passage for adults and children, the cheapest of which was transport to Quebec, with a minimum fare of £3 3*s*. per statute adult.[54] Children under 14 were counted as a half statute adult and therefore would be charged half of the adult fare and allocated half of the statutory provisions, including bedding and cooking utensils, for the voyage.[55] From the outset of the scheme, as confirmed by this itemized list on a scrap of notepaper, the available evidence strongly suggests its double-edged nature. The deserving poor would be given a new lease on life, while the cheap fares would save the estate Poor Law payments and, at the same time, free up acres for its re-development. There has been the suggestion, albeit still unproven by hard evidence, that the townlands selected by the Major and his agent may have been chosen to provide a cleared corridor for the new Irish railway which was currently being built to link Dublin to the west coast, via Mullingar.[56] Serious talk of the proposed railway was not recorded until 1853 and 1854, six to seven years after the migration scheme and the murder of Major Mahon.[57] This line eventually bypassed Strokestown and never crossed the Shannon into Roscommon.

By early April, John Ross Mahon rapidly commenced the proposed emigration scheme. Despite the repeated attempts of the Major to ship the migrants from Sligo,[58] the agent won out again in his own preference of Liverpool. John Ross Mahon's other instructions were generally followed, including a few selected townlands for the "first batch" and a focus on townlands that were overcrowded and where he acknowledged the land was "miserably bad."[59] By mid-April the invitations to emigrate were sent to tenants who might normally be served with *haberes*; upon their promise of extinguishing their leases, levelling their cabins, and receiving compensation for their existing crops and chattels, the landlord pledged to provide the willing subscribers with food and transportation from Dublin to Liverpool and from Liverpool to the British North American port of Quebec.[60] It is also evident from contemporary newspapers that the tenants were told that they were going to Upper Canada, at that time one of the burgeoning farming frontiers in the British-held Province of Canada.[61] Once Liverpool, not Sligo, had been chosen as the port of departure, John Ross Mahon's Dublin office negotiated with firm of J. and W. Robinson in Liverpool for the charter of ships to accommodate two groups of immigrants. Denis Mahon warned his agent in early May to make sure that the assisted migrants were healthy because the Government Order-in-Council was soon to tighten health regulations on the Dublin steamers to Liverpool.[62] In late May, a Dublin newspaper, reprinted in the Quebec *Berean*, reported the arrival of the first batch of Mahon tenants at Custom House Quay in Dublin, "presenting marks of comfort not recognizable in the bulk of people fleeing from the famine."[63] This report confirmed that the voluntary migrants were well outfitted by the landlord for their journey, and may have possessed some means prior to signing on to the scheme.[64]

Major Denis Mahon's plans for the scheme were clear and were now left for John Ross Mahon and his bailiffs to execute. Tenants on specified estate townlands would be approached with the offer to emigrate, with their costs of travel and food being assumed by Mahon from Strokestown to Dublin, from Dublin to Liverpool, and finally on chartered vessels from Liverpool to Quebec (Lower Canada), in British North America. The landlord would also compensate for crops and animals left behind, on the condition that the tenant would agree to the toppling of the cabin. This latter action was to acknowledge that the tenant was not to return to the area and the agreement was final. The tenants who agreed to the scheme cancelled their leases but would be permitted to remain on their former tenancy until their departure for Dublin. During that period, they would be known as "caretakers" and not as "tenants."[65] John Ross Mahon compiled detailed lists for the townlands covered of the families who agreed to leave, the acreage surrendered, and the amount of compensation. Rough drafts and final lists kept in the Strokestown Estate Papers indicate that the holding pattern, between tenant and caretaker, served a few wavering tenants well. On the Cregga Townland (House Division), for example, nine families agreed to accept the initial offer. Shortly thereafter, the agent recorded that the families of John Egan, James Duffy, and Michael Beirne decided not to depart and presumably stayed put. It remains puzzling why Duffy and Beirne remained. In 1840, both had appeared on a list of tenants accused of stealing timber and Beirne was found guilty.[66] Evidently, such crimes were not sufficient in the mind of either landlord or agent to be rid of these tenants and they were permitted to rescind their initial agreement. In the final drafts of the agent's list, 271 family units (single and multiple person) from 32 townlands agreed to leave the estate and begin a new life in Canada.[67]

The assisted migrants appeared to be removed methodically from the estate townland-by-townland in two distinctive waves. By 14 May 1847, 31 of the 47 volunteering families from the Kilmackenny Townland, in the civil parish of Lissonuffy, were duly registered and were moved *en masse* towards Dublin, presumably with members of families from townlands in the civil parish of Kilglass. These latter emigrants were identified by parish when they arrived at the port of Dublin later in May. These are the travellers identified in the *Berean* as having been better off than most famine migrants seen thus far in the capital, with at least 15 carts of baggage accompanying them.[68] A cross referencing of the names of the Kilmackenny tenants with the lists of maize distribution on the estate suggests that very few of these hopeful travellers had availed themselves of the free maize, but some had been actually able to pay for the maize when it was offered for sale.[69] Yet, as indicated in Chapter 1, four migrating families from the Dooherty Townland had availed themselves of the cheap maize in July 1846. Thus, it appeared that even in this first wave in the scheme there was a curious mix of several classes of tenants.

While the physical clearing of the estate and the assistance to willing tenants went relatively smoothly, the second principal concern of Mahon, maintaining the right kind of tenants on the estate, did not meet expectations. The Kilmackenny situation certainly provided proof of this setback. While the early letters reflected a wish that the poorest be assisted to Canada, John Ross Mahon reported, with some regret, that many of the better off tenants were volunteering for the scheme.[70] This was not news that Denis Mahon wanted to hear, particularly since he had given explicit instructions that the poorest tenants be given priority, and that those suspected of being in "combination" could pay their own expenses. Having reviewed many of the names, he responded: "I think the first class for us to send is those of the poorest and worst description. They would become a charge on us for the Poor House outdoor relief."[71] The landlord trusted that John Robinson, the chief bailiff on the estate, would be able to recognize any of the tenants who were part of the rent "conspiracy" and not permit them to join in the pilgrimage to Dublin. Nevertheless, the operation did not work out as either the Major nor his agent had planned, as there was a mixture of those the Mahon's described "first class" and other tenants on the final lists. In fact, those tenants who voluntarily surrendered their holdings may not have been the poorest, as the reports the first wave arrived in Dublin with so many carts of baggage in tow.

Late April and early May threw the estate agency into a sense of urgency, when it appeared that the Robinson Company in Liverpool could accommodate as many potential passengers as Mahon's estate might send. Denis Mahon's own demeanor took on a tone of greater anxiety and alarm that the first vessels might depart Liverpool without the Strokestown migrants. Assisted migrants from the townlands of Kilmackenny, Cregga House, Cregga Plunkett, and Cloonrain were cleared, and Denis Mahon scrambled among the banking houses of London to secure the money to pay for their passage and their stores. As late as 24 May, when the first wave of emigrants has set out from the estate, accompanied by the estate bailiff, John Robinson, the Major reported that he had paid for up to 390 (statute adult) places on the *Virginius*, in addition to £200 in stores and provisions.[72] Three days later, he wrote to the agent telling him he had raised £550 to pay for the "first batch" and he was pleased that John Ross Mahon was to be in Liverpool to see the first group depart.[73] The landlord himself mentioned several times to his agent that he would make himself available in Liverpool if his assistance was needed in the final stages of the scheme.

Denis Mahon and John Ross Mahon did rendezvous in Liverpool anticipating the arrival of both waves of assisted migrants. On 28 May, John Ross Mahon was present when the *Virginius* sailed with 476 passengers, and on 1 June when the remainder of the first wave of assisted tenants departed on *Erin's Queen*. Denis Mahon was also in Liverpool to finalize arrangements and he indicated to John Ross Mahon that he might be found at the affluent Adelphi Hotel,[74] should he be needed. The Major's letters reveal that much of his time in England was being spent raising money for what he thought might be as a many as 400 statute adults in the second group.[75] He reported to his agent that week that he had raised an additional £1,400 *16s 7d* to subsidize the 405.5 statute adults who sailed on the *Naomi*, on 15 June, and the overflow of 55 statute adults who were dispatched on the *John Munn*, a day later.[76] By mid June, Denis Mahon had accepted an additional £3,590 16*s* 7*d* in debt to finance the two waves of the migration scheme.[77]

The first wave of assisted emigrants set the pattern for the orderly departure from the estate. First, the willing participants in the scheme were gathered in their townlands by the bailiffs under the direction of John Robinson. Once gathered in a group, the families proceeded on foot with their carts to Tarmonbarry, crossed the Shannon, and began their 160-kilometer trek to Dublin along the banks of the Royal Canal. While it has all the appearances of a pleasant walk today, the scene along side the Royal Canal was anything but peaceful in 1847. The canal had been built in the eighteenth century and it, and its southern iteration, the Grand Canal, were designed to link the hinterland interior counties of Ireland to Dublin, and to provide a water transportation corridor that linked Dublin to the Shannon, and eventually via the Shannon to Limerick and the Atlantic. In 1847, the scene on the canal would have been a cacophony of children crying, bargemen yelling and swearing, horses moving their way along the banks towing the barges, and joined at various villages by mobs of travellers, from many counties, fleeing the ravaged land of the interior in hopes of food, lodging, and work in Dublin. The crowding would have been made worse by the fact that the canal banks were narrow, often elevated above the canal on one side, and above the fields, farms, and bog land on the other. One can imagine parents trying to corral their children from wandering off in the throng, falling into the canal, climbing into the bog, being trampled by the horses that shared the pathway, or foully sloshing though the horse dung that littered the pathways. Robinson knew the deadline to have them in Liverpool, as he herded the assisted Roscommon folk on their way, making up as much time as possible, and making sure the potential emigrants chose not to migrate off the route to Longford, Mullingar, or Maynooth, only to double back to the estate to squat.

By June, there were 1,490 assisted immigrants accounted for in the Mahon Emigration scheme.[78] Denis Mahon and John Ross Mahon, however, were not finished. As the second wave was pouring into Dublin, the landlord and his agent were plotting to send more. It was clear to Denis Mahon that with the mixing of preferred migrants and those whom he had wish to keep on the estate now departed, his mind returned to assisting the poorest tenants while punishing those in "combination." The latter became Mahon's obsession, particularly those tenants with large holdings, who did not pay rent. Mahon wanted a third batch of migrants to exclude any tenants he suspected of participating in the "rent strike" and include those deeply in arrears who could not hope to pay. The townland most frequently mentioned in their correspondence is Castlenode, which the Major wanted cleared in a similar fashion to the previous two groups of migrants. Denis Mahon had another Liverpool ship in mind, the *Champion,* which was scheduled to sail in early July. He assured John Ross Mahon that the Robinson Company was holding 100 spaces on the ship, at a cost of £3 5*s* per statute adult; like the previous four vessels, the *Champion* was bound for Quebec.[79] Unfortunately, there is little evidence to suggest whether the *Champion* fulfilled Denis Mahon's hope that another contingent of tenants could be transported to Canada. The simple truth of the matter is that Mahon was back in Ireland in July, first in County Louth visiting family, and finally, by 12 July, in Strokestown.[80] As a result, there exists no written evidence of the scheme since, in practical terms, there was little need to write to an agent when he was on site. What is known is that the Castlenode townland tenants did not end up in a "third wave" of assisted migration.[81] The estate records at Strokestown Park indicate that the tenants who had been in arrears at Castlenode were still living in the townland after 1847.[82]

The question arises, however, if the Castlenode tenants were not on the *Champion*, were other Mahon tenants on the ship? Death registers from the quarantine station at Grosse Ile, near Quebec, record several deaths aboard the *Champion*, but none of the surnames seem indigenous to Castlenode or other townlands on the Mahon estate. Nevertheless, there is one thread of evidence that suggests that some of Mahon's people may have been on the *Champion* when it arrived at Quebec. Emigration officials reported that the ship arrived at Quebec City on 28 August, after 42 days at sea from Liverpool, and there were 422 steerage passengers, of whom 29 died at sea and 65 in quarantine.[83] The *Quebec Chronicle* was dismayed and disgusted that: "The passengers of the Champion [sic] are more of the wretched, miserable tenantry of Major Mahon and are equally squalid and filthy as those coming out on the Virginius [sic] and Naomi [sic]."[84] While there is little one-to-one correspondence between names of the dead from the *Champion* and names from Strokestown, it was certain that Canadian authorities considered them Mahon's tenants and they were not impressed.[85]

What is known is that two waves of assisted migrants from Mahon's estate arrived at Custom House Quay in Dublin in late May and early June. As has been noted earlier, local newspapers reported their arrival and were surprised by the state of "comfort" in which they appeared. Bailiff Robinson was to report later that he had not lost any of them on route. He had their transit papers checked at the Custom House, and then prepared for the next leg of the journey—passage across the Irish Sea to Liverpool. There are no available records of how long they waited for the steam ferries to take them from Dublin, nor are there any reports of any migrants "jumping ship" just prior to departure. What is known is that they had a goal in mind. They were heading for a new life in Upper Canada, which had been a prime destination for tens of thousands of Irish migrants before the blight had struck in 1845. Canada held out the prospect of work on the canal systems that were being built to circumnavigate the mighty Niagara Falls. There was also the possibility of clearing the forests of the colony and creating farms, upon which they would have no landlord to oversee their labours and take from the fruit of their harvests. Canada also held out the possibility of moving farther afield to the United States, where Roscommon people had already travelled and started new lives in a Republic free from the British Crown. Most members of these 271 families had never left their own townlands, let alone their own county. The sight of Dublin, the big city, would be awe-inspiring. The sight of the Irish Sea, which they were about to cross, would be terrifying. The vision of the Slieve Bawn, the long hill that towered over the Mahon Estate in Lissonuffy, would be but a memory from now on.

For Denis Mahon, however, the legacy of what happened to these former tenants would haunt him for months and, perhaps, take him to his early grave. It is tempting to read the events of the migration scheme backwards from the time of his assassination on 2 November 1847, thereby creating trajectories that may actually be exercises in the historical fallacy of *post hoc ergo propter hoc*. As has been seen in this chapter, the letters between Denis Mahon and John Ross Mahon help to identify the multi-layered concerns of a landlord, who tried to balance financial self-interest and keeping up the social expectations of his class, with a regard for the health and livelihood of the poorest of his tenants. Mahon was deeply concerned for the sustainability of his estate and making certain that defaulting tenants were brought to justice, but he also wanted to lighten the burden of the poor. These two principal concerns did not work at cross-purposes since the emigration scheme to Canada was seen as a means of assisting poor tenants in starting a new life in a presumably better environment, while clearing a significant financial burden from the estate books and opening up the vacated lands for new possibilities. When advisors to Major Mahon suggested that it might have been cheaper to relocate the tenants in Great Britain, even John Ross Mahon conceded that he thought the relocation of tenants to England was "not so charitable or so liberal a plan as sending this [sic] poor creatures to America."[86]

For both the 1,490 assisted tenants, and their landlord, Denis Mahon, the next stage of the journey would have tragic consequences. The events of the next six months would put an indelible mark on the Strokestown story.

NOTES

1. The United Service Club was a private gentlemen's club in London reserved for senior officers, active and retired, in the British Army. The Duke of Wellington was one of its most prominent members.
2. Lindsay Proudfoot, "Landlords," in S.J. Connolly, ed., *The Oxford Companion to Irish History* (Oxford: Oxford University Press, 1998), p. 297; James S. Donnelly, jr., "Mass Evictions and the Great Irish Famine: The Clearances Revisited," in Cathal Póirtéir, ed., *The Great Irish Famine* (Dublin: RTE/Mercier, 1995), pp. 156–7; Cecil Woodham-Smith, *The Great Hunger: Ireland, 1846–1849* (New York: Old Town Books, reprint 1989, original 1962), p. 326.
3. Susan Hood, "The Strokestown Park House Archive," *History Ireland* 3, no. 4 (Winter 1995), 12. Hood indicates that there are 18,000 estate documents at Strokestown Park and approximately 5,000 documents in the Pakenham-Mahon Papers in the National Library of Ireland, Dublin (hereafter NLI). This correspondence under discussion in this paper is in MS 10,138, Denis Mahon's Migration, and MS 10,102 (1) to MS 10,102 (4).
4. Donnelly, p, 169; a similar link between Mahon's actions in the migration scheme and his murder is offered in John Kelly, *The Graves are Walking: A History of the Great Irish Famine* (New York: Henry Holt and Co., 2012), pp. 284–5.
5. Anne Coleman, *Riotous Roscommon: Social Unrest in the 1840s* (Dublin: Irish Academic Press, Maynooth Studies in Local History, no. 27, 1999). Charles E. Orser Jr, "An Archaeology of Famine-Era Eviction," *New Hibernia Review* 9, no. 1 (Spring, 2005), p. 52.
6. Padraig Vesey, *The Murder of Major Mahon, Strokestown, County Roscommon, 1847* (Dublin: Four Courts, Maynooth Studies in Local History, no. 80, 2008), p. 13; Kelly, *The Graves are Walking*, pp. 284–5.
7. Peter Duffy, *The Killing of Major Denis Mahon: A Mystery of Old Ireland* (NY: Harper, 2007), pp. x-xi.
8. Robert James Scally, *The End of Hidden Ireland: Rebellion, Famine & Emigration* (NY: Oxford University Press, 2005); Mary Lee Dunn, *Ballykilcline Rising: From Famine Ireland to Immigrant America* (Amherst: University of Massachusetts Press, 2008).
9. Michael Huggins, *Social Conflict in Pre-Famine Ireland: The Case of County Roscommon* (Dublin: Four Courts, 2007), pp. 156–61.
10. Enda Delaney, *The Great Irish Famine: A History in Four Lives* (Dublin: Gill & Macmillan, 2014), pp. 195–6; Stephen J. Campbell, *The Great Irish Famine: Words and Images from the Famine Museum, Strokestown Park, County Roscommon* (Strokestown: The Famine Museum, 1994), pp. 47–8.
11. Ciarán O'Murchadha, *The Great Irish Famine: Ireland's Agony, 1845–1852* (London: Continuum, 2011), p. 10; Proudfoot, p. 297.
12. Vesey, *The Murder*, p. 13.
13. Thomas Bartlett, *Ireland: A History* (Cambridge: Cambridge University Press, 2010), p. 295.
14. Terence Dooley and Christopher Ridgeway, eds., *The Irish Country House, Its Past, Present and Future* (Dublin: Four Courts Press, 2015), p. 15.
15. O'Murchadha, *The Great Irish Famine*, p. 11.

16. Susan Hood, "The Famine in the Strokestown Park House Archive," *The Irish Review*, no. 17/18 (Winter, 1995), pp. 110–12. Strokestown Park Archive (hereafter SPA), Box STR 88, Census of 21 March 1847. This local census counted 68 townlands with 2,237 families constituting 11,958 persons.
17. Mary Kelly, "The Great Famine in County Roscommon," in Richie Farrell, Kieran O'Conor and Matthew Potter, eds., *Roscommon: History and Society* (Dublin: Geography Publications, 2018), p. 389. Kelly estimates that the average amount of land held by tenants and sub-tenants was between one and five acres.
18. Huggins, *Social Conflict*, pp. 13–16 and pp.113–4.
19. Vesey, 13–14.
20. NLI, MS10,102, John Ross Mahon to Denis Mahon, 18 September 1846.
21. SPA, STR/1A/111, Denis Mahon to Thomas Conry, 28 June 1846. Copy.
22. SPA, STR/1A/91, List of Names of Rents owed in Gurtoose and Kildalloge, 1846.
23. SPA, STR/1A/104, Extract, Strokestown Relief Committee, 8 August 1846.
24. SPA, STR/1A/111, Denis Mahon to Thomas Conry, 10 July 1846. Copy.
25. Ibid.
26. NLI, MS10,102, John Ross Mahon to Denis Mahon, 18 September 1846.
27. SPA, STR/1A/111, Denis Mahon to Thomas Conry, 10 July 1846. Copy.
28. SPA, STR/1A/105, Cloonahee Petition, 22 August 1846.
29. NLI, MS10,102, Denis Mahon to John Ross Mahon, 27 December 1846.
30. Ciarán Reilly, *Strokestown and the Great Irish Famine* (Dublin: Four Courts, 2014), 49–78; Mark G. McGowan, "Old Sources, new discoveries: in search of the 1,490 assisted immigrants from Strokestown to Canada, 1847," *Archivium Hibernicum* LXXI (2019): 374–96; Mark G. McGowan, "Migration, mobility, and murder: assisted immigration from the Mahon estate, Strokestown, County Roscommon, Ireland, 1847," *Breac*, an online journal of Irish Studies, Notre Dame University (2017).
31. Gillian O'Brien, *The Darkness Echoing: Exploring Ireland's Places of Famine, Death, and Rebellion* (London: Penguin & Doubleday Ireland, 2020), pp. 146–7.
32. National Library of Ireland [NLI], Mahon Papers, MS 10,102 (1), Denis Mahon [DM] to John Ross Mahon [JRM], 4 May 1847. The Major proposed to stay in Liverpool's Adelphi Hotel and meet the agent there.
33. NLI, MS 10,1002 (2), John Ross Mahon to Guinness & Mahon, 19 November 1846.
34. Susan Hood, "The Famine in the Strokestown Park House Archive," *The Irish Review*, no.17–18 (Winter 1995), pp. 110–1.
35. NLI, MS 10,102 (2), DM to JRM, 21 November 1846. *Roscommon Journal*, 5 December 1846 referred to rent reduction as the sign of "a good landlord."
36. NLI, MS10,102, DM to JRM, 2 March 1847.
37. Reilly, *Strokestown*, pp. 26–7; SPA, STR 88, "Charitable Loan Fund."
38. SPA, STR/1A/122, Attached #8 Book, Indian Meal, 6 August 1846; Yellowstone File, List of Persons who were relieved with meal, 22 June 1846.
39. NLI, MS 10,102 (4), DM to JRM, 29 January 1847.
40. NLI, MS 10,102 (3), DM to JRM, 26 February 1847.

41. NLI, MS 10,102 Denis Mahon to John Ross Mahon, 2 March 1847.
42. NLI, MS 10,102 (3), DM to JRM, 14 April 1847.
43. SPA, STR/1A/122, Attached #8 Book, Indian Meal, Given "Gratuitously", 6 August 1846.
44. NLI, MS 10,102 (2), DM to JRM, 3 January 1847 also DM to JRM, 21 November 1846.
45. NLI, MS 10,102 (1), DM to JRM, 14 June 1847.
46. NLI, MS 10,1002 (2), DM to JRM, 19 November 1846; DM to JRM, 21 November 1846; and DM to JRM, no day specified, December 1846; and MS 10,102 (4), DM to JRM, 18 December 1846.
47. NLI, MS 10, 102 (2), JRM to DM, 28 February 1847 (copy).
48. NLI, MS 10.102, Memorandum of John Ross Mahon to Major Denis Mahon, 23 July 1847.
49. NLI, MS 10,102 (2), DM to JRM, 7 March 1847.
50. A migration scheme had been proposed to the Devon Commission by Denis Mahon's brother John as early as 1843. Duffy, *The Killing*, p. 54.
51. NLI, MS 10,102 (1), DM to JRM, 28 March 1847.
52. NLI, MS 10,102 (2), DM to JRM, 30 March 1847.
53. NLI, MS 10,102 (2) DM to JRM, 2 April 1847.
54. NLI, MS 10,102 (1), Unknown (presumably JRM) to Mr. Samuel Gale, 8 April 1847. Children under 14 years of age usually were counted and charged as half a statute adult. Gale was likely from the Dublin land surveying firm of Brassington and Gale, which had been retained by the estate. SPA, STR/1A/146 and STR/1A/199 include correspondence between the Estate and the firm between 1847 and 1849.
55. Ibid., Queries about Assisted Emigration, 8 April 1847.
56. Ciarán Reilly, "Strokestown and the Pakenham-Mahon Estate," in Farrell, O'Conor, Potter eds., *Roscommon*, pp. 375–6.
57. SPA, STR/1A/362, Letters from John Ross Mahon to Thomas Roberts, Strokestown House, 3 March to 21 November 1853; STR/1A/375, file of letters to Thomas Roberts, January to December 1854; STR/1A/381, File of Letters from John Ross Mahon, January to December 1854; and STR/1A/388, Thomas Roberts, Farn Cottage to Henry Pakenham Mahon, 21 October 1854. The proposed railway extension from Longford is raised several times. It would cross the Shannon from Longford, and run through Scramogue, eventually entering Farn, with a station at Cloonfree.
58. NLI, MS 10, 102 (2), DM to JRM, 13 April 1847.
59. SPA, STR/1A/150, Memorandum of Agreement of Tenants on Strokestown Estate, 14 May 1847; Memorandum of John Ross Mahon to Major Denis Mahon, 23 July 1847.
60. SPA, STR//1A/150, Agreements With 31 Tenants witnessed by Michael Dalton, 14 May 1847; Reilly, pp. 65–7. In retrospect, after Major Denis Mahon's murder, John Ross Mahon outlined the entire scheme in some detail. NLI, Microfilm, N558 P928, "Memorandum of the Management of the Strokestown Estate by Ross Mahon," 8 November 1847.
61. *Berean*, 24 June 1847.
62. NLI, MS 10,102 (3), DM to JRM, 11 May 1847.
63. *Berean*, 24 June 1847.
64. John Ross Mahon itemized a list of additional provisions purchased by the Major for each

statute adult, in addition to the government allowance: 6lbs sugar, 10 oz tea, shellcoose [sic] 2 lbs, rice, 8 lbs, oatmeal, 14lbs, herring, 1 dozen, 1lb soap, 1 pint vinegar, pepper and salt; each child under 14 was allocated half of that amount. NLI, Microfilm, N558 P928, "Memorandum of the Management of the Strokestown Estate by Ross Mahon," 8 November 1847.

65. NLI, MS10,102, Denis Mahon to John Ross Mahon, 11 and 14 May 1847.
66. SPA, STR/1A/51, Trial of Cregga Tenants, 14 October 1840.
67. SPA, STR/1A/148, Original Lists of Tenants Assisted, 1847. These were compiled by Dr. Ciarán Reilly and form the corpus of the names on the memorial glass wall, listed by townland, at Strokestown Park.
68. *Berean*, 24 June 1847.
69. SPA, STR/1A/122, Box STR 88, Attached #8 Book, Indian Meal, Given "Gratuitously," 6 August 1846.
70. NLI, MS 10,102 (2), JRM to DM, April 1847.
71. NLI, MS 10,102 (3), DM to JRM, 14 April 1847.
72. NLI, MS 10,102 (2), DM to JRM, 24 May 1847.
73. NLI, MS 10,102 (3), DM to JRM, 27 May 1847.
74. *The Albion*, 10 May 1847, p. 5.
75. NLI, MS 10,102 (2), DM to JRM, 5 June 1847.
76. NLI, MS 10, 102 (3), DM to JRM, 13 June 1847; http/the shipslist.com/1847/index.html
77. NLI, MS 10, 138, Invoice from J&W Robinson, June 1847.
78. The list was compiled in 2014 by Dr. Ciarán Reilly based on SPA, STR/1A/148, Lists of Assisted Tenants by Townland, 1847.
79. NLI, MS 10, 102 (2), DM to JRM, 21 June 1847 and MS10,102 (1), DM to JRM, 25 June 1847.
80. NLI, MS 10,102 (1), DM to JRM, 30 June 1847 and MS 10,102 (2), DM to JRM, 6 July 1847.
81. SPA, STR/1A/134, Mahon to John Ross Mahon, 6 July 1847.
82. Email message from Dr. Ciarán Reilly to the author, 31 March 2020, indicating that there is documentary evidence dated 13 September 1847, in the Strokestown Park Archive, attesting to the fact that the Castlenode tenants were evicted, but readmitted to the townland as caretakers.
83. Marianna O'Gallagher and Rose Masson Dompierre, *Eyewitness Grosse Isle: 1847* (Sainte-Foy, Que: Carraig Books, 1995), Appendix, Table 8, p. 353.
84. *Quebec Chronicle*, 24 August 1847.
85. André Charbonneau and Doris Drolet-Dubé, eds., *A Register of Deceased Persons at Sea and on Grosse Île in 1847* (Ottawa: Canadian Heritage, Parks Canada, 1997); *Freeman's Journal*, 29 April 1848.
86. NLI, MS 10,102 (2), JRM to DM, 8 June 1847 (copy).

CHAPTER THREE

LIVERPOOL AND THE MISSING 1,490

Christine Kinealy

If Major Denis Mahon had remained true to his original idea of sending his tenants to Canada via the port of Sligo, the subsequent history of the "Strokestown 1,490" could have been very different.[1] Sligo town was located approximately 48 miles (almost 80 kilometres) to the east of Strokestown and ships that arrived in Quebec from the Irish port in the summer of 1847 recorded little to no disease or deaths during the journey.[2] However, at the encouragement of John Ross Mahon, the newly appointed estate agent, the Strokestown emigrants sailed from Liverpool, a journey that entailed a walk of 100 miles (160 kilometres) to Dublin, a sailing to Liverpool across the notoriously rough Irish Sea, spending time in the overwhelmed city of Liverpool while awaiting a transatlantic sailing, and a further journey onward to Canada, with untold days in between spent walking or sleeping out of doors. In this way, the city of Liverpool unwittingly became part of the Strokestown story. Moreover, as thousands of poor refugees from the Famine arrived in the city every day, their individual experiences became part of a wider narrative of suffering and survival that extended far beyond the island of Ireland.

Liverpool in 1847 was the second largest city in Britain. It was also the main port for transatlantic sailings but had passenger and trading links with all parts of the globe. The city had grown rapidly following the ending of the Napoleonic War in 1815. In the decade 1821 to 1831, the population had increased by 40 per cent. Two decades later, it had grown to approximately 250,000.[3] For its inhabitants, Liverpool represented a tale of two cities, with extreme poverty co-existing alongside conspicuous wealth and grandeur. A parliamentary committee in 1840 had confirmed that the city was the unhealthiest in the United Kingdom.[4] At that stage, approximately 60,000 people, almost 25 per cent of the city's population, were Irish born, and they overwhelmingly lived in overcrowded, unsanitary cellars or in high density, back-to-back, poor quality "courts."[5] Perhaps not surprising, they accounted for 50 per cent of all patients seeking medical relief.[6] Just as disturbing was the perception that the Irish accounted for almost half of all criminals in the city.[7]

In contrast with the abject poverty, Liverpool was flourishing, largely as a result of its maritime activities. Since 1815, the wealth of the city had increased by an estimated 136 per cent.[8] As Dr. William Duncan informed a parliamentary committee in 1840, "the external appearance of the place, whether from its docks, from its warehouses, or the general aspect of the buildings in its surrounding districts, is that of the most prosperous description."[9] The dock area was expanding—a new custom house had been opened, and property prices were rising with the wealthy inhabitants living in villas on the outskirts of the city surrounded by pleasure grounds. From the 1820s, a number of the local "merchant princes" settled in the newly developed and highly prestigious Abercromby Square.[10] Only 20 years later, these "respectable" residents would object to the local authorities about the opening of fever sheds in the vicinity of their expensive homes.[11] Liverpool was divided in other significant ways, namely by religion and politics. In the 1840s, the city's governance was controlled by Tories, who were overwhelmingly Protestant and conservative. This dominance extended to the Poor Law Guardians, referred to as the Select Vestry, who administered the local Poor Law. By the 1840s, the Liverpool Workhouse contained a disproportionate number of Irish Catholics and it became a battle-ground for many of the sectarian confrontations being fought in Ireland.[12] These divisions were intensified by the exodus precipitated by the Famine.

In the early nineteenth century, Liverpool had established its role as the hub of the passenger trade from Ireland and to the rest of the world. Consequently, the city was the first port of call for many emigrants escaping from the Famine, as a place of refuge or as a staging post for travelling to other places in Britain or taking a longer journey overseas, be it North America or Australia. The city's economy and infrastructure were geared towards this rapid inflow and outflow of people but its resources were stretched to the limit following the second and more devastating failure of the potato crop in 1846. The reappearance of blight, far earlier in the harvest season, unleashed an exodus from Ireland that would not begin to abate until 1853. The impact was overwhelming; in the week ending 19 December 1846, 13,471 passengers arrived from Ireland, compared with only 888 a year earlier. A worried Select Vestry petitioned the Home Secretary to stop the influx. He refused to intervene.[13] The *Times* of London—no friend to the Irish poor or to Irish landlords—entered the debate on behalf of the beleaguered city, claiming, "the anticipated invasion of Irish pauperism has commenced, 15,000 have already, within the last three months, landed in Liverpool and blocked up her thoroughfares with masses of misery."[14]

The impact on the city was visible and increasingly deadly. By the end of January 1847, soup kitchens in the city were feeding between 25,000 and 26,000 daily, "out of which number, more than 22,000 were destitute Irish persons."[15] The Select Vestry again petitioned the London parliament to intervene and stop the influx, pointing out, "the people of Ireland as well as the people of England should be compelled to support their own poor."[16] Even at this stage, the Liverpool authorities were blaming the "landed proprietors of Ireland" for a dereliction of their duty.[17] Their anger was increasingly focused on those in Ireland who enabled this influx by paying the fares across the Irish Sea, thus shifting the burden from Irish to English taxpayers. Prominent in this list were Irish landlords, although several Irish boards of guardians were also blamed. During a heated discussion by the Select Vestry in April, when government intervention was again sought, the chairman pondered, "whether it would be lawful if the inhabitants of Liverpool were to subscribe and send 10,000 Irish paupers up to London?"[18] These debates suggested that even as people were dying in Ireland and in the ports of Britain, a scapegoat was being sought, and Irish landlords were more and more the main culprits.

The issue of Irish immigrants in Liverpool and other British ports was discussed frequently in Westminster in the early months of 1847.[19] A connection was being made both locally and within parliament between mass evictions in the west of Ireland and the arrival of poor Irish in Liverpool.[20] During a debate on this issue in the House of Lords, the Marquess of Westmeath defended his fellow Irish proprietors, protesting "against the aspersions and imputations that were constantly cast upon the Irish landlords."[21] Again, the government chose not to intervene either to stop the evictions or the emigration. Despite acknowledging the pressure that this immigration was putting on Liverpool, the number of Irish continued to rise throughout 1847, with May and June recording the highest number of arrivals in the port—26,943 and 25,456 respectively.[22]

Typhus, known as Irish fever, had appeared in the city in February, with newspapers reporting that "fever is following on the heels of famine."[23] Within weeks, three poor law officials had died and two more were "dangerously ill." Irish immigrants were blamed.[24] Only two months later, deaths would become commonplace. At the recommendation of Dr. Duncan, three fever sheds were opened between Brownlow

Hill (the site of the local workhouse) and Mount Pleasant. The location was a short distance from some of the most prestigious homes in Liverpool, prompting the calling of public meetings and the signing of petitions demanding their removal. A Memorial was sent to the Home Secretary "against the occupation of the obnoxious sheds with fever patients and thanks were voted to the public press for their advocacy of rights and feelings of the aggrieved inhabitants."[25] Despite numerous protests, over the ensuing months the number of fever sheds in the city increased with additional ones opened in Great Howard Street adjoining the Clarence Dock, where the passenger ships from Ireland first docked.[26]

By the time the first emigrants from Strokestown arrived in Liverpool, any initial sympathy for the Irish had turned to anger and despair as the streets of Liverpool had become thronged with paupers, fever sheds were being erected in central locations, the workhouse was full and poor rates had risen from *2s 1d* to *4s 1d*.[27] Adding to the general antipathy towards the Irish presence were frequent reports in the local newspapers about Irish people pretending to be destitute. In late April, a local newspaper ran an article entitled "More thriving pauperism" about three different Irish people (two men and one woman) who had applied to the Relieving Officer on the grounds that they were destitute, but when searched, had been found to be in possession of relatively large amounts of money. They were all imprisoned for their deception.[28]

In May, following months of appeals from the local authorities for financial support, the government finally took some action, including an order that ships arriving from Ireland should be monitored for disease before docking. They also allowed two quarantine ships, the *Akbar* and *Newcastle*, to be used as floating hospitals. Two more vessels were subsequently added.[29] It was not enough to stop the spread of disease and the measures fell far short of the repeated requests for paupers to be prevented from leaving Ireland. Moreover, the cost of these additional facilities fell largely on the ratepayers of Liverpool. The death of the captain of the *Akbar*, followed shortly by that of his assistant, would have inspired little faith in the efficacy of the hospital ships.[30] At the end of May, the Health Committee of the Select Vestry reported that mortality had risen to 20,000 a year, compared with the ordinary mortality of 8,000 annually. Immigration into Liverpool peaked in June, bringing with it more deaths. The death of front-line care-givers was becoming commonplace. St Patrick's church had lost three priests to "Irish" fever, while a fourth priest was "seriously indisposed."[31] The usual Sunday masses had to be suspended. By the end of June, eight Roman Catholic priests had succumbed to fever, in addition to the barber who worked in the fever sheds, and several more relieving officers.[32] While fever was the major cause of mortality, Dr. Duncan reported that smallpox had reached epidemic proportions. This was attributed to the influx of the Irish, "for their children seldom underwent the operation of vaccination when at home."[33] Duncan also warned the Select Vestry that that "so long as the influx of Irish paupers continued unchecked, no amount of work done, or exertion made [would] arrest the progress of fever." Inevitably, it was the poorest who were most at risk, with the highest number of deaths occurring in the Exchange, Vauxhall, and St. Anne's Wards—all close to the Clarence Dock and all with large Irish populations.[34] It is likely that many Irish immigrants, including those from Strokestown, would have stayed in the dockland area while awaiting their transatlantic passage from the nearby Waterloo Dock.

While Liverpool was struggling to deal with wave after wave of immigrants, Major Mahon, from the comfort of his various clubs and hotels in England, was paying careful attention to the preparations regarding the movement of what he hoped would be between 2,000 and 3,000 poor from his estate. As he signed the notices to quit in early April, from his club in the prestigious Pall Mall district of London, Mahon's main regret appeared to be that it was 'the better sort of tenant' who wanted to emigrate from his estate.[35] It was no surprise, therefore, when he told Ross Mahon, his newly appointed estate agent, that the first batch of emigrants should be tenants of "the poorest & worst description."[36] Cost was an ongoing concern and Major Mahon quizzed Ross Mahon on, amongst other things, the cheapest passages, the amount, type and quantity of provisions to be provided on the voyage, and the cost of accommodation and stores while they were waiting to sail. The Atlantic crossing represented the main expense and Mahon was assured by Ross Mahon that the cost of a passage from Liverpool was "much the same" as departing from an Irish port.[37] Mahon's letter of 13 April suggested that both men were in agreement that the emigrants should sail from Sligo.[38] Yet, for some reason this decision was reversed. At the end of April, Ross Mahon was in Liverpool making preparations for the first consignment of emigrants to arrive there and then travel onwards to Canada.[39] Why did the Major change his mind? Why was the longer and more arduous journey chosen that entailed spending time in the fever-ridden city of Liverpool? Did the casual observation regarding cost made by Ross Mahon seal the fate of the Strokestown emigrants? Whatever the reason for Liverpool being chosen over Sligo, the Strokestown emigrants now had to walk over 100 miles (160 kilometers) before even boarding a ship.

Ross Mahon was briefly joined in Liverpool by Major Mahon, who arrived from London by train on the evening of 5 May.[40] At the time of their meeting in the Adelphi Hotel, the initial batch of emigrants were preparing for the first leg of the journey to Dublin. The Adelphi Hotel—the accommodation favored by Major Mahon—had opened in Liverpool in 1826, with the ambition of becoming one of the most luxurious hotels in Europe.[41] It soon established its position as the preferred hotel for nobility, royalty and the rich and idle when in the city.[42] When Major Mahon had his face-to-face meeting with Ross Mahon in the hotel in early May, they were seated only half a mile from the newly opened—and extremely controversial—fever sheds. The residents who lived in the space between the hotel and sheds had protested vociferously, but unsuccessfully, to have the sheds relocated.[43] The health of the city, and the prevalent of "Irish Fever," was frequently discussed in the press and in parliament, so both men must have been aware of the risks to emigrants, even those who only stayed for a short time while awaiting their transatlantic passage. On 8 May, from London, Mahon informed his former land agent, Thomas Conry, that he expected that the first batch of Strokestown emigrants would arrive in the English port before the end of the month—"Detachment to be at L'pool [Liverpool] for Embarkation on the 25th or 26th."[44]

During Mahon's brief stay in Liverpool, he signed a memorandum with a local shipping firm, J. and W. Robinson. The agreement was that 200 to 300 "statute'" adults would be taken to Canada at the cost of £3–2–6*d*. The cost rose to between £3–12*s* and £3–15*s* when the passage and provisions for the journey from Dublin to Liverpool was factored in. Children aged under 14 would travel at half price.[45] By the 1840s, there were 21 licensed passenger brokers in Liverpool. Because of the competition in the trade, fares could vary from day to day, even from hour to hour, fluctuating from as low as £3–10s to over £5 for a passenger in steerage.[46] Even before blight had appeared in Ireland, the Robinson brothers, through their agent Denis Delany, had established a market presence in Ireland.[47] Irish emigrants were assured that on board their ships from Liverpool to North America, all passengers "will be supplied with good bread stuffs, and pure water, at the daily rate of one pound of bread stuffs and three quarts of water per adult and ... all persons who are detained in Liverpool, after the time of sailing, will be allowed subsistence money." Moreover, prospective passengers were told that there would be "Medicine supplied Gratis."[48]

Back in London, Mahon kept a close eye on his tenants' movements and the costs being incurred, especially as he was having to find the money to finance the journeys. He was particularly concerned that the first batch of emigrants would be speedily and efficiently got "over the line,"[49] possibly being worried that if this did not happen, it would be a disincentive for subsequent batches to leave Ireland. In expectation that the emigrants would have to spend some time in Liverpool, Mahon agreed to pay the Robinsons £200 for accommodation and "stores."[50] Unfortunately, in the context of Liverpool in the 1840s, accommodation meant the already overcrowded and disease-ridden cellars.[51] Mahon was clearly concerned that there could be sickness on the ships sailing from Dublin to Liverpool. This was particularly worrying to him as, on 5 May, Orders in Council had been passed, requiring that ships arriving in the River Mersey be searched, and sick passengers be moved to a lazaretto, that is, ships that had been designated as quarantine stations.[52] By these new regulations:

> All passenger vessels arriving from Ireland shall be boarded by the tide surveyors, who shall cause the yellow flag to be hoisted and kept flying at the mast head, until such vessel shall have been examined by the medical staff appointed for the purpose, and until the sick, if there be any such on board, shall have been removed direct to the lazaretto.[53]

Additionally, the commanders of all passenger vessels from Ireland were informed that should any of their vessels arrive in Liverpool a second time with sick people on board, their vessels would be quarantined for an indefinite length of time. By these orders also, two of the lazarettos already in the river were to be used as hospitals for the sick[54] As Mahon would have realized, these new regulations could seriously interfere with his plan for a swift transition through Liverpool, he warning both Ross Mahon and the Robinsons:

> This in itself will cause a few days delay, therefore be so kind a to make allowance for it, we must avoid sending any that are ill or likely to be reported as "Fever Cases" when inspected at Liverpool.[55]

When Mahon was persuaded to send his emigrants through Liverpool this was an added complication he could not have foreseen and, in retrospect, made this route even more problematic.

As the emigrants made their slow progress from Strokestown to Dublin and onward to Liverpool, Mahon was monitoring their movements through a frequent correspondence with Ross Mahon. By 11 May, Mahon had adjusted the arrival date of the first batch to 23 or 24 of May. He was also expressing some reservations about using the Robinson company for all of his tenants, telling Ross Mahon:

> I am of opinion that in the 1st instance the 300 are sufficient to send at present & have no doubt from what we agreed on in our Conversation at L'pool you will be of the same Opinion—I shall not answer M Robinson's letter as to the sending any more than the 300 until I hear from you, what answer you may be inclined to send him.[56]

More concerning, perhaps, was Mahon's awareness of the prevalence of disease, he informing his agent that, "I fear the Passage to L'pool will have sickness at least so the papers say."[57]

In mid-May, Mahon used much of his time in London raising the money to pay the Robinson company. He was already thinking about subsequent groups of emigrants but clearly wanted to use different shipping agents, telling Ross Mahon, "I trust you may be able to get some of them to Quebec on better terms than we made with Messrs. Robinson."[58] His trust in his agent was evident when he added, "I am satisfied you will make the best terms you can."[59] At this stage, Ross Mahon was preparing to return to Liverpool, possibly to oversee the safe and full dispatch of the emigrants to Canada and ensure there was no slippage when they reached the bustling English port. Even as preparations for their departure were being made in Strokestown, Ross Mahon was negotiating with different shipping agents in Liverpool—Shaws Company—regarding their terms for passage to Quebec.[60] These discussions appeared to have come to nothing as Mahon continued to send money to the Robinsons. Moreover, Ross Mahon remained dutifully in Liverpool to oversee the first group of emigrants who sailed on the *Virginius* at the end of May, with the "surplus" sailing a few days later on *Erin's Queen*.[61] A few weeks later, the *Naomi* and the *John Munn* would carry the next batches of emigrants from Strokestown to Quebec, J. and W. Robinson having made all the arrangements.

In early June, as a fresh batch of Strokestown immigrants arrived in Liverpool and disease and mortality continued to increase, members of the Select Vestry, accompanied by Dr. Duncan and two local MPs, Lord Sandon and Sir Howard Douglas, travelled to London to plead with the government to stop the Irish inflow.[62] There, they met with the Home Secretary to discuss the deteriorating health of their city.[63] Estimates of the number of Irish paupers who had landed at Liverpool since the beginning of the year varied greatly, with one Irish politician placing it at 236,000, while the Select Vestry believed it was closer to 300,000.[64] The British government acknowledged its reluctance to stop the Irish from emigrating, but they did introduce legislation that made it easier for Poor Law officials in Britain to return them to Ireland. Yet again, it was a measure that placed the burden—and the cost—on local authorities, and not on the central government. In the face of government inaction, some people in Liverpool and other British ports suggested that the solution to the problems they were facing was to return the Irish poor back to their country. This was a slow and costly legal process.

The concept of "settlement," which had been part of the English and Welsh Poor Law since the time of Elizabeth I, meant that the Irish poor had no legal right to poor law relief unless they could prove residency. Removal, however, was a complex and costly process that involved serving a summons and the deportees appearing before a magistrate, who could order their removal by signing a warrant.[65] Towards the end of April 1847, the Select Vestry in Liverpool petitioned the House of Commons asking that the pauper influx from Ireland to ports like Liverpool and Glasgow be controlled.[66] They pointed out that since the beginning of the year, only 48,136 of the Irish who arrived in Liverpool had emigrated. Of those remaining, they believed that the vast majority had come with the expectation of seeking relief, not employment. Although they could be removed under poor law legislation, both the cost and the bureaucracy proved prohibitive. As the weather improved, they expected the numbers to grow. Many who came were ill, and it was not simply paupers who were dying, but medical officers and nurses. They added that while they wanted to extend justice and charity to Ireland, they believed the people of Liverpool deserved the same. A thousand copies of the petition were printed for distribution in the town.[67] In the acrimonious debate that followed in the House of Commons, Fitzstephen French, the MP for Roscommon, defended the Irish immigrants, saying:

> The English would allow the poor Irish to come in and cut the harvest, or assist in the manufactures of the country, when anything could be got by using the labour of Irishmen; but the moment their crops failed, or trade became dull, they would throw them back for subsistence to their own country.[68]

His was a minority voice and in June 1847, an act was passed that simplified and expedited the process of removal.[69] As a consequence, removals from Liverpool immediately increased and, by August, between 400 and 500 Irish were being shipped home each week, which was far higher than from any other British port.[70] The Liverpool authorities hoped that the new policy would deter any fresh arrivals from seeking relief. It was amidst this atmosphere of hostility and fear that the Strokestown emigrants and thousands of other Irish poor had arrived in the city.

In September 1847, Dr. Duncan was able to provide the Select Vestry with some good news—since August, the number of fever cases had been declining and the city was returning to its ordinary state of health.[71] Following the peak in June, the number of arrivals from Ireland was also falling, helped by a rigorous application of the power to return them, which appeared to have deterred people from lingering in Liverpool or applying for poor relief. The Select Vestry responded to the improving health situation by closing some of the auxiliary fever sheds and emergency medical stations, while refusing the government's offer that an additional quarantine ship be placed in the Mersey.[72] A new disease, "ship fever," was identified as the source of the problem, it arising from "the combined influence of imperfect nutrition, vitiated air, filth, and moral depression," all of which was exacerbated by "the gross personal uncleanliness of the Irish poor especially ... increased by the apathy arising from want of physical strength and of proper food."[73] It was a gloomy insight into the state of Irish emigrants who were travelling beyond Liverpool. By this time, the vessels that had carried the Strokestown 1,490 to Canada had all arrived, but in a condition that would cause shock and outrage on both sides of the Atlantic. The same newspaper that carried Duncan's encouraging report, included a long article about mortality on passenger vessels to North America and the need for fever sheds to be erected on the other side of the Atlantic. In the early months of 1847, the port of Liverpool had been at the center of many discussions about Irish emigration. By summer, the focus was shifting to Canada as the colony's ports became the new frontier of Famine suffering.

The year 1847 is enshrined in Irish history as "Black '47." However, the horror of that year extended far beyond Ireland. Between mid-January and mid-December 1847, almost 300,000 people arrived in Liverpool from Ireland.[74] More shocking than the sheer number of arrivals, was the description by Edward Rushton, the city's Stipendiary Magistrate, that 40 per cent of them were "half naked and starving."[75] More graphically, Dr. Duncan described Liverpool in that year as "the city of plague."[76] He believed the unprecedented levels of disease and death resulted from the "hordes of sickly and half-starved Irish" flooding into the city and spreading fever.[77] The medical journal, the *Lancet*, referring to the impact of the Irish exodus, described the "starving and fever-stricken" migrants who arrived in the first six months of 1847: "80,000 ... located themselves in dog-kennels and cellars, and remained to glut the labour market and propagate a wretched mode of life. In this unhappy year, 60,000 persons were attacked with fever, and 40,000 with dysentery."[78]

The timing of the Famine influx was inauspicious as there was a trade slump throughout the United Kingdom in 1847, that resulted in widespread unemployment and short hours in many industries. Regardless of the existence of the United Kingdom with one central government, Ireland was treated differently, especially regarding poverty. This was evident from the draconian Irish Poor Law introduced in 1838.[79] Moreover, the use of the settlement laws to summarily return people to Ireland was a clear signal that the "United" Kingdom existed in name only. For the emigrants from Strokestown and elsewhere, Canada offered a sanctuary that was not offered to them in Britain. Sadly, what faced them after Liverpool was equally grim. On 9 June, around the same time that the second batch of Strokestown emigrants were arriving in Liverpool, Archbishop Joseph Signay of Quebec issued a circular letter to the Catholic Archbishops and Bishops of Ireland, which opened by warning of "the dismal fate that awaits thousands of the unfortunate children of Ireland who come to seek in Canada an asylum from the countless evils afflicting them in their native land." He ended by asking that the Irish bishops "use every effort to dissuade your diocesans from emigrating in such numbers to Canada."[80] The warning was too late as Irish landowners and the British government aligned in their desire to clear Ireland of its poorer classes. For his part in this clearance, Major Mahon would pay with his life, being assassinated on 2 November 1847 as he returned from a meeting of the Roscommon Board of Guardians.[81]

The experience of Liverpool reinforced the fact that the British government's response to the poor Irish was tardy, limited, and piecemeal, they preferring to place responsibility on local authorities, whether they were in Ireland, Liverpool, Montreal, Toronto, or Glasgow. Lack of enforceable legislation, especially when it came to travel by sea, compounded the problem of people fleeing from a crisis.[82] Emigration had long been regarded as a palliative to Ireland's endemic poverty and the government did not want to slow down the process. Thus, the Strokestown 1,490, and hundreds of thousands of other Irish poor famine emigrants, found themselves caught in the middle of a longer term and ongoing debate about poverty in Ireland.[83] Consequently, appalling conditions on the passenger steamers to Britain and those vessels that sailed further afield were tolerated. Liverpool, a city with its own problems, was caught in the middle of this maelstrom. For many refugees from famine, the city was only one step in a much longer journey of sorrow and misery. The deaths of so many tenants of Major Mahon, which shocked opinion on both sides of the Atlantic, was further testimony to a system in which the poor Irish were expendable.

What happened to James and William Robinson who were a central part of the Strokestown and Liverpool story? In a business where defrauding passengers had become commonplace, the Robinson brothers had an unenviable reputation. The name of their company and its location changed often but in 1847, they were operating out of 48 Waterloo Road in Liverpool.[84] The brothers were no strangers to the local court rooms. A newspaper article in June 1846 entitled "Important to Emigrants" had reported that they had been found guilty of over-selling passenger tickets to New York. For this misdemeanor, they were ordered to repay the fares and three guineas to each of the three accusers.[85] It may not have been a surprise, therefore, that over summer 1847, the Robinson Company remitted money to Major Mahon for overcharging him for passengers who had left on the *Virginius* and the *John Munn*—the first and the final of the four ships carrying the Strokestown emigrants, which had sailed on the 28/29 May and the 16/17 June, respectively. Mahon used this money to pay for a number of his tenants to emigrate to New York.[86]

The Robinson business appeared to flourish. The *Naomi,* one of the ships that had achieved notoriety in August 1847 for the appalling condition of its passengers, reappeared later in the year, the Robinson brothers advertising her as "the splendid new ship *Naomi* under Captain Wright", which was about to undertake her third voyage to New York.[87] Shortly after this, the brothers moved location and by May 1848, a year after the fateful events of previous year, they were operating out of the Baltic Buildings on Redcross Street. The same month, they advertised that "the very superior ship *Naomi*" would be soon sailing to Quebec. The *Naomi* was now described as "not two years old; a remarkably fast sailer; and in all respects a most desirable conveyance."[88] The Robinsons reemerged in another way when they inserted themselves into a national debate regarding emigration. In a letter to the President of the Board of Trade in early 1848, they object to new measures being considered to address the issue of the previous year's mortality amongst emigrants to Canada. The letter from the Robinsons, which was widely reprinted, provided a frank insight into the health of those people being removed in this way:

> They were dispirited and heart-broken, and having neither physical strength nor mental vigour to resist the first feeble attack of disease, they speedily became a sacrifice to its ravages. Great and fearful was the mortality even among this class, it must be borne in mind, that it was equally great among the same class at home in Ireland. What humanity requires of government appears to us to be, *special regulations* for the emigrants cleared off Irish estates, and sent out at the expense of the landlords—and not new and needless, but expensive, regulations affecting emigration generally.[89]

In light of what happened to the Strokestown 1,490, their intervention in such a forum might be considered a public rebuke to the then dead Major Mahon—or perhaps they were absolving themselves from any culpability? Changes were made that had an impact on the Robinsons. In 1850, legislation was tightened up regarding granting licenses for "passage brokers," they now having to provide two sureties to the value of £200.[90]

It is impossible to know precisely how long the Strokestown emigrants spent in Liverpool, or to what extent their stay in the city or conditions on board the emigrant ships contributed to disease and mortality after they left the port. One London newspaper, written following the assassination of Major Mahon, suggested that the Strokestown emigrants had been delayed in Liverpool and during that time they had come under the influence of "evil" Jesuits, who made them dissatisfied that they had been forced to leave their homes.[91] Seeing the emigration through the retrospective prism of Mahon's murder may serve to obfuscate rather than elucidate what happened to the Strokestown emigrants during their time in Liverpool. Much remains unknown and unknowable about their fate. It is possible, however, that if they had journeyed to Canada via Sligo, many lives could have spared, including that of Major Mahon.

NOTES

1. National Library of Ireland (NLI), Mahon Papers, MS 10,102 (9), Denis Mahon to Ross Mahon, Coburg Hotel, Charles Street, London, 2 April 1847; Ibid., MS 10,1002 (5), Denis Mahon to John Ross Mahon, United Service Club, Pall Mall, London, 13 April 1847.
2. Ship arrivals at the port of Quebec in 1847,' www.theshipslist.com/1847/shipsaug1847.shtml
3. Evidence of Dr. Duncan, *Report from the Select Committee on the Health of Towns; together with the minutes evidence taken before them, and an appendix, and index*, BPP (London: House of Commons, 17 June 1840), p. 141.
4. Ibid.
5. Ibid., qu. 2522, p. 150.
6. Ibid., qus 2536, 2539, 2540, pp. 150–1.
7. This opinion was stated by Augustus Campbell, Chairman of the Select Vestry in 1849, BPP, *Select Committee on Poor Removal and Settlement* (XVII, 1854*)*, qu. 4954.
8. "The Health of Towns Association," *Liverpool Mail*, 12 December 1846.
9. Evidence of Dr. Duncan, *Report from the Select Committee on the Health of Towns*, qus 2529, 2530, 2531, 2532, p. 150.
10. "The history and building of Abercromby square, Liverpool," at: www.yoliverpool.com /forum/showthread.php?95122-The-History-and-Building-of-Abercromby-Square-Liverpool.
11. "Liverpool and the Irish. The Health of the Public," *Manchester Courier and Lancashire General Advertiser*, 12 May 1847.
12. Thomas Burke, *Catholic History of Liverpool* (Liverpool: C. Tinling and Co., 1910).
13. Select Vestry to Sir George Grey, Home Secretary, 24 December 1846, BPP, *Relief of distress in Ireland* (Board of Work Series, House of Commons, 1847, vol. 6), pp. 435–436.
14. *Times*, 5 January 1847.
15. Lord Brougham, "Distress in Ireland," *Hansard,* House of Lord Debates, 28 January 1847, vol. 89, c. 502.
16. Ibid., "Irish Paupers in Liverpool," 1 February 1847, vol. 89, c. 612.
17. Ibid., c. 614.
18. "Meeting of the Select Vestry," *Liverpool Mercury*, 30 April 1847.
19. "Irish Poor in Liverpool," *Hansard,* House of Lord Debates, 4 February 1847, vol. 89, cc. 770–1; Ibid., "Irish Poor in Liverpool," 16 February 1847, vol. 90, cc. 1–3.
20. Ibid.
21. Ibid., 1 February 1847, vol. 89, c. 615.
22. "Select committee on settlement and removal" (1854), was created at behest of Edward Rushton, qu. 4954.
23. "At Liverpool," *Home News for India, China and the Colonies*, 8 March 1847.
24. "Fever in Liverpool,' *Leeds Times*, 27 February 1847.
25. "The Fever Sheds in Mount Pleasant," *Gore's Liverpool General Advertiser*, 29 April 1847; "The Fever Sheds', *Liverpool Mercury*, 30 April 1847; "The Fever Sheds," *Liverpool Mail*, 1 May 1847; "Select Vestry,*" Liverpool Standard and General Commercial* Advertiser, 4 May 1847.
26. "Health Committee," *Liverpool Mail*, 5 June 1847.

27. Evidence of Edward Rushton, stipendiary magistrate, *Select Committee on the Settlement and Removal of Paupers*, BPP, 1847, xi, qus 4328–34.
28. "More thriving pauperism," *Gore's Liverpool General Advertiser*, 29 April 1847.
29. "Another Casualty from Fever," *Liverpool Mail,* 10 July 1847.
30. Ibid., "Deaths from Fever," *Liverpool Mail*, 28 August 1847.
31. "Death of another Roman Catholic clergyman in Liverpool," *Dublin Evening Post*, 29 June 1847. A memorial erected in St Patrick's Church in 1898 identified 10 "Martyr Priests" who died in 1847. For more, see, "Memorial to the Martyr Priests," at: liverpoolmonuments .co.uk/pat01.html
32. "Death of another Roman Catholic Priest," *Liverpool Mercury*, 29 June 1847.
33. "The Health Committee," *Liverpool Mail,* 17 July 1847.
34. Ibid., 5 June 1847.
35. NLI, Mahon Papers, MS 10,102 (8), Denis Mahon to John Ross Mahon, US Club, Pall Mall, London, 14 April 1847.
36. Ibid.
37. Ibid., (4), Denis Mahon to John Ross Mahon, 8 April 1847.
38. Ibid., (5), Denis Mahon to John Ross Mahon, US Club, Pall Mall, London, 13 April 1847.
39. Ibid., (9), Denis Mahon to John Ross Mahon, Belmont Hotel, Hereford, 30 April 1847.
40. Ibid., (4), Denis Mahon to John Ross Mahon, Mivarts Hotel, Brook Street, London, 4 May 1847.
41. "The Adelphi," at: bbc.co.uk/liverpool/localhistory/journey/lime_street/adelphi/hotel.shtml #:~:text=The%20first%20Adelphi%20Hotel%20on,acquired%20and%20rebuilt%20 the%20Adelphi.
42. "Arrivals at the Adelphi", *Saunders's News-Letter*, 25 October 1836.
43. See, Christine Kinealy, 'A City of Plague. Dr. Duncan of Liverpool', in Christine Kinealy, Jason King and Gerard Moran, *Heroes of Ireland's Great Hunger* (Hamden: Quinnipiac University Press, 2021), chapter nine.
44. Strokestown Park Archive, (SPA), STR/1A/111, Dennis Mahon to Thomas Conry, from United Service Club, 8 May 1847.
45. NLI (8), Mahon Papers, MS 10,102, Notes by Denis Mahon, made while in Liverpool, 6 May 1847.
46. "Emigration from Liverpool," *Illustrated London News*, 6 July 1850.
47. "Packet ships for New York," *Dublin Weekly Nation,* 8 March 1845, 11 March 1848.
48. Ibid., "Line of packet ships," 19 July 1845.
49. This phrase was used in letter from Denis Mahon to John Ross Mahon, NLI, Mahon Papers, MS 10,102 (8), Mivarts Hotel, London, 12 May 1847.
50. Ibid., (7), 24 May 1847.
51. A report by Dr. Duncan and others in 1840, revealed the average life span of people in Liverpool's cellars was 15 years of age, *Report from the Select Committee on the Health of Towns; together with the minutes evidence taken before them, and an appendix, and index* (London: House of Commons, 17 June 1840), p. xi.
52. Letter from William Bathurst, Council Office, Whitehall, London, 5 May 1847, reprinted in *Liverpool Mail*, 8 May 1847; NLI, Mahon Papers, MS 10,102 (8), Denis Mahon to John

Ross Mahon and Robinson, Mivarts Hotel, London, 11 May 1847, in which the Major expressed his concern at this new development.

53. "Liverpool and the Irish. The Health of the Public," *Manchester Courier and Lancashire General Advertiser*, 12 May 1847.
54. Ibid.
55. NLI, Mahon Papers, MS 10,102 (8), Denis Mahon to John Ross Mahon and Robinson, Mivarts Hotel, London, 11 May 1847.
56. Ibid., Denis Mahon to John Ross Mahon, 12 May 1847.
57. Ibid.
58. Ibid., 20 May 1847.
59. Ibid.
60. Ibid., (7), John Ross Mahon to Shaws of Liverpool, Strokestown, 20 May 1847.
61. Ibid., (8), Denis Mahon to John Ross Mahon, Mivarts Hotel, London, 27 May 1847.
62. "Irish Fever in Liverpool," *Vindicator* (Belfast), 30 June 1847.
63. "Health of the Town," *Liverpool Standard and General Commercial Advertiser*, 22 June 1847.
64. The first figure was provided by the Earl of Wicklow in the debate regarding Settlement, and the second by the Select Vestry: Poor Removal (England and Scotland) bill, *Hansard,* House of Lords Debates, 7 June 1847, vol. 93 c. 174; "The Health Committee," *Liverpool Mail*, 17 July 1847.
65. The passing of the Five Years Residency Act in August 1846 (9 and 10th Vic., cap. 66), before the impact of Famine emigration became felt, had further complicated the matter.
66. "To the Honorable the Commons of Great Britain and Ireland," *Liverpool Mercury*, 30 April 1847.
67. Ibid.
68. "Poor Removal (England and Scotland) bill, *Hansard*, House of Commons Debates, 7 May 1847, vol. 92, cc. 546–53.
69. The Poor Removal Act (10 and 11 Vic., c. 33); "The Irish Fever in Liverpool," *Vindicator*, 30 June 1847.
70. "Select Vestry," *Liverpool Mail*, 7 August 1847.
71. "Health of the Town," *Liverpool Standard and General Commercial Advertiser*, 21 September 1847.
72. "Select Vestry," *Liverpool Mail*, 7 August 1847.
73. "The late Dr. Andrew Combe on the mortality in emigrant vessels, its causes, and mode of prevention," *Liverpool Standard and General Commercial Advertiser*, 21 September 1847.
74. These figures were provided by Rushton to the Home Secretary, the former having placed police at the Clarence Dock for the purpose of counting arrivals from Ireland, and charging them with the virtually impossible task of categorizing arrivals as "poor" or as "pauper."
75. *Select Committee on Removal* (1854), qu. 4954.
76. Lancashire Record Office, Medical Officer of Health Reports, W. H. Duncan, Report to the Health Committee of the Borough of Liverpool, on the Health of the Town during the Years 1847–48–49–50 (Liverpool: 1851), p. 7.

77. Ibid.
78. Report of the *Lancet* Sanitary Commission on Relapsing Fever in Liverpool, and on the General Sanitary Condition of the Town," no. II, "The Site and the Sewers," *Lancet,* 19 November 1870, 710–713, p. 711.
79. Christine Kinealy "The Operation of the Poor Law During the Famine," *Atlas of the Great Irish Famine*, eds., John Crowley, William J. Smyth, and Mike Murphy (Cork University Press, 2012), pp. 89–92.
80. *Circular letter to the Catholic Archbishops and Bishops of Ireland, dated 9 June 1847* [S.l.: s.n.]. Available online at: https://babel.hathitrust.org/cgi/pt?id=aeu.ark:/13960/t1xd1rn8f&view=1up&seq=5
81. See the Chapter 7.
82. Oliver McDonagh, *A Pattern of Government Growth 1800–1860: The Passenger Acts and their Enforcement* (London: MacGibbon & Kee, 1961), despite being published over 60 years ago, it still remains an authoritative text on this subject.
83. See Christine Kinealy, *This Great Calamity. The Irish Famine 1845–52* (Dublin: Gill and Macmillan, 2006), which argues that the Famine provided an opportunity for the government to effect long-desired changes in land holding, pp. 342–59.
84. "Packet Ships for New York," *Dublin Weekly* Nation, 8 March 1845, 11 March 1848.
85. "Important to Emigrants," *Manchester Courier and Lancashire General Advertiser*, 20 June 1846.
86. Ciarán Reilly, *Strokestown and the Great Irish Famine* (Dublin: Four Courts Press, 2014), pp. 76–77.
87. "Liverpool to New York," *Gore's Liverpool General Advertiser*, 18 November 1847.
88. "British America," *Liverpool Standard and General Commercial Advertiser*, 30 May 1848, 13 June 1848.
89. "Emigration. The Government Passengers' bill," *Londonderry Sentinel*, 4 March 1848.
90. "Emigration from Liverpool," *Illustrated London News*, 6 July 1850.
91. "Terrorism in Ireland," *Saint James's Chronicle*, 21 December 1847.

CHAPTER FOUR

"PILED UP IN THE BOTTOM OF THE HOLD"

From Liverpool to Quebec[1]

Mark G. McGowan

Mrs. Cox was deeply troubled about the whereabouts of her son Patrick. In May 1847, the "Widow" Cox and her children joined 270 other families from the Mahon estate and left Liverpool on the next leg of their journey to what they hoped would be a new life in Canada. After experiencing a short delay, facing all the miserable challenges Liverpool could offer, the Cox family boarded the *Virginius*, as did most of the other migrants from their townland of Culliagh. On route to their destination, 158 of these famine refugees, or one-third of the registered passengers, perished at sea; 109 more died of infectious disease at the quarantine station at Grosse Île, some 50 kilometres northeast of Quebec on the St. Lawrence River. Patrick Cox had taken ill, and local medical authorities removed him from the *Virginius* to the fever sheds at Grosse Île, with the hope that, after his recovery, he might eventually catch up to the rest of his family as they moved to the interior of Canada. After two months had passed since his last sighting, Patrick's nearly frantic mother posted a notice requesting any information about her son, and directing any correspondence to Hamilton, Canada West, where the family was staying.[2] The Cox's were now over 900 kilometres to the west of where they last laid eyes on Patrick.

The trials of the Cox family speak vividly to the experiences of the Mahon migrants as they made the perilous journey from Liverpool to Quebec. As the assisted migrants from Roscommon made their first venture on the open sea, on board four ships of questionable quality, no one in their company knew what tragedy lay ahead of them. Young Thomas Quinn, who had left the townland of Curhouna, with his family, described his experience on the *Naomi* as being "piled up in the bottom of the hold of an unhealthy ship" (see Chapter 6). Of the entire Quinn family of six, only he and his brother Patrick would survive the ordeal as typhus spread among the passengers and crew when they were at sea. The experiences of the Cox and Quinn families put a human face on the oft-depicted faceless impoverished masses, the hundreds of thousands of Irish who left Ireland for North America, during the Famine. Theirs are among the few stories of the Mahon migrants who survived the voyage and then quarantine at Grosse Île, and, as such, they add new testimony to other pathetic stories of transatlantic migration, previously focused on New Brunswick, Vermont, and New York City.[3] While not all ships travelling to North America in 1847 could be categorized as coffin ships, it is clear that the four ships chartered by John Ross Mahon through the Robinson brothers in Liverpool, could be classified as some of the worst vessels to put to sea during that sailing season. Families like the Cox and the Quinns would be subject to inhumane conditions, poor food, infectious disease, poor weather, and the accompanying sea sickness. As a result, many of the Mahon families would never see Canada, or have the opportunity, should they land, to make a new life for themselves.

The first "batch" of Mahon's assisted migrants left on board two ships departing Liverpool—the *Virginius* and the *Erin's Queen*. The former allegedly was boarded exclusively by Mahon passengers, with the overflow boarding the *Erin's Queen*. The *Virginius* left Liverpool on 28 May 1847, under the direction of Captain Thomas Austin, with 476 statute adults on board. Captain Joseph Davidson's *Erin's Queen* left four days later, on 1 June, with a steerage complement of 493 statute adults, with 100 of these being listed as Mahon's people.[4] John Ross Mahon prepared for a second "batch," the largest group, 350.5 out of 421 statute adults, which set sail under Captain Thomas Wilson on the *Naomi* on 15 June, while the overflow 55 statute adults, sailed on Captain James Watt's ship, the *John Munn*, the following day.[5] Since children under the age of 14 were considered half of a statute adult, and infants were included free of charge, the number of passengers from the Mahon estate would have been far greater than the passenger manifest of the ships' attest. Since no passenger lists survive for any of the four ships, one will likely never know how many of Mahon's people were on board these vessels. The best estimate, based on the ledgers provided by John Ross Mahon, suggest as many as 1,490 persons were part of the scheme. While the actual number may have been more, or perhaps less, it is "The Missing 1,490" which has stuck among historians and locals at Strokestown, as the working collective noun for the migrants in the scheme.

The crossing of the Atlantic of at least three of the ships—*Virginius*, *Naomi*, and *John Munn*—confirm the inherent problems of trying to reconstitute a cargo vessel for one that hauls passengers. These ships, like many others returning to North America from Liverpool, were not properly outfitted for passenger travel. Most of the vessels transporting Famine migrants and others in 1847 were essentially cargo ships that normally would unload their timber, grain, and raw materials in Liverpool and other United Kingdom ports and then make the return trip to North America with rocks or salt as their ballast. Both the *Virginius* and the *Erin's Queen* had recently arrived at Liverpool, having left New Orleans, likely filled with cotton and foodstuffs.[6] For the *Erin's Queen*, the New Orleans to Liverpool run appeared to be its regular trade route, with this Quebec voyage appearing as a brief detour.[7]

During the Famine migration the steerage compartments were refitted with makeshift bunks to allow for human cargo to serve as ballast for the journey back to North America. With hundreds of passengers crammed below deck, in poorly lit areas, and whole families consigned to a single bunk, their living space may have measured eight feet by six feet, with an allowance of 18 inches per person. Additional passenger regulations mandated that these bunks could be stacked not more than two tiers, with six feet of clearance between upper and lower berths, and lower berths at least six inches off the deck.[8] Under such cramped conditions, the ocean voyage was a misery, particularly if one embarked in Liverpool or Cork, which soon gained the reputation of being the unhealthiest ports from which one could depart.

The Colonial Land and Emigration Commission was clear in what these passenger vessels were required to carry in terms of supply. While the length of the voyages, depending on the weather, could vary from as few as 38 days from United Kingdom ports to Halifax, and as long as 46 days from these same ports to Quebec, every ship was required to take on board provisions for 70 days.[9] Given the amount paid per passenger by Mahon, between £3 and £4, the passengers would be provided with the minimum daily rations outlined in the Passenger Act, as opposed to the "full allowance of provisions," that a £4-£5 fare would have fetched. In addition to the provisions supplied by Mahon in the "carts of baggage" that accompanied them, Mahon's tenants, when on board ship, were to be provided with:

> At least three quarts of water per diem … a supply of provisions, not less than twice a week at the rate of 7 *lbs* of bread stuffs per week, half at least to be bread, or biscuit, the other half may be potatoes, of which 5 *lbs* are to be reckoned equal to 1 *lb* of bread stuffs.[10]

The *Guide to Emigrants* advised that if they were not part of the comprehensive victualing plan, as provided by the maximum fare, they were advised to bring with them provisions of meat, fish, split peas for soup, vinegar, tea, mustard, and pepper. Passengers were advised to bring at least two pounds of soap per person.[11] Medicines and medical supplies were also to be stocked on board ship, although the presence of a surgeon or doctor was not required. The sale of alcohol was strictly forbidden and any transgression of this section of the Act could bring a fine of £100 on the offender. In general, any ship found in violation of the Passenger Act faced a fine of £50.[12]

Denis Mahon's passengers on board the *Virginius*, and presumably the other three ships, had their provisions supplemented by the landlord. According to J.H. Prior, RN, the Assistant Emigration Officer at Liverpool, his inspections of the *Virginius* confirmed that no passengers were sick, and Mahon had given "moderate" supplies of food. His report to the Government Emigration Office was detailed:

> I was on board the "Virginius" on the 27th May as well as on the 28th. The passengers, 476 souls equal to 397 adults, were, generally speaking, a less robust, as well as poorer class than usual, but had no appearance of disease whatever amongst them, that I am aware of, after a most minute inspection, and no death took place, as stated prior to her sailing. Many of her passengers were sent out by the late Major Mahon, who caused them to be supplied with a moderate supply of tea, coffee, sugar, rice, oatmeal, dried fish, and vinegar in addition to the usual bread stuffs of the ship.[13]

Prior's testimony also hints that not all of the passengers on board the *Virginius* were from the Mahon estate, as previously believed. While he confirms that no passengers were sick or ill-supplied, Prior does suggest that typhus was rampant in Liverpool and it is not impossible to believe that it appeared on board ship, well into its journey.

It should not be assumed, however, that all ships crossing the Atlantic from the British Isles to the Americas in 1847 were coffin ships. The quality of one's passage could vary greatly according to one's port of departure, the perspicacity of port officials to health conditions, the provisioning of ships, and the extent to which captains adhered to even the basic regulations of the Passenger Act regarding fresh water, medical attention, adequate passenger space, sanitation, and food spoilage. All of these factors were within human control and there were many conscientious port agents, ships captains, medical officers, and booking agents who made certain that passenger health and safety were priorities. In the case of the port of Limerick, which sent more ships to Quebec than any Irish port in 1847, 50 out of 441 arrivals at Quebec (11.3 per cent), had one of the lowest rates of passenger deaths at sea, or 4.2 deaths per ship. Cork, on the other hand, possessed the worst record of any Irish port for deaths aboard its trans-Atlantic vessels during "Black 47" at a staggering rate of 26.9 deaths at sea per ship. (See Table 4.1). Liverpool's casualty rate was close to that of Cork's, with the British port recording an average of 25.8 passenger deaths per ship. Liverpool also launched the most ships headed to Quebec during the sailing season of 1847, at 72 vessels, or 16.3 per cent.[14] In the case of Limerick and the conditions of its ships, the reports to the Colonial officials credited the diligence of Mr. R. Lynch, RN, the chief government agent of the port, for making certain that ships were properly outfitted and passengers were healthy when boarding.[15] Evidently, even Earl Grey at the Colonial Office admitted that such strictness to the rules was not the practice in Liverpool, and that became the misfortune of Mahon's 1,490.[16]

Table 4.1: Selected British & Irish Ports and Migration to Quebec, 1847[17]

Port	Ships	Total Cabin Steerage	Average Per Ship	Assisted	Percentage Assisted	Sick Average	Dead at Sea
Liverpool	72	27,039	375.5	512	1.9	43.4	25.8
Limerick	50	9,174	183.5	1,287	21.06	4.0	4.2
Cork	33	10,322	312.8	680	11.13	50.3	26.9
Glasgow	30	2,019	67.3	0	0	2.7	2.0
Dublin	27	6,568	243.3	2,079	34.03	18.8	8.9
Sligo	26	5,732	220.5	802	13.12	14.9	14.2
Belfast	21	6,913	329.2	5	0.07	10.1	6.7
London	19	1,985	104.5	0	0	0.3	3.3
New Ross	15	4,395	293	251	5.71	16.1	7.8
Waterford	14	3,050	217.9	64	2.10	4.6	2.6
Derry	11	3,526	320.6	156	4.41	18.4	5.6

Source: André Charbonneau et André Sevigny, 1847 *Grosse Île: A Record of Daily Events* (Ottawa: Canadian Heritage Parks Canada, 1997), p. 21.

A ship's captain, however, could not be blamed for the weather or the changing conditions while at sea. In the spring and summer sailing the north Atlantic could be perilous. Prevailing winds and the Gulf Stream naturally moved from west to east, necessitating that ship tack against the current and the trade winds. At this rate, the voyage from Liverpool to Quebec could take from six to eight weeks. Cooking fires were only permitted on deck and only when weather permitted, which meant food was often eaten raw and cold, when passengers were able to eat at all. It is safe to say that none of Mahon's tenants had ever been to sea; they easily became seasick spending much of their time vomiting, urinating, and defecating below decks. The smell in steerage was ungodly, and the lack of sanitation made for horrendous conditions. The mandatory water supplies often became contaminated, and biscuits could become infested with maggots or be soiled by vermin. Rats became a common travelling companion, spreading disease and biting the young and the sick.

In such conditions disease flourished. Diarrhea, malnutrition, and dysentery were common on these ships. The deadliest problem below decks could be the outbreak of typhus or "ship's fever." The *Rickettsia prowazeki* bacteria[18] often lived in the feces of the common louse. Lice abounded in the conditions on board these ships. When a louse bit a passenger, it defecated at the site of the wound. When the wound became itchy, an unsuspecting victim scratched the affected area, which effectively rubbed the bacteria into the lesion, and it invaded the victim's system. One effectively became the agent of one's own infection. A further problem was that the bacteria was very hardy. It could survive for days on clothing, bedding, on bunks, and on surfaces where it might come in contact with other passengers. Once infected, the victim would not know symptoms for the better part of a week or more. In that time the bacteria were multiplying in one's body and attacking vital organs. Soon, victims would display a high fever, head aches, abdominal pain, profound thirst, rashes, skin lesions, and a dopiness or fuzziness (hence the name typhus, the Greek word for smoke or cloud). The condition ran its course in two weeks and most of those who contracted typhus died. In today's medicine, typhus can be treated with antibiotics, but in 1847, doctors attempted a variety of remedies—poultices, plasters, brandy, milk—without much success.[19] For thousands of Famine migrants, including Mahon's families, typhus would end their journey to a new life in America.

There have been several published dairies or travelogues of the journeys of coffin ships on the Atlantic in 1847, most of dubious authenticity and origin.[20] One reliable account of the voyage of famine refugees has been recorded by Stephen DeVere, a landlord who accompanied his passengers from Limerick to Quebec. The trans-Atlantic journey with his tenants forms part of a series of handwritten diaries, composed by DeVere in 1847, and now deposited in the archives of Trinity College in Dublin.[21] DeVere's ability to take this experience and return to the United Kingdom and address a Parliamentary Committee demanding reform of the Passenger Acts make his testimony credible; as a landlord, he had nothing to gain by such raw testimony to Parliamentarians, based on his own experiences.

> Wednesday 16th June. Arrived at Grosse isle [sic] Quarantine about 7 am. Detained waiting for dr till evening, when he inspected & gave us clean bill of health – abt. 40 ships detained there—villages of white tents on shore for the sick. Daily mortality about 150 One ship, Sisters of Liverpool, in with all passengers & crew in fever of this ship, all but the Cap'n and one girl died. Laid alongside of "Jessy" in which Many ill. Water covered with beds Cooking utensils refuse of the dead. Ghastly appearance of boats full of sick going ashore never to return. Several died between ship and shore. Wives separated from husbands, children from parents. Ascertained by subsequent enquiry that funds in agents hands altogether insufficient for care.[22]

George Mellis Douglas, the chief medical officer at the Grosse Île quarantine station, was perhaps more shocked when he reported to superiors that: "I never saw a people so indifferent to life, they would continue in the same berth with a dead person until the seaman or captain dragged out a corpse with boat hooks."[23]

In the wake of the sailing season, Canadian politicians, medical officials, and civil servants were highly critical of the British government for allowing this massive emigration of impoverished and sick Irish emigrants. The horrible state of passenger ships was often singled out by Canadians as being among the worst aspects of the suffering endured by the migrants in Black '47. In a stinging public letter to Earl Grey (Lord John Russell's Secretary of State for Colonial Affairs), Adam Ferrie, a Legislative Councillor from Canada, lambasted the British for their hand in creating the misery that year:

> Many thousands of these unhappy beings have fallen victim to that cruel system of marine imprisonment which, in crowded vessels and the impure atmosphere twixt decks, induces contagion and produces that endemial disease which so rapidly spreads over the mass of its congregated victims. Vast multitudes have died on the passage out, while a still greater proportion of them have reached our shores in such a sickly and debilitated state as to defy the penetration of medical skill, and to find wholly unavailing all the attentions and nursing care of their humane and faithful attendants. ... I must here, my Lord, express my deep regret that men pretending to be Christians, and especially that Britons could be guilty of such barbarity, evidently for the paltry purpose of freeing themselves from the natural and just burden of assisting to support and provide for their own poor.[24]

Ferrie's missive expressed the outrage of many Canadians for whom it was evident that not only did the United Kingdom appear to be dumping the poor and destitute onto its colonies, but that Canadians were going to have to pay for relief, and essentially compensate for the greed and indifference of landlords like Denis Mahon.

As Ferrie was writing, the Governor General of Canada, Lord Elgin, attempted to recoup the costs of the entire sailing season, its quarantine station expenses, transportation costs, salaries, and food distribution from the Imperial Government. After protracted arguments with the Russell administration, and particularly Earl Grey, Elgin demanded compensation of £35,729 5*s* 10*d*, which was the balance remaining on total expenditures on assisting the destitute migrants. By January 1848, the demand was for £71,529 sterling, which was the remaining balance on the £164,895 19*s* 2*d* for the entire year of 1847.[25] By early 1848, negotiations had exceeded Elgin's expectations, as the Imperial government remitted the entire sum to compensate for the expenses incurred by the Legislature of the United Province of Canada. In future, however, the Imperial authorities devolved control of emigration and admissions on the Canadians, themselves, who would assume control of disembarkation standards and taxes at Quebec.[26]

This crowding on board the ships, as Ferrie had complained, had similarly disastrous effects for Mahon's migrants. The *Virginius* did not sink as was assumed by some local people in Roscommon,[27] although it did sail off course and its complement of dead was as high as reported later by both Canadian and British newspapers.[28] Data from the death registers reveal that of the 476 passengers recorded on the ship, of which children under 14 were counted as half a person, there were 267 (56.1 per cent) deaths. Of the known 271 household heads that represented the entire 1,490, 31 either died at sea on the *Virginius*, or once the ship disembarked its sick at Grosse Île (See Table 4.2). Included among the dead was Captain Austin of the *Virginius*, and almost all his officers.[29] On the other hand, the overflow passengers from Mahon's estate on the *Erin's Queen* fared somewhat better: 100 of its 493 registered passengers were from Mahon's 1,490. Of these, only 14 appear in the death registers at Grosse Île, included therein are only 2 household heads from the original 271 assisted families. The death rate on the *Erin's Queen*, when all passengers are considered, was 136 or 27.6 per cent, still startling, but half of the deaths on the *Virginius*. If you had been in Mahon's overflow group, you might have counted yourself as lucky.

Beyond the numbers representing the casualties in the "first batch," were men, women, and children. Notable were the families who lost their principal breadwinners and household heads. The family cohorts from the townland of Culliagh, Bumlin Parish, witnessed nine of its 19 household heads perish on the *Virginius* or die as a result of the disease contracted on board the ship. The deaths of James Green Sr., John Mullen, John Lyons, Luke Lyons, Martin Green, Michael Hopkins, Darby Cox, Patrick Feeney, and James Lyons left 46 women and children to fend for themselves.[30] The aforementioned "Widow" Cox, who ended up in the city of Hamilton, but without her son Patrick, was among the seven household heads from the townland who survived and can be traced in their journey inland. Similarly, of the 47 families who left the townland of Kilmackenny, Parish of Lissonuffy, nine lost their household head because of their passage on the *Virginius*.[31] While only a few of Mahon's household heads perished on the *Erin's Queen*, the case of passengers from the village of Mullivetron offers an example of cruel irony.[32] Eight families from this village agreed to Mahon's terms but it appears that the families were split between the *Virginius* and the *Erin's Queen*; only two household heads perished, one on the *Virginius*, Michael Donlon, and one on the *Erin's Queen*, Michael Lannon. Most of the other families appeared to have settled or sojourned in Upper Canada.[33] While it is not known how or why the families from Mullivetron were split up in Liverpool, the better survival rates for Mahon's people on the *Erin's Queen*, suggests that most families from Mullivetron, except the Donlons, were dispatched from the *Virginius* because it was already full.

The second batch of Mahon's families fared little better than their kinsmen and neighbours on the *Virginius*. Of the 196 dead on the *Naomi*, 126, or 35.9 per cent of the ship's passenger list, were from the Mahon estate—a shocking statistic, but nevertheless, not the numbers that were reported back to the estate in the fall of 1847. On the *John Munn*, 26, or just under half of the Mahon passengers either died at sea or at Grosse Île. In total, about 41 per cent of the *John Munn's* passengers perished. When the death rates on board these two ships are added to the dead among the first wave of migrants who left in May, about 387 migrants of the 1,490 perished, or just over one in every four. Similarly, 58 of the 271 household heads, or just over one in five heads of families never realized the "new start" that had been promised them in Upper Canada. (See Table 4.3) While the numbers of dead do not jibe with the dead of popular memory, the death toll is still a testament to horrific conditions on board the four ships and account for the blame that would be laid at the feet of the landlord. It is no small coincidence that after the reports of the dead reached Ireland in the autumn of 1847, Major Mahon became a marked man.[34]

Table 4.2: Deaths of Household Heads by Ship Recorded for the Mahon Estate, 1847

Ship	Estimated Passengers	Strokestown Assisted	Estimated Total Deaths	Strokestown Deaths, Verified	Strokestown Household Head Deaths
Virginius	476	476	267 (56.1%)	221 (46.4%)	31
Naomi	421	350.5	196 (46.6%)	126 (35.9%)	16
Erin's Queen	493	100	136 (27.6%)	14 (14.0%)	2
John Munn	452	55	187 (41.4%)	26 (47.3%)	7
At Sea Not defined					2
Total	1,842	981.5	786 (42.7%)	387 (39.4%)	58 of 271 (21.4%)
Total if 1,490		1,490 Includes children under 14		387 (26.0%)	

Source: Strokestown List prepared from the Strokestown Park Archive and put in a database by Dr. Ciarán Reilly of Maynooth University. The 274 families appear on the glass memorial in front of the Strokestown Park Museum; Canadian data is from Marianna O'Gallagher and Rose Dompierre, *Eyewitness: Grosse Isle 1847* (Ste-Foy, Quebec: Livres Carraig Books, 1995); André Charbonneau and Doris Drolet-Dubé, eds., *A Register of Deceased Persons at Sea and on Grosse Île in 1847* (Ottawa: Canadian Heritage, Parks Canada, 1997). See also The Morning Chronicle (Quebec), 24 December 1847.

Table 4.3: Status of Mahon Households in British North America, 1847

Status of the Household Head	Number	Percent
Died at Sea or in Quarantine	58	21.2
Confirmed Not Travelling	3	1.1
Located in Canada	71	25.9
Located in the United States	29	10.6
Location/Status Unknown	113	41.2
Total Located or Identified	161	58.8
Total From Estate	274	100

Source: Census of Canada, 1851–1852; Registers of Catholic Parishes in Canada East and Canada West (online Familysearch.com); Library and Archives Canada; RG 19 D-5, v.2532, Department of Finance, Travel Vouchers and Expenses, 1843–1854; André Charbonneau and Doris Drole-Dubé, *A Register of Deceased Persons at Sea and on Grosse Île in 1847* (Ottawa: Canadian Heritage, Parks Canada, 1997).

The quarantine station at Grosse Île presented another grim chapter of the journey of Irish families to Canada during the Irish Famine. Established in 1832 as a quarantine station during the cholera epidemic, Grosse Île was the first Canadian stop for the surviving Mahon families. Located in the St. Lawrence River approximately 50 kilometers northeast of Quebec City, Grosse Île's quarantine facility was under the supervision of Dr. George Mellis Douglas and his medical staff. The island had been inundated with unprecedented numbers of migrants from Ireland in 1846 (32,753) and Douglas anticipated a similar if not greater flow of migrants to the station in 1847.[35] To prepare Grosse Île appropriately, he petitioned the Canadian Government for £3,000 to outfit the island. The station had several sheds for the sick, a hospital, and quarters for the physicians and workers. Not sensing the urgency of Douglas, the Government responded with a warrant of £300 and use of the steamship *St. George* to ferry healthy emigrants from the island to Quebec City.[36] Decisions made in the ports of entry in the United States to levy heavy fines on captains carrying infirm emigrants, and a larger levy on each passenger landed, would make Quebec and Saint John, New Brunswick, cheaper and more advantageous destinations for those financing and outfitting transatlantic vessels. While the United States did not ban emigration from Ireland,[37] they certainly made it more difficult, and Canada became the alternative.

Early in the shipping season, the arrival of numerous ships with hundreds of sick and dying passengers proved Douglas' prognostications correct.[38] The island was quickly overwhelmed, and ships had to anchor by the dozens until an attending physician could inspect the passengers on board. In late May, the *Montreal Herald* reported that "the forebodings of evil with respect to emigrants arriving in the St. Lawrence, are at this moment too sadly verified."[39] In the first few weeks of receiving the arrivals, Douglas boarded the ships to assess who would have to be taken to the island for treatment. When they learned of this practice, Canadian government officials insisted on the letter of the law, forcing Douglas to disembark entire shiploads of passengers, sick and healthy, to the station, for inspection. When it became clear that Douglas and his staff and their small facility could not handle the crush of emigrants, the Government rescinded its order and permitted quarantine to take place on board ships, without disembarking all passengers.[40] Matters were made worse by the fact that waiting passengers were drinking water directly from the St. Lawrence, causing numerous cases of dysentery.[41] By summer, new sheds were being built on Grosse Île, tents were erected as temporary shelters, more physicians were sent by the Government,[42] and the army was deployed to the island to keep order. But the result was much the same because doctors were unable to treat most of the typhus cases. Thousands died. In 1847 alone, 3,238 emigrants died in quarantine, and 5,424 emigrants in total (from ships and hospitals) were buried on Grosse Île, including Thomas Brennan's wife, Bridget, and his young son, from the Kilmackenny Townland, who had been passengers on the *Virginius*.[43]

The eyewitnesses on the island—clergy, medical staff, and military personnel—all left records of the horror faced by those forced to land on Grosse Île, and, in one sense abandon hope. Father E.A. Taschereau, a future Archbishop of Quebec and Canada's first Cardinal, served on Grosse Île with many Catholic priests and Anglican ministers, during the summer of 1847. When writing to his Archbishop, Joseph Signay, Taschereau offered a heart-rending testimony:

> The number of orphans is very great and sadly enough we could not do anything more for them than entrust them to a few mothers of families and give them some money to buy food. Most of them will die like the others; happy to have not known their misfortune here! I saw a child playing with the hand of his mother who had just died! It had always seemed to me that the presence of a dead body in a ship must arouse some kind of feeling, but I have already seen many that have been pointed out to me with sort of indifference when I passed by their beds or where we lay them while waiting for coffins to be ready; I have seen this as a new mark of degradation caused by an excess of suffering and misfortune.[44]

One month later, George Mountain, the Anglican bishop of Montreal, reported to T.C. Aylwin, the Chair of the Special Commission of Enquiry into Grosse Île, that "the accommodation for the sick was, in many instances, wretched in the extreme, and the attendance so deficient that their most crying wants were often unsupplied."[45] Mountain, who had visited the island, praised the work of the overwhelmed Douglas and the medical team, but told Aylwin that "the impression produced upon my mind was that of the hopelessness of doing anything effectual to stay the consequences of such a visitation from the hand of God."[46]

The four ships chartered by Mahon could not have landed at a worse time. By late July and early August, the island quarantine station was overcrowded with the sick and dying emigrants. The Strokestown passengers faced lazarettos and tents filled with 831 men, 745 women, and 572 children.[47] If one survived the horrendous voyage—the *Virginius* did not land at Grosse Île until 31 July, after having spent 51 days at sea—the quarantine station was the next risk to one's life. Both the *Erin's Queen* and the *Naomi* arrived at Quebec in advance of the Mahon's lead ship.[48] It is difficult to distinguish between the burials of Mahon's assisted immigrants at sea, or on the actual quarantine station. First, the two extant registers of the dead at Grosse Île do not consistently identify the death of an individual as being at sea or in quarantine.

Secondly, Mahon's assisted passengers were mixed with other Irish migrants on the *Naomi*, *Erin's Queen*, and the *John Munn*, which makes it impossible to parse out the Strokestown from non-Strokestown migrants in the aggregate statistics on mortality from each of these ships. Not even surname is a fool-proof identification since Irish names common to the Strokestown estate can be found in other parts of Ireland. Even the notorious *Virginius*, which was supposed to have been filled entirely with migrants from Mahon's estate, was not what it seemed in terms of passengers. The Grosse Île registers reveal dead migrants from the *Virginius* who are not listed among the 271 families who left Strokestown under the auspices of the Mahon scheme. Evidently, some of the Mahon families had swapped their tickets with other migrants while waiting for their embarking on the ill-fated ship in Liverpool.

The basic truth of the experience of the Mahon migrants on Grosse Île is that many died. As Table 4.4 indicates, many of those who died on board the anchored *Virginius* or on the quarantine island itself were from Mahon's estate.

Table 4.4: The Dead Passengers On-Board Mahon's Chartered Ships

Vessel	Passengers	Deaths at Sea	Landed Sick	Deaths on Quarantined Ship	Deaths on Grosse Île	Survival Rate	Total Dead
Virginius	476	158	106	19	90	15%	267
Erin's Queen	493	45	130	20	71	45.4%	136
Naomi	421	78	100	31	87	13%	196
John Munn	452	59	100	11	117	-17%	187

Note: The deaths represented on this table are the aggregate numbers of both Mahon's assisted passengers and all other passengers. Source: Marianna O'Gallagher & Rose Masson Dompierre, *Eyewitness Grosse Isle* (St-Foy: Carraig Books, 1995): Table 8; André Charbonneau et André Sevigny, 1847 *Grosse Île: A Record of Daily Events* (Ottawa: Canadian Heritage Parks Canada, 1997), pp. 171–99.

Given that Douglas was allowed to evacuate just the sick from the ships to the quarantine station by July 1847, the discrepancy between those who landed sick and those who died on the island supports the idea that those who landed at Grosse Île had very little hope of survival. On the *Virginius*, 106 passengers, presumably most from the Mahon estate, had a survival rate of 15 per cent. The rate of survival was close to the same on the *Naomi*, at 13 per cent. The rate of death on the *John Munn* was worse likely because, when space became available, they continued to unload the sick from the ship and place them in the available facilities on the island. The number of dead, who died on ships as they sat anchored off Grosse Île, not only testifies to the extent of the spread of disease, but also the general overcrowding of medical facilities on the island that could not manage to accommodate all of the sick pouring into the country.

Once again, the *Erin's Queen* was an anomaly. Its crew and Douglas' team landed about 130 sick passengers but, unlike the three other chartered vessels, just under half survived their quarantine. The reason for this high rate of survival may be the product of only fallible speculation. The *Erin's Queen* arrived about 20 days before the other vessels, but the heat of the summer was no less oppressive and the medical structures on Grosse Île still appeared to be filled to capacity and beyond.[49] Auxiliary Bishop of Quebec, Pierre F. Turgeon, wrote to Lord Elgin on 10 July, explaining to the Governor General "that the sick languished in the holds of vessels because of a lack of space at the station to receive them." He added that "a large number of sick are already under canvas on the island. Consumed by heat in this weather, they breathe morbid air, which is equally deadly for them."[50] It was possible that Douglas' staff and military guards were more expeditious in dealing with the *Erin's Queen*, because it had been reported that Captain Davidson and his officers had abandoned ship, and there was a need to take direct control of the vessel.[51] Finally, it may have been a case that typhus was not the principal cause of illness on the ship, although there is no surviving evidence of the specific type of disease that afflicted passengers. Once again, passengers on the *Erin's Queen* fared better than the rest.

What one can conclude about the experience of the Mahon passengers at Grosse Île was that death was as likely to strike them in quarantine as at sea. At least 387 passengers recorded as embarking the ships chartered by Mahon died either at sea or in the quarantine station at Grosse Île. What has been firmly established is that 58 household heads from the estate were included in this number (Table 4.3). Often their partners died with them, leaving the surviving children in the family without parents when they arrived at Quebec. The most conservative estimate possible, based on the available data, suggests that perhaps as many as 300 children may have died on route from Mahon's estate to Quebec City. The fact that often infants were not included by name in the counts complicates matters, as does the fact that John Ross Mahon's records indicate that 1,490 tenants agreed to participate in the migrations scheme, while only 981.5 statute adult passengers are officially recorded on board these ships. Although any firm number of dead is pure speculation, there were far more children under the age of 14 on these ships, than what the official record implies. The death toll could be far higher than the official death records suggest.

The fate of the "1,490" did not go un-noticed. When word of the devastating loss of life was reported back to Roscommon, via a short article reprinted from the Toronto

Globe which focused on the *Virginius*, there was general outrage in Strokestown, particularly from the pulpit of the local Catholic parish. It may have been no coincidence that in November 1847, while returning from a meeting regarding local Poor Law Union business, Denis Mahon was gunned down (see chapter 7), becoming the first Irish landlord to be assassinated during the Famine.[52] It was unfortunate that the *Globe* had recorded only part of the story; research into the records of Grosse Île reveal that while the *Virginius* casualties were accurate as reported, overall mortality may only have been around 39 per cent, if based on the actual statute passengers recorded, or 26 per cent if based on the entire original number of 1,490, or just 21 per cent if based on the household heads alone, on board all four ships.

The vilification of Mahon was evident in Canada as it would be in Ireland. Adam Ferrie, in his fiery missive to Earl Grey, blamed Mahon by name, among other landlords, for the "fearful destitution" of his tenants who migrated.[53] Similarly, the passengers on board the *Champion,* which may have carried a third "batch" of Strokestown tenants, became yet another opportunity to blame Mahon for neglect and cruelty. The *Quebec Morning Chronicle* was dismayed and disgusted that: "The passengers of the Champion are more of the wretched, miserable tenantry of Major Mahon and are equally squalid and filthy as those coming out on the Virginius and Naomi."[54] Upon close scrutiny of the available records from Grosse Île, there is little one-to-one correspondence between names of the dead from the *Champion* and names of tenants from Castlenode.[55] Whether or not the ship contained any passengers from Mahon's estate, Canadian authorities would not forget the horrendous state of some of his assisted emigrants as they landed at Grosse Île.

The question remains whether Mahon is culpable for this catastrophe at sea and in the quarantine station. The booking agents certainly made the cheapest arrangements possible, cutting corners which seemed to be part of John Ross Mahon's economizing on behalf of the estate. Clearly, the passengers were not inspected carefully when boarding the ships, there were not sufficient supplies of fresh water and edible food for the passengers registered, and, in the case of the *Virginius,* the navigators were handicapped by weather and currents and ended up off course. If the *Berean* newspaper article (see chapter 2) on the positive state of the Mahon migrants is to be treated with any weight, it appears that at least the first wave of migrants from the townlands that included Kilgraffy, Culliagh, Tully, and Kilmackenny, Mahon had done his due diligence in supplying them with food and providing wagons for the cartage of their personal belongings.[56] Invoices in Mahon's papers indicate that he was liable for not only the fares for each of the passengers but also for considerable baggage.

The story of Widow Cox and her family tends to serve as a microcosm of the fate of some of the Mahon immigrants. Like many other passengers on board the four ships, Patrick Cox was ill, and was forced by Dr. Douglas, the chief medical officer on the island, to evacuate to the lazarettos of Grosse Île. Douglas was present enough to the disembarking migrants that Mrs. Cox would be able to cite him by name in her eventual plea for any knowledge of her lost son. In 1852, the Census of Canada West reported that "widow" Susan Cox was living in a "hovel" on Queen Street, St. George's Ward, in Hamilton. At 45 years of age Susan was employed as a "knit worker" and her children were gainfully employed. Two sons were labourers and a daughter, Nancy, was working as a servant, which was a popular choice of work for young Irish women.[57] The youngest of the three children, 15-year-old Patrick, had somehow survived Grosse Île, and likely through the agency of fellow Irish travellers, clergy, and civil officials, miraculously was re-united with his family. Amidst the hundreds of dead from the Mahon estate, the Cox family survived and began the new life promised them when they left Strokestown. Having survived the long voyage, the sickness, and death, Susan Cox and over 100 of Mahon's families began the equally difficult journey of starting their lives over.

NOTES

1. Archives of the Richmond County Historical Society, Melbourne, Quebec, Thomas Quinn Fonds, 03-G-F–26.62, Monsieur Abbé Thomas Quinn, 1841–1923, "Souvenirs D'Enfance (Arrivé au Canada), translated from "entassés dans le fond de cale."
2. *Hamilton Gazette*, 27 September 1847.
3. Of particular note are Bruce Elliott's pioneering work *Irish Migrants in the Canadas: A New Approach* (Montreal & Kingston: McGill-Queen's University Press, 1988), in which he tracked 775 Protestant Irish families from Tipperary to their resettlement in central Canada, before the Famine. Jim Rees *Surplus People: From Wicklow to Canada* (Cork: The Collins Press, 2000) traces the assisted migrants from Lord Fitzwilliam's estates in Wicklow between 1847 and 1856, over which time some six-thousand tenants migrated to Quebec and later to the colony of New Brunswick. Tyler Anbinder's, "From Famine to Five Points: Lord Lansdowne's Irish Tenants Encounter North America's Most Notorious Slum," *American Historical Review* 107, no. 2 (April 2002): pp. 351–87, is a meticulous study of Lord Lansdowne's assisted migrants from Kerry to the Five Points neighborhood in New York. Robert Scally's *The End of Hidden Ireland: Rebellion, Famine, & Emigration* (New York: Oxford University Press, 1995), is a detailed examination of the migrants of the Ballykilcline estate, adjacent to Denis Mahon's lands at Strokestown. Similarly, Mary Lee Dunn's *Ballykilcline Rising: From Famine Ireland to Immigrant America* (Amherst: University of Massachusetts Press, 2006) continues the story of this townland tracking several families to Rutland, Vermont.

4. *Belfast Newsletter*, 8 June 1847. Joseph Davidson was only 36 years old. *Belfast Commercial Chronicle*, 1 April 1848.
5. Ships List: http//www.shipslist.com/1847/index.htm
6. *Belfast Newsletter*, 7 and 21 May 1847.
7. *Belfast Newsletter*, 12 January 1847 and *Belfast Commercial Chronicle*, 1 April 1848.
8. Library and Archives Canada (LAC), Colonial Office Papers, CO384/79. Letter to the Right Honourable Earl Grey from the Honourable Adam Ferrie, Member of the Legislative Council, Chairman of the Executive Lay Commission for Emigration, 1847, Montreal, 1 December 1847, p. 199.
9. LAC, Colonial Office Paper, CO384/80, Guide for Emigrants to British North America, By Order of S. Walcott, Secretary, Colonial Land and Emigration Commission, March 1847, p. 197.
10. LAC, Colonial Office Papers, CO384/80, Guide for Emigrants to British North America, By Order of S. Walcott, Secretary, Colonial Land and Emigration Commission, March 1847, p. 198.
11. Ibid., p. 197.
12. Ibid., p. 198.
13. J.H. Prior to S. Walcott, Government Emigration Office, Liverpool, 12 January 1848, in *Journals of the Legislative Assembly of the Province of Canada,* Vol. 7, 1848, Appendix W. The letter was retained because it refuted Dr. George Mellis Douglas' claim (at Grosse Île) that the passengers were not ill with dysentery or fever when boarding the ship at Liverpool.
14. Charbonneau & Sevigny, *Grosse Île*, p. 21.
15. Lynch was a member of the Royal Navy and the chief government agent at Limerick. LAC, Colonial Office Papers, CO384/80, Guide for Emigrants to British North America, By Order of S. Walcott, Secretary, Colonial Land and Emigration Commission, March 1847, p. 197. Also, CO384/80, T. Fred Elliot and C. Alexander Wood, Colonial Land and Emigration Office to James Stephen, Colonial Office, 11 June 1847. The letter commends Lynch for taking care of passengers on board the *Vesta*, which had departed from Limerick but then put into Baltimore, Cork, because the ship was "in distress." It returned to Limerick and Lynch personally made arrangements and "personally attended to their comfort" as they boarded another vessel. LAC, Colonial Office Papers, CO 384/81, Plans for the Eighth General Report, of the Colonial Land and Emigration Commissioners, London: William Clowes and Sons, 1848, p. 14.
16. British Parliamentary Papers, (1947–48), hereafter BPP, House of Commons, Emigration, Papers Relative to Emigration to the British Provinces in North America and the Australian Colonies, Part 1, Earl Grey to Lord Elgin, Governor General of Canada, 1 December 1847. This criticism of Liverpool and Cork is echoed in the UKPP, Enclosure #20, Report of the Colonial Land & Emigration Office, 20 November 1847.
17. BPP, vol. 17, Buchanan Report. And Andre Charbonneau & Andre Sevigny, *1847 Grosse Île: A Record of Daily Events* (Ottawa: Canadian Heritage, Parks Canada, 1997), p. 21.
18. O'Gallagher and Dompierre, *Eyewitness Grosse Isle*, p. 52.

19. Bishop Michael Power of Toronto commented on the "insidious character" of the disease for which there seemed to be no cure. It eventually claimed his life on 1 October 1847. *Mirror*, 22 September 1847 and 19 November 1847.
20. Mark G. McGowan, "Famine, Facts, and Fabrication: An Examination of Diaries from the Irish Famine Migration to Canada," *Canadian Journal of Irish Studies* (Spring 2009); Jason King, "The Genealogy of *Famine Diary* in Ireland and Quebec: Ireland's Famine Migration in Historical Fiction, Historiography, and Memory," *Éire-Ireland*, vol. 47 (Spring/Summer 2012).
21. Stephen De Vere's Famine diaries in Canada in 1847 and 1848 have been digitized and transcribed at https://irishfaminestories.ca/en/bearing_witness.
22. Trinity College Dublin MS 5061. Stephen De Vere Unpublished Famine Diary Vol. 1 April 29 – December 1, 1847.
23. BPP, 1847–48, Enclosure 3, document 3, A.C. Buchanan to Major Campbell, Civil Secretary, 9 June 1847. Buchanan cites Douglas verbatim.
24. LAC, Colonial Office Papers, CO 384/79, Letter to the Right Honourable Earl Grey by the Hon. Adam Ferrie, Montreal, 1 December 1847, p. 394 (original pp. 8–9)
25. LAC, Colonial Office Papers, CO384/81, W. Murdoch to Herman Merivale, Colonial Land and Emigration Office, 15 January 1848; BPP, 1847–48, Enclosure 3, Document 14, Lord Elgin to Earl Grey, 9 October 1847 and Grey to Elgin, 1 December 1847. The Bank of England's inflation calculator estimates the £164,895 19*s* 2*d* is roughly the equivalent of £1.2 million in 2021 sterling.
26. Leslie Anne Hunt, "The Canadian Response to the Irish Famine Migration of 1847" (Unpublished Master of Arts Thesis, University of British Columbia, 1973), pp. 168–76.
27. Desmond McCabe, "Denis Mahon," *Dictionary of Irish Biography* (Cambridge: Cambridge University Press & Royal Irish Academy), p. 200 and p. 295.
28. Duffy, pp.129–30. *The Belfast Newsletter*, 3 September 1847 reported that 158 passengers died at sea and 186 were ill upon landing at the quarantine station. *The Belfast Commercial Chronicle*, 4 September 1847, reported 178 dead and 186 sick. The "Return of the Passenger Ships" provided by Emigration Agent A.C. Buchanan, at Quebec, records that the *Virginius* lost 158 at sea, 19 at quarantine, and 90 in the quarantine hospital to a total of 267 dead.
29. *The Armagh Guardian*, 7 September 1847. Reprinted from the Quebec *Morning Chronicle*.
30. SPA, STR/74, List of Tenants Assisted, Townland of Culliagh, 1847.
31. Ibid, Townland of Kilmackenny, 1847.
32. One very interesting exploration of the material history of Mullivetron see Katherine Hull, "Material Correlates of Pre-Famine Agri-Social Hierarchy: Archaeological Evidence from County Roscommon, Republic of Ireland" (PhD dissertation, University of Toronto, 2004).
33. SPA, STR/74, List of Tenants Assisted, Townland of Mullivetron, 1847.
34. See Jason King, "In the Footsteps of Strokestown's Famine Emigrant to Niagara: Transatlantic Press Coverage and Retribution for Major Denis Mahon's Coffin Ships," in Christine Kinealy and Gerard Moran, eds., *Irish Famines before and after the Great Hunger* (Hamden, Connecticut and Cork: Quinnipiac and Cork University Press, 2020).

35. Cited in O'Gallagher and Dompierre, *Eyewitness*, p. XX. Derived from UK Parliamentary Papers, Volume 17, Canada, Sessions 1847–1848, p. 540.
36. Leslie Anne Harvey, "The Canadian Responses to the Irish Famine Migration of 1847," (Unpublished Master's Thesis, University of British Columbia, 1973), p. 63.
37. They received 119,000 emigrants from UK ports in 1847. Donald H. Akenson, *The Irish in Ontario: A Study in Rural History* (Montreal & Kingston: McGill-Queen's University Press, 1884), p. 30.
38. *St. Catharine's Journal*, 3 June 1847. Reprinted from *Montreal Courier*. Also, *Quebec Morning Chronicle*, 7 August 1847; *The Belfast Commercial Chronicle*, 4 September 1847.
39. Cited in, *The British Colonist*, 28 May 1847.
40. Harvey, pp. 72–5.
41. *British Colonist*, 4 June 1847.
42. *British Colonist*, 15 June and 13 July 1847.
43. Charbonneau and Drolet-Dubé, *A Register of Deceased Persons*, 66. O'Gallagher and Dompierre, *Eyewitness: Grosse Isle*, Table B, 384 and 394.
44. E. A Taschereau to Archbishop Joseph Signay, 3 June 1847, cited in O'Gallagher and Dompierre, Eyewitness, pp. 85–6.
45. George J Mountain to T.C. Aylwin, 25 July 1847 as cited in O'Gallagher and Dompierre, *Eyewitness*, p. 204.
46. Ibid., p. 205.
47. Quebec *Morning Chronicle*, 7 August 1847.
48. O'Gallagher and Dompierre, *Eyewitness Grosse Isle*, pp. 349 and 352.
49. André Charbonneau et André Sevigny, 1847 *Grosse Île: A Record of Daily Events* (Ottawa: Canadian Heritage Parks Canada, 1997): pp. 125–6.
50. Archives of the Archdiocese of Quebec, 210A, RL, vol. 22, pp 31–32, P.F Turgeon to Lord Elgin, 10 July 1847 as cited in O'Gallagher and Dompierre, *Eyewitness*, p. 158
51. Reported in Charbonneau and Sevigny, *Grosse Île*, p. 140.
52. Reilly, *Strokestown*, pp. 91–8; Duffy, *The Killing*, pp. 131–4. *Globe* (Toronto, Canada) 14 August 1847; Campbell, *The Great Irish Famine*, pp. 48–9.
53. LAC, Colonial Office Papers, CO 384/79, Letter to the Right Honourable Earl Grey by the Hon. Adam Ferrie, Montreal, 1 December 1847, p. 395 (original p.10) See also BPP, *Papers Relative to Emigration, Emigration to the British Provinces in North America* (London: William Clowes, 1848) Enclosure in No.2, Letter from George M. Douglas, MD to Governor General, Lord Elgin, 27 December 1847, p.7. Douglas singles out Mahon, but mistakenly claims his estate is in County Tyrone. He cites the horrors on the *Naomi* and *Virginius* by name.
54. Quebec *Morning Chronicle*, 24 August 1847.
55. André Charbonneau and Doris Drolet-Dubé, eds., *A Register of Deceased Persons at Sea and on Grosse Île in 1847* (Ottawa: Canadian Heritage, Parks Canada, 1997); *Freeman's Journal*, 29 April 1848.
56. *The Berean*, 24 June 1847.
57. Census of Canada, 1851–1852, Canada West, Hamilton, St. Georges Ward, Queen Street, Susan Cox, image e002380593.

CHAPTER FIVE

SETTLERS, SOJOURNERS, AND ORPHANS

Mark G. McGowan

By August 1847, the survivors among Mahon's assisted migrants were prepared to leave their dead behind on Grosse Île and move forward into the wilds of Upper Canada. Of the original household heads, one in five was dead. Of the 1,490 passengers who boarded the four ill-fated ships in Liverpool, only about two-thirds were to continue the journey. Some of the healthy survivors waited at the new pier at Grosse Île, for the steamer *St. George* to take them to Quebec City. Others would have to wait for their original vessels to be cleaned before they could re-board and leave for Quebec.[1] From this point onward in their journey, the record of their travel becomes incomplete, spotty, and even non-existent. At least 400 kilometers (250 miles) lay between them and the first port of call in Upper Canada and during that time more of them would disappear from the routinely generated records of the day. The dead along the way would be placed in unregistered common graves, unmarked cemeteries near fever sheds and hospitals, and wherever they could be buried when their time came, far from a city or town, or along some Canadian roadside. Without a collection of accurate records, preserved from the 1840s and 1850s in Canada, the identities of Mahon's migrants are difficult to trace and, for the historian, there are only slender threads to follow as one attempts to discover the fate of those who left the Strokestown estate. The Mahon migrants are not unusual in this regard; immigrants to the Canadas in this period were constantly on the move, more often sojourning than settling, and thus hard to pin down in any location for a long period of time.[2]

Nevertheless, at least three patterns emerge in the existing fragmented records as to the fate of the Mahon migrants: some settled and sojourned in Upper Canada (also known as Canada West/Ontario), availing themselves of cheap land on the frontier or wage work in the towns and cities; a second group pushed further into the United States, reconnecting with family and friends, or striking out into the broad American frontier; a final group, the orphaned children of Mahon's 271 assisted families, found themselves unofficial wards of the Catholic Church as they were placed involuntarily with Canadian families. With these three possible clusters in mind, tracking the Mahon migrants is not an impossible exercise, just a very difficult one. Few ship's manifests of passengers exist for this period in Canada and many Boards of Health did not prepare detailed records, including names, for the thousands of migrants who passed through their jurisdictions. The so-called Canadian Census of 1851 was actually enumerated in 1852, almost five years after the coming of Mahon's people. Moreover, the census records that survive are sloppy, often inaccurate, plagued by misspellings and carelessness, and some key areas of the country have no records at all. Toronto, Kingston, and parts of Montreal are simply just lost to history. It is little wonder that the search for Mahon's people can be likened to trying to find needles in a proverbial haystack or making bricks without straw.

What can be known about the survivors of the 1,490 can be traced to the general pattern of Irish migrant movement in the Canadas in 1847 and 1848. Mahon's migrants' first stop was at the docks of Quebec City's lower town near to Champlain Street, ironically a Quebec neighbourhood heavily populated by Irish immigrants from pre-Famine times. At his offices close by, A.C. Buchanan, the Chief Emigration agent for the Province of Canada (both East and West sections), would have his team inspect the incoming migrants and triage the sick to the General Marine Hospital at St. Roche, not far from Quebec's "Lower Town." Hundreds of Irish migrants, many of whom only began to display the symptoms of typhus after departing Grosse Île, would be sent to the hospital. Dozens of the sick travellers would be admitted to the hospital weekly and many of these, who were unable to recover from the "ships' fever," dysentery, diarrhea, and even smallpox, would be buried in the hospital cemetery nearby. Without a register of the dead surviving, it is impossible to know how many of Mahon's migrants ended their journey here.

Children left orphaned on Grosse Île or at the General Marine hospital were also inspected and led by clergy to the Orphan's Asylum on Prince Edward Street, run by the Charitable Catholic Ladies of Quebec.[3] Ironically, much more is known about these children, of whom at least 40 were from the Mahon estate, because the

Ladies kept a comprehensive ledger of all the orphans in their care. In addition to the names of their deceased parents, counties and parishes of origin, ship's name, age, and religion, the ledger also included the name of the Canadian individual or family with whom they were placed. For the Mahon orphans, their new life would not begin in Upper Canada, but in Lotbinière, Portneuf, Montmorency, Rimouski, Nicolet, and St-Grégoire—names that would have sounded most strange to Irish children. Unlike the rest of their friends and neighbours from the Mahon townlands, the orphan children's movements would be limited to regions near Quebec. Their dream of Upper Canada would remain unrequited, at least for the foreseeable future.

Table 5.1: Counties of Origin of Irish Famine "Orphans" at Quebec, 1847–1848 N=619

County	Number	Percentage	County	Number	Percentage
Roscommon	52	8.4	Meath	7	1.1
Tipperary	33	5.3	Limerick	7	1.1
Clare	26	4.2	Louth	6	0.9
Fermanagh	20	3.2	Armagh	4	0.6
Queen's	20	3.2	Antrim	3	0.5
Leitrim	20	3.2	Donegal	3	0.5
Mayo	18	2.9	Derry	3	0.5
Kildare	17	2.7	Monaghan	3	0.5
Tyrone	16	2.6	Waterford	2	0.3
Kilkenny	16	2.6	Carlow	2	0.3
Sligo	13	2.1	Kerry	2	0.3
Galway	11	1.8	King's	1	0.2
Wicklow	11	1.8	Longford	1	0.2
Cork	11	1.8	Non Irish	5	0.8
Westmeath	11	1.8	Unknown	259	41.8
Cavan	10	1.6	**Total**	**619**	**100.0**
Wexford	7	1.1			

Source: Marianna O'Gallagher, *Grosse Île: Gateway to Canada, 1832–1937* (Ste-Foy: Carraig Books, 1984), Appendices. Note neither Dublin nor Down were represented. Non-Irish consisted of two each from of England and Scotland and one from Quebec.

For their first few weeks in Quebec, the Mahon orphans would be housed by the Charitable Catholic Ladies in their asylum at Prince Edward Street. It was from there that their patrons would arrange, through the local Catholic clergy, their placement in Catholic homes. Archbishop Joseph Signay had been adamant to his priests and lay parishioners that the Catholic faith of these children be preserved and that his flock open their homes to these Irish children.[4] Coordinated by Signay's Vicar General, Father Felix Cazeau, numerous parish priests from the Archdiocese of Quebec ventured to the Prince Edward Street Asylum, collected Irish children, and placed them in private homes, small businesses, and farms in their home parishes.[5] The image of the French-Canadian largesse was immortalized by John Francis Maguire in his monumental *The Irish in America* (1880) when he wrote:

> Half-naked squalid, covered with vermin generated by hunger, fever, and the foulness of the ship's hold, perhaps with germs of the plague lurking in their vitiated blood, these helpless innocents of every age—from the infant taken from the bosom of its dead mother to the child who could barely tell the name of its parents—were gathered under the fostering protection of the Church.[6]

Despite Maguire's rather dramatic and romanticized description of the Irish orphans and their so-called adoption, further scrutiny of the historical record produces a different picture of the events in 1847 and 1848.

The orphan placements were not exclusively in French-Canadian homes, and the Mahon orphans, like their other Irish fellow travellers, were also placed in the homes of Irish-Canadian families as well. At least six Mahon orphans were placed among Irish Canadians, while the majority went to French-Canadian homes, or made their way directly to the United States. Five simply died in the care of the Ladies, before they could be placed (see Table 5.3). It should also be noted that none of these children were legally adopted by the families with whom they were placed.[7] While the term "adoption" had been used colloquially in Canada since colonial times in New France, there was no legal provision for adoption in the Province's civil law until the twentieth century.[8] These Irish children were simply "placed" and there was no legal obligation of the families that took them in, nor were these Irish children legally entitled to any share of the family inheritance. Even the Canadian census provided categories pertaining to family members of those inscribed in its rolls; these Irish children were normally categorized as "non-family."

Of the Mahon orphans traceable through the Canadian Census, it is evident that these children were used as domestic servants, farm labour, and day labourers by their placement families. This situation does not entirely diminish the generosity and charity exhibited by many of the Canadian families, but it does underscore nineteenth-century attitudes about idleness in children. In the minds of mid-nineteenth century social leaders, children were either to be schooled or put to work, in order to be moral, upstanding, and productive members of society. It was not uncommon in Canada that local authorities and the Churches established schools in orphan asylums and would also advocate that children work to avoid them descending into a life of criminality or dependency. Houses of Industry became agencies to place the able-bodied youth into positions wherein they could learn a trade, assist in household chores, or labour at an honest day's work. In Upper Canada, for example, apprenticeships "were the only legislative provision for poor or orphaned children from 1799 to 1851."[9] In the Maritime Provinces (Nova Scotia, Prince Edward Island and New Brunswick) children could be auctioned off to serve on farms or other local businesses. In Montreal, Canada East (now Quebec), children were expected to work in order to support their impoverished working-class families.[10] It is not surprising then to see colonial orphanages, hospitals, and houses of refuge release children so that they might apprentice, undertake domestic service, do manual labour, go to school, or as was sometimes the case in the Catholic Church, be recruited into the religious life, either as sisters or in the clerical estate (see chapter 6).

Table 5.2 Placement Locations of the Irish Orphans of 1847-1848 N=420

Location	Number	Percentage
Quebec City & Region	107	25.5
Rimouski & Area	57	13.6
Nicolet & St. Grégoire	56	13.3
Lotbinière & Region	25	6.0
United States of America	22	5.2
Upper Canada	19	4.5
Montreal & Region	5	1.2
Other Placement Areas	129	30.7
Total	**420**	**100.00**

Source: Marianna O'Gallagher, *Grosse Île: Gateway to Canada, 1832-1937* (Ste-Foy: Carraig Books, 1984), Appendices. Many of the "other" placement areas involved less than three children per place.

Table 5.3 Placement Locations of the Strokestown Orphans of 1847 N=40

Location	Number	Percentage
Quebec City & Region	2	5.0%
Rimouski & Area	10	25.0%
Nicolet & St. Grégoire	5	12.5%
Lotbinière & Region	4	10.0%
United States of America	7	17.5%
Died Prior to Placement	7	17.5%
Place not Recorded	5	12.5%
Total	**40**	**100.00**

Source: Marianna O'Gallagher, *Grosse Île: Gateway to Canada, 1832–1937* (Ste-Foy: Carraig Books, 1984), Appendices.

None of the stories of the Strokestown orphans who were traceable in the Canadian records endured exactly the same life experiences in their new homes. As Table 5.3 suggests, they were placed within the four major clusters of settlement, as dictated by the parish origins of the priests who collected them from the Charitable Catholic Ladies' Asylum. Strokestown orphans could be found near the towns of Nicolet/St-Gregoire, Lotbinière, and Rimouski.[11] The latter town, Rimouski, perhaps saw the largest placement of Strokestown orphans, with one in every four children sent there. Thus, Rimouski provides a good laboratory in which to study orphan placement because the census records for 1851–52 are complete, as are the registers for the Catholic parish of St. Germain. By contrast, Lotbinière County, another area of heavy placement, is frustrating to study because of the fragmentary nature of the census data for huge swathes of the county.

The county of Rimouski is located about 300 kilometers (187.5 miles) north east of Quebec City, with its northern boundary forming part of the southern shore of the St. Lawrence River, as it widens into the Gulf of St. Lawrence. It is primarily hilly terrain, an extension of the Appalachian mountain chain, punctuated by lakes and rivers which ultimately empty into the St. Lawrence.[12] Given its potential as home base for fishermen and with the promise of some agriculture on the coastal plain and in the river valleys, the French Crown ceded this remote seigneury to Renée Lepage de Sainte Claire in 1688 and the village, later to become the town of Rimouski, was founded eight years later and soon became the primary centre of seigneurial life.[13]

At the time of the arrival of the Famine orphans, the region had a growing population of over 3,600, about three-quarters of whom were farmers.[14] The rise in population was certainly facilitated by the completion, in the late 1830s, of the King's Road from the village of Trois Pistoles, west of Rimouski. Ironically, when the Irish children arrived in the region, local farmers were facing their own food crisis: local harvests had been poor and there were critical food shortages in the region. The other, perhaps pleasant, irony for the Irish children was that they would likely meet other Celtic settlers in Rimouski; a group of Scottish migrants had already settled in the Parish of St. Germain.[15]

Table 5.4 Sample of Strokestown Orphans Placed at Rimouski, 1847 N=10

Name	Age	Father	Mother	County	Placement	Religion	Ship
Andrew Dalton	13	William Dalton	Onah Tierney	Roscommon	Joseph Marcheterre	RC	*Erin's Queen*
Susan Dalton	16	William Dalton	Onah Tierney	Roscommon	Pierre Coté	RC	*Erin's Queen*
Peter Egan	16	Bryan Egan	Bridget Casey	Roscommon	Agapit Belanger	RC	*Erin's Queen*
George Cox	9	Martin Cox	Mary Maloney	Roscommon	Andre Gauvreau	RC	*Virginius*
Mary Cox	7	Martin Cox	Mary Maloney	Roscommon	Andre Gauvreau	RC	*Virginius*
Michael Hanley	12	Edward Hanley	Mary Egan	Roscommon	Germain Langis	RC	*Virginius*
Bridget Holden	14	Henry Holden	Bridget Mahan	Roscommon	Auguste Lavoie	RC	*Naomi*
Henry Holden	9	Henry Holden	Bridget Mahan	Roscommon	August Lavoie	RC	*Naomi*
Catherine Nugent	10	John Nugent	Sally Nally	Roscommon	Charles Paquet	RC	*Naomi*
John Dalton	5	William Dalton	Onah Tierney	Roscommon	Pierre Coté	RC	*Erin's Queen*

Source: O'Gallagher List; Census of 1851–1852, Canada East, District of Rimouski.

It was the curate of St. Germain Parish,[16] 31-year-old Father Antoine LeBel, who would be primarily responsible for bringing the Mahon orphans to this remote part of the diocese. Responding to Archbishop Signay's call for help to assist the refugees, LeBel served on Grosse Île for eight days between 3 August and 10 August 1847. He witnessed the human devastation first-hand, burying at least 123 migrants during his short sojourn on the island. His encounters with the Irish also included the conversion and marriage of two sailors who wished to be wed to two young Catholic passengers from County Longford.[17] His short time on the island left an indelible impression on him. With the assistance of Father Cazeau, LeBel pledged himself to honour the archbishop's request for orphan placement and took 30 Irish children to Rimouski, with the promise to return to the asylum for more.[18] Within the year, LeBel's superior at St. Germain, Father Thomas-Ferruce Picard-Destroismaisons, reported to the archbishop that the Irish children were adapting well to their new surroundings, while keeping their Irish surnames although converting their Christian names to a French equivalent.[19]

While local historians estimate that as many as 60 Irish children were placed in Rimouski,[20] the Asylum List indicates that 57 children, or 13.6 per cent of the 420 traceable locations on the list, were relocated there (see Table 5.2). Of these 57 children, only 24 were traceable to the 1851–52 census, ten of whom were from the Mahon cohort of orphans. Admittedly, almost five years elapsed between the placement of the Irish children and the taking of the census and much can happen in this short time to account for the number of missing orphans when census enumerators came to call. Children on the cusp of adulthood, like Peter Egan and Susan Dalton, both 16 in 1847, could have easily left their placements, seeking friends and relatives in other parts of British North America or the United States. Some may have left for other districts adjacent to Rimouski. Other children may have died, although if they had done so their deaths occurred outside of the parish, since the records of St. Germain do not register any burials of Irish children, including Mahon's orphans, during these intervening years. Nevertheless, the "disappearance" of these children from the public record, so soon after placement, casts considerable doubt on even their "de facto" adoption by French-Canadian farmers. Life on the frontiers of the future province of Quebec was merely a way station for these orphaned Irish children, as they eyed independence and betterment elsewhere.

All ten of the Mahon orphans who can be traced through the census were placed in French-Canadian Catholic homes. None were listed as family members, thus confirming that there was no adoption per se, but a living arrangement in which Irish orphans would help supplement the family workforce on the farm. Irish girls assisted

French-Canadian women with domestic and farm chores and the caring for little children. Boys worked in the barns and fields. The census confirms that boys were listed as *journalier* or day workers or labourers, and one as a farmer. What is clear from the census, however, that in a fashion not atypical within nineteenth century family life, these orphan children were expected to work. The story of George and Mary Cox, 9 and 7, originally from the Parish of Bumlin on the Mahon estate, reflected the patterns of rural placement experience among Irish orphans generally. They had survived passage on the notorious ship *Virginius*; parents Mary and Martin had not survived the voyage or quarantine; the children were placed with the Gauvreau Family in St. Luce, in Rimouski County; Mary jr. remained with the Gauvreaus, while George worked as a day labourer on the neighbouring farm of Eusèbe Lavoie. There is no record of either in the Rimouski area after 1852. One difference experienced by the Cox siblings from the other Mahon orphans was that they had a little money. After their parents' death, they were bequeathed the modest sum of £1 2s, the children's only means of survival.[21]

Such was not the case with Bridget and Henry Holden, aged 14 and 9, from the townland of Farnbeg. They were orphaned after leaving Grosse Île, because neither of their parents, also Henry and Bridget (Mahan), appear on the Grosse Île registers as having died at sea or in quarantine. The Holden siblings also lost two brothers, John (6) and Matthew (16) in the Quebec asylum. Henry and Bridget Holden, the younger, were both taken by Auguste Lavoie, dit Samson, a farmer in Rimouski; in the census they are listed as "Olden", likely a mistake made by a French-Canadian enumerator, when the children did not aspirate the "H" in their surname, when identifying themselves; neither Holden child was considered a member of the family. In 1852 Henry was listed as a *journalier*—or day worker on the farm. The Holdens are significant in that they were among the few orphaned siblings, from any region in Ireland, who were conscientiously placed in the same home.

The stories of Mahon orphans taken to other areas of Quebec all have different twists. Thomas and Patrick Quinn were placed with Georges Bourque, who was the gatehouse keeper of the seminary at Nicolet. Both orphan boys became Catholic priests in the diocese of Nicolet (see chapter 6). Michael Hanley was actually placed twice. His first placement, in August 1847, was with Olivier Donneau in Nicolet. Something must have caused Hanley not to live up to Donneau's expectations and he was returned to Quebec. In May 1848, he was sent to Germain Langis, a farmer in Rimouski. Hanley left the farm and was reported to have died in the United States in 1860. Anne Kilmartin, originally from Lissonuffy, was one of two orphans from her family who were left in the care of the Catholic Charitable Ladies. Her older sister Catherine (12) died in September 1847, and Anne (10) was placed in the farm of elderly Jacques Bourgeois of St-Grégoire, near Nicolet. Unlike her other orphans from the Mahon estate, the Bourgeois family considered Anne a family member. In 1871, Anne could still be found in St-Grégoire, and was living with the Brassard family, where she appears to have been a "day worker" likely occupied by taking care of the seven Brassard children, ranging in age from 2 to 14.[22]

Finally, as chapter six will reveal, Daniel and Catherine Tighe, also from Lissonuffy, may have become the most famous of Mahon's orphans. Having lost their widowed mother, Mary, three siblings, and their uncle's family on the trans-Atlantic voyage, Father Edouard Faucher collected them from the Prince Edward Street orphan asylum in Quebec and took them to his home county of Lotbinière. He dropped 12-year-old Daniel at the farm of François Coulombe and his wife, a childless couple in search of a young man to work their farm. They got more than what they bargained for. Nine-year old Catherine put up such a fuss at the thought of being separated from her brother that the Coulombes graciously took both children. In time, François secured the services of a notary, who drew up documents that would allow Daniel to inherit the farm. Since there was no legal adoption, title to the farm could not be assumed by Daniel, unless another legal provision was made for inheritance. Catherine eventually moved into the home of the Coté family, as a means of working as a housekeeper for Father E.B Cotè, of St-Croix Parish. Daniel was the first of four generations of Tighes to work the former Coulombe farm (see chapters 6 and 8). Daniel Tighe was unique to the Mahon orphans, whose life was transformed, and dreams of prosperity fulfilled.

While the Mahon orphans would be jockeyed between farms and local patrons, the rest of the Mahon emigrant survivors continued their journey into the interior of the continent. Mahon's migrants would be loaded on steamships in Quebec, one ironically bearing the name of one of their coffin ships, the *John Munn*, and make the 250-kilometer (156 mile) journey to Montreal, Canada's largest city and its industrial and commercial hub. There is no record of the steamers stopping at points in between so it can only be assumed that the survivors among the 1,490 went directly to Montreal. By August, Montreal had already experienced thousands of migrants pass through its ports. Many of the Irish who became sick after leaving Quebec were landed in the port of Montreal and taken to hospital sheds that had been constructed at Point St. Charles in the western suburbs of the city, on the waterfront. Here the sick, with all manner of disease were cared for by doctors, volunteers, and several Roman Catholic religious orders including the Sisters of Charity of Montreal (Grey Nuns),[23] the Sisters of Providence, the Sisters Hospitallers of St. Joseph, and the

Sisters of the Good Shepherd.[24] Clergy also served as chaplains to the fever sheds and at least four died, having contracted typhus from the migrants. Even the Bishop of Montreal, Ignace Bourget, was stricken with typhus having served in the sheds, but he survived. His Vicar General, Msgr. Prince, was not so fortunate and became the highest-ranking cleric in the city to die of the disease.

A report originally published in Montreal, but reprinted in Armagh, Ireland, was clear about the horror awaiting migrants and first responders in the sheds:

> All is consternation here. Those who recollect the visitation of cholera here some sixteen years since, pronounce that day terrible, but was light compared to the actual occurrences and heavy forebodings of the present. Such is the mortality among the people in the emigrant sheds, that coffins can with difficulty be got to made to cover or hearses to carry away the dead. I have seen a wretched looking native of Ireland with the remains of his deceased relatives on his back carrying them to the place of *sepulture*. And women may often be observed bearing the bodies of their children to the grave, with perhaps no-one to assist at the internment. ... Business is dull, the death and disease having a most blighting influence on the full trade.[25]

For their part, the Grey Sisters, with attending priest Father Jean Richard, arranged that a separate shed be set aside for the children, so that they did not need to be treated near infected adults, or be witness to the death and destruction in the main sheds.[26] By the end of the season, almost 6,000 migrants, unnamed, were buried in mass graves at Point St. Charles.

At Montreal there were five possible "next steps" for Mahon's people. Some elected to stay in the city, where there was already a significant Irish population, an Irish mission parish, and public acceptance of the Catholic fact. The Diffily family from the Kilmackenny townland chose this route and settled in the Irish section of the town. In 1856, a child was born to them, and the baptism was recorded in the registers of the basilica parish. The baptismal register reveals that Margaret, daughter of John Diffily and Catherine Monahan, of the Kilmackenny townland, was baptized in the presence of witnesses named Donnoghue and Reynolds. The convergence of these four Roscommon surnames, all included in the original Strokestown List, appears more than just a coincidence. Perhaps some of the Strokestown survivors re-founded a community together in the urban Irish villages that made up the wards of Montreal, and their settlement there made perfect sense. The city was one of the first major urban centers where immigrants could make contact. It provided employment and housing, albeit often in filthy neighborhoods, and it was for the most part a Catholic city, where the faith had a prominent public presence, entrenched in law. What the baptismal register entry confirms is that some of Mahon's families decided to stay together and recreate life in Montreal, taking advantage of the availability of employment, an established Irish community, and a clear sense of being part of a church that had status, in what had been more commonly considered a Protestant Empire.

A second possible destination for the Mahon migrant children, who were left orphaned by the ravages of typhus on their Canadian journey, might also be to sojourn in Montreal until such time as they were placed in Canadian homes and farms, as had been the case in Quebec. The Grey Sisters gathered the orphans of the Famine together in a separate shed at Point St. Charles, and those who they did not care for in their own facilities, were sent to the care of the Sisters of Providence in downtown Montreal, and their newly established St. Jerome Emilien Asylum, [27] named after the Catholic patron saint of orphans.[28] From St. Jerome, sick orphans would be treated in the adjoining St. Patrick's hospital or placed with local French and Irish Canadian families. Priests such as Father Calixte Marquis placed many of the orphans among families in his home parish of Becancour, east of Montreal on the road to Trois Rivières. Overflow girls were sent to the Sisters of the Good Shepherd who accommodated close to 100 orphans, many of them sick and dying. Of the Mahon families, perhaps only one, James Flood, was left abandoned as an orphan in Montreal. He appears on a list of orphans placed in the care of Bishop Bourget in 1847. Flood had accompanied his father and mother, James and Mary Flood, and his seven siblings from the Cregga Feehilys Quarter townland on the Mahon estate. There is a record of at least three of his siblings dying at Grosse Île, but no record of what had happened to the rest of his family. Presumably, the surviving Floods had arrived at Montreal, only to be stricken by the typhus bacteria, which during its incubation period gave them the semblance of health, appeared after they arrived at Point St. Charles. Only the records of young James remained and even he is described in them as being very sick. In the absence of any surviving records from Point St. Charles and the omission of county of origin in the official ledgers of the St Jerome Emilian Asylum, it is unlikely that we will ever know who and how many of Mahon's people passed through Montreal or perished there.

A third possible journey made by Mahon's people may have been to the north west, up the Ottawa River towards the lumber town of Bytown, now called Ottawa and currently serving as Canada's capital. In the 1840s Bytown was little more than a dirty colonial backwater where logs were driven either on to Quebec, or to the mills that dominated both sides of the river. Named after Colonel John By, the town was also the northern terminus of the canal built by the Colonel, his engineers and Irish navvies, thus transforming the Rideau River system into a safe transportation route that avoided the border (and unwanted military encounter) with the United States.

The Ottawa Valley had been a known place of settlement for the Irish long before the Famine. Irish Protestants had carved out farmsteads in Pontiac County, on the Canada East shore of the river, and had settled the townships in Carleton and Renfrew counties on the Canada West side of the river. Irish Catholics, many from Kerry and Limerick, had also become farmers in the area, who supplemented their incomes in the winter by working in the timber shanties of the upper valley, harvesting the first growth stands of red and white pine. For Famine migrants, such as Mahon's people, the Valley would be known for its Irish settlements and its potential for cheap land and work in the forests and canals. Admaston Township, in Renfrew County, for example, became a target to Famine migrants, particularly drawn to its cheap but marginal agricultural lands.[29] Had Mahon's migrants chosen this route "up the Valley" the town of Bytown would have been their principal stop, whether they had travelled up the Ottawa River, or via the Rideau Canal, which linked the upper Ottawa Valley with the upper St. Lawrence Valley.

At Bytown, the Irish would be greeted with much of the same tragedy that awaited them in Quebec and Montreal. Irish migrants who began to show symptoms of typhus and other diseases were herded into sheds near Barracks Hill, now the site of Canada's Parliament buildings.[30] Once again it was the Bytown branch of the Grey Nuns, the Sisters of Charity led by Mother Elizabeth Bruyère, that assumed primary responsibility for the Irish migrants. As had been the case all along the Canadian journey, Irish Catholics found themselves in a town where the Catholic Church was a prominent minority with an established health and social service infrastructure operated by Catholic women religious. The Grey Sisters also created an orphanage in their convent-hospital, accommodating just over 60 orphans in 1847, and using it as dispersal point for local French-Canadian families who requested a young Irish boy or girl for domestic service or farm labour.[31] To date, the surviving records of the Grey Sisters' orphanage and the lists compiled by James Allison, the emigration agent who monitored the Montreal to Ottawa migration route, contain no surnames from the Strokestown list. If Mahon's people passed through Bytown, on route to the upper valley, they did so without leaving a trace in the surviving local records.[32]

A fourth route available to Mahon's migrants, once they reached Montreal, was use of the roads and river systems south to the United States via the Richelieu River and the town of St. Jean. The Richelieu could lead prospective migrants to the northern shores of Lake Champlain in Upper New York State, and then southward to the Hudson River, which empties into the Atlantic at New York City. This was a well-known route used by landlord Stephen DeVere in 1847, when he made a brief visit to Troy, New York, after leaving part of his entourage in Montreal. DeVere had accompanied many of his tenants who were leaving the estate in Limerick to begin new lives in North America. Another access point from this route was for migrants to travel down the Hudson and then proceed east, overland through Massachusetts to Boston. In both these American centres, Strokestown survivors would find members of extended family or acquaintances within the growing Irish urban enclaves that historically distinguished these American ports. American-bound migrants from Roscommon might also use the Lake Champlain route to access sections of Vermont, particularly the town of Rutland, where many of the migrants from the Crown townland of Ballykicline, adjacent to Mahon's estate, would eventually settle.[33]

There is considerable evidence drawn from the American censuses of 1850 and 1860 to suggest that some of Mahon's migrants made temporary homes in Troy and Albany, both in New York State, and in New Jersey and Vermont. This was likely the route taken by the six Sheridan children of the townland of Curhouna. Their parents James Sheridan and Mary Sheridan perished by the time the children had reached the Quebec orphan asylum on Prince Edward Street. Yet on 2 October 1847, led likely by the eldest sibling Catherine, age 20, the surviving children, Mary (19), Anne (15), Owen (14), Ellen (12), and Patrick (10), made their way to Lockport, New York, on the Erie Canal. They likely employed the Montreal to Albany route, then followed the Erie Canal, as did the Fury family from the Culleen Park townland. It is also likely that these Mahon migrants were attracted by the possibility of canal work, but perhaps even more lured to the area in the knowledge that a Roscommon-born priest, Father John Sheridan, rode circuit in the area.[34]

The fifth option before the Irish emigrants was to journey further into the interior into what had been their promised destination: Upper Canada. The Mahon survivors would board steamers at Lachine, at the west end of Montreal Island, and shooting across the Lachine rapids moving up the St. Lawrence to Cornwall. At each stop thereafter, Boards of Health were in place to take care of the increasing numbers of sick and dying. Kingston, the former capital of the Upper Province, was a major disembarkation place. What would have greeted the Mahon migrants was little different from what they had experienced in Quebec and Montreal. For public health reasons, landings of emigrants were restricted to a single pier, Brewery Wharf. The sick passengers were removed from the ships and dockyards and ushered to makeshift sheds at King and Emily Streets. Unfortunately, the city workers built the sheds too close to the residential area of the town, which sent local citizens into panic, fearing the spread of disease and the odors emerging out of the sheds in the heat of the summer. While the town was primarily Protestant and had been referred to as the "Derry of Canada," the local Irish-born Catholic Bishop, Patrick Phelan, and the town's Mayor Thomas Kirkpatrick, created a cooperative environment, which was imitated by others who were directly responsible for emigrant assistance. Notable was the co-operation between Kingston's Religious Hospitallers of St. Joseph, who operated an orphanage and the Hôtel Dieu Hospital, and the Protestant women who managed the Kingston General Hospital.[35]

With the census data for Kingston missing for 1851–52, it is difficult to ascertain how many of the Mahon migrants passed through Kingston. It is clear that there were 989 deaths of Catholic migrants in the city, and at least 328 (one-third) were identified by county, 13 of whom were from Roscommon. Included in the latter were names that might be linked to Mahon's migrants: Anne Beirne (20), Patrick Noon (20), James Difly (17), Catherine Kelly (23), and Patrick Mahon (24).[36] The list of orphans recorded in the records of the Hospitaller Sisters offers no names of the Roscommon families. In December 1847, however, the city created a House of Industry for the local population and emigrants who were destitute. The House provided shelter for families, the aged, and children, who were then despatched to various places of potential employment. It is here in the ledgers of the House of Industry that some names common to Mahon's migrants can be found, identified by their Roscommon origins, who surrendered themselves on the charity of Kingston citizens. It is uncertain whether these Roscommon families, predominantly women and their children, were either stranded in Kingston, after the loss of their family head, or were part of the Emigrant Agent Anthony Hawke's consolidation of all refugees from the eastern part of the Province to Kingston, for the winter of 1847–48.

It is entirely possible that members of the Mahon emigrant group wintered in Kingston at the House of Industry. At least 32 persons in the House were listed as having come from Roscommon, and half of these shared surnames from the lists of migrants prepared by John Ross Mahon and his agents in advance of the migration scheme: Feeney, Burn (Bierne), Noone, Hanley, Madden, and Green. Most of these migrants appear to be single or widowed women with small children or teenagers. If they had been part of Mahon's migrants they would have been only identified as a "female over 14 years of age" on the ship's records, since the Mahon List usually only identifies the male household head, not the spouse. Is it possible that these women survived the loss of their husbands after Grosse Île, only to find themselves completely destitute and dependent of the charity of the people of Kingston? One such example is that of 40-year-old Nelly Feeney and her two children Jane (14) and Anne (7).[37] There were at least four Feeney households among the 271 families assisted off the Mahon estate. Could Nelly have been the widow of Michael Feeney of Scramogue, who died on the *Virginius*, leaving a wife and three children?

Or could she have been the widow of 42-year-old Patrick Feeney, of the Culliagh townland, who died on the *Virginius* as well, but who emigrated with several Green families, the remnants of whom appear at the Kingston House of Industry, shortly after the arrival of Nelly. Margaret Madden arrived at the Kingston refuge shortly after Nelly. It is possible she lost her husband John, of Goortose Murray townland, at Grosse Île, but managed to bring their sons John (3) and Michael (1) as far as Upper Canada. Unfortunately, John was hospitalized, and the baby died that winter. With the census records missing for Kingston, one might never be able to make a firm conclusion as to what happened to these fragments of Mahon's migrants in Kingston.

Irish migrants used Kingston as a diving board into the Upper Canadian interior. Since the Canadian Shield juts down prominently to the north of Kingston in a rocky "land-o-lakes" wilderness called the Frontenac Axis, Mahon's migrants would have found little opportunity to engage in agricultural work to the north of the city. The best opportunities were available in the farmlands bordering Lake Ontario, and in the hinterlands of port towns west of Kingston. Lake boats and Royal Mail steam packets would collect passengers, at the expense of the Canadian government, in Kingston and transport them to small ports on the north shore of the great lake—Cobourg, Port Hope, Darlington, and Whitby—or to Toronto, the Niagara Peninsula on the south shore of the Lake, or to Hamilton, at the western head of Lake Ontario. From the small lake ports emigrants could venture inland to agricultural areas near Peterborough, and farmland in what are now the Durham Region, Victoria and Northumberland Counties, and lands near Lake Simcoe. In this way, Brian O'Hara of the Kilgraffy townland was recorded as farming in Northumberland by 1861, and Michael Reilly was doing the same near Peterborough that same year. Similarly, Michael Duffy of Laughboy townland could be found in 1851 was sojourning in Hope Township, Durham County.[38] Michael Mullooly of Lower Culliagh townland was on the move until many years later, he settled in Victoria County. Given that much of the farmland in the counties and townships directly adjacent to Lake Ontario's north shore had filled with settlers in the 50 years prior to the Famine migration, the suggestion of several days' walk, or by hired cart, on the poor roads heading into the "Great Pine Ridge" may have been sufficient deterrent to many of the surviving Mahon migrants to keep moving west, lured by better prospects.

The city of Toronto was the hub of economic activity in Canada West. Located on Lake Ontario some 250 kilometres (156 miles) to the west of Kingston, it possessed a fine natural protected harbour, numerous industries, and accessible transportation to points north, south, and west of the city. With a population of only about 20,000 in 1847, the city was completely overwhelmed between June and November that year by over 38,000 emigrants, most of whom were Irish fleeing the Famine conditions in Ireland. The city had established its Board of Health as early as February, in anticipation of a busy sailing season, but certainly the Mayor and Council never anticipated processing the near equivalent of twice the city's population. Mahon's migrants, with all the others, would be landed at Dr Reese's Wharf, where they would be triaged by the police and local Emigration Agent Edward McElderry. The sick would be sent by cart to the Toronto General Hospital at King and John Streets, a place transformed into an emigrant hospital with up to 14 outdoor "fever sheds." Hundreds crowded into the sheds daily and, by the end of the season, 1,124 persons were recorded on the death registers by the hospital staff. Those who recovered from a variety of ailments, including typhus, were then transported to a Convalescent Hospital west of the sheds, where they were prepared for re-entry into society, or returned to the Emigrant Hospital if they had suffered a relapse of their sickness. McElderry sent the healthy packing both from the Convalescent Hospital and the arrival shed at Reese's Wharf. Those travelling inland were given Government-subsidized travel vouchers to travel to the farming townships north of Toronto, or to towns to the west: Brantford, Hamilton, London, St. Thomas, and Sandwich (Windsor).[39] Other healthy emigrants were placed back on steamers and Durham boats and transported directly by water to Hamilton or Niagara. From Niagara, it was a short journey to western New York State, Pennsylvania, Ohio and the American Midwest. Sandwich was also a potential entry point to the American Northwest—Michigan, Wisconsin, the Upper Mississippi, and destinations as varied as Iowa and New Orleans.

The problem with Toronto is that almost no Mahon migrants appear in the routinely generated records. None appear among the dead at the fever sheds, nor in the fragmentary records of the Catholic cemetery, or the Church of England burial ground. No names from Mahon's estate are evident in the ledger of admissions for the Convalescent Hospital, and no widows and orphans from the estate are recorded among the 197 entries in the register for the Widows and Orphans Asylum. In Toronto, the care for Irish orphans was done through the co-operation of the major churches, to preserve the Protestant and Catholic faiths among the children of each group. The priests of the Diocese of Toronto arranged for orphans to be contracted out to "upstanding" Catholic farmers in the hinterlands of the province's commercial centre, once again placing over 100 Irish boys and girls in steady jobs, with shelter, and a monthly wage.[40] The city of Toronto marks a notable departure from other British North American centres in that agreements of indenture were formally drawn up and periodically inspected by municipal authorities. Yet, where Mahon orphans were found in reception centres to the east in Canada, none were in Toronto. This absence is complicated by the fact that the Census for Toronto, in 1851–52, is lost. While, 2,000 famine migrants remained in Toronto, after touching down at Reese's Wharf, there is little evidence to suggest that Mahon's people were among them. At a time when migrants and Upper Canadians were "on the move," it is not improbable that the Mahon migrants followed suit.

There is evidence of Mahon migrants sojourning in three areas, for which Toronto would have been a natural hub. First, travel vouchers and existing census records reveal that they were in the rural hinterlands north and west of Toronto. Secondly, there is strong evidence pointing to Mahon migrants recreating community on the Niagara Peninsula, particularly along the Welland Canal. Finally, they may also have been attracted by the cheap but potentially fertile lands of the Huron Tract, lands adjacent to Lake Huron, one of the largest of the Great Lakes. The gaps in the surviving records are enormous, but from time-to-time other evidence—newspapers, court documents, work ledgers, and official receipts—allow the historical detective a chance to pick up the "scent" again.

In an effort to relieve population pressure and the cost of relief in the main towns, local emigration agents provided vouchers for free transportation for migrants to rural and frontier areas. In Toronto, Edward McElderry was particularly effective in clearing out the healthy Irish migrants by hiring a great variety of carters to take them out of the city. Vouchers for baggage and families were presented to private drivers and waggoneers to take Irish emigrants to what is now York County. One popular destination was the Holland Marsh, north of Toronto on Yonge Street, where the fertile soils were providing increased need for agricultural labour. It is possible that Bridget Brannon of Gortoose Murray townland was subsidized on her journey from Toronto west to the township of the Gore.[41] Similarly, Edward Duffy, and his family of five, from Aghadangan townland, Peter Dempsey, and his family of seven from Cloonrain townland, and Martin Brannon and his wife, also from Cloonrain, may have been taken to Holland Landing, after having landed in Toronto.[42] Reflecting the emigrant mobility of the era, however, Duffy, by 1852, seemed to have relocated to Durham County to the east of Toronto.[43]

There was also a small clustering of Mahon migrants near or close to Hamilton, at the head of Lake Ontario, west of Toronto. In May 1847, the "Widow" Cox and her children made the journey from the Culliagh townland in Bumlin parish and persisted all the way to Hamilton (see chapter 4). Her youngest son, Patrick Cox, however, had taken ill, and recovered on Grosse Île, reappeared with his family, in Hamilton, in the Census of 1851–1852.[44] Susan Cox, a "knit worker" was living in what enumerators described as "a hovel," with her three children.[45] The Cox family were not alone among the Mahon migrants in clustering around the Hamilton area: Peter Brannon of Ballyhubert worked in the city as a labourer, as did John Coleman of the Curhouna townland. Patrick Tighe and Michael Donnelly both from Dooherty townland, were listed as labourers in nearby Haldimand County in 1851. John McNamara, also from Dooherty, was listed as a labourer in nearby Brantford. It is curious how so many from the same townland may have ended up in a similar region of Upper Canada, perhaps a testimony to the region's economic opportunities or a degree of agency among the Mahon migrants. It is also not coincidental that when Susan Cox left an address for any correspondence about her son, inquiries were to be sent to Lawrence McNamara, a mason, in Hamilton. One suspects that the region may have been already known to Strokestown families before their departure from Ireland.

Perhaps one of the most attractive areas of settlement to Irish emigrants in the 1840s was the Huron Tract in the western region of Upper Canada. Through the agencies of Lord Goderich, the British Chancellor of the Exchequer, the Westminster Parliament prepared legislation, in 1826, to form a joint stock company, the Canada Company, to administer and sell the 1.1 million acres recently "acquired" from the Chippewa First Nation on the Huron Tract, and 42,000 acres of the Halton Tract, near the current city of Guelph.[46] The Canada Company was headed by a London-based Commission of Directors (after whom all the townships were named) although the Chief administrator on the ground was John Galt, a Scottish-born novelist, historian, and entrepreneur, who from his headquarters in Guelph, Canada West (Upper Canada), was tasked with surveying and allocating the lands of the Huron Tract. Competition from cheaper lands in the American Midwest and bordering territories to Canada West provided serious challenges for the Canada Company, and subsequent failures to attract large groups of settlers had Directors and Parliamentarians questioning the continuation of its charter. In 1839, Galt's successor, Frederick Widder adopted a new strategy: advertise the lands more effectively in the provincial newspapers and create a lease-to-own scheme, which might be more attractive to prospective settlers. A new extended lease period of ten years was created, with no down-payment required. Fifty and 100 acre lots were available for five pence an acre rent per year with six per cent interest. Average annual rent would be around three pounds.[47] The settler could fix the final price in advance and could be awarded the deed once the balance was paid. The lands were widely advertised in the major points of entry and by word of mouth.

Irish immigrants, particularly Famine migrants, would have been aware of this deal awaiting them on the Canadian frontier. Moreover, with the established presence of some pre-Famine Irish in the region, there may have been personal links pre-existing between Famine migrants and those who had gone before them, simulating the characteristics of chain migration. With access to good roads out through London, Canada West, the townships of Biddulph, Hibbert, and McGillivray began to fill as early as 1842 (Table 5.6). The townships of Usborne, Fullarton, and Hay, would be serviced by the Huron road from Guelph, Wilmot, and Stratford, eventually connecting to Goderich, which accounted for the slower rise of these areas. Irish migrants were well represented, comprising between one-quarter and one-third of the non-Canadian born in each township, except for Biddulph, where the Irish constituted four in every five foreign-born household heads.[48] While the total numbers of Irish Catholics and Irish Protestants varied from township to township, Hibbert was overwhelmingly Catholic, while Protestantism was prominent among Irish settlers elsewhere in the Tract.[49]

It is toward this new Irish homeland that three of Mahon's migrant families may have been drawn. In 1852, James Carroll, his wife Bridget and at least three children were living in McKillop Township, in Huron County. While little is known about them, other than their farming activities, they may be the same family that Mahon had assisted off Dooherty townland. The Carrolls appear to remain in the area and elude the census takers, although a James Carroll does emerge later in the century as sheriff in nearby County Middlesex. Similarly, there is evidence to suggest that William Cain, of the Killinlosset townland, may have also landed in McGillivray Township in the Huron Tract as early as 1848. Census data for 1852, however, sees Cain having moved to nearby Bentick Township, in Grey County.[50] Perhaps much easier to track is Patrick Boland, from Tully in the civil parish of Kilglass, who appears to settle in the McGillivray Township. While the name is transcribed incorrectly as Bohan, on the commemorative glass wall at Strokestown Park, the original archival records list him as Boland. The Canadian Census of 1911 confirms that his year of migration was 1847. The Bolands eventually acquired two 50 acre lots in McGillivray, which was a staggering amount of land compared to the few acres they subsisted on in Tully, while paying rent to Mahon.[51] The Bolands remained in the area for generations, with their activities reported in the local press until the 1940s, almost a century after their arrival. As such, Patrick and his family defied the usual characteristic of Irish settlers being on the move, during the period immediately after their arrival in British North America.

Table 5.5: Settlement By Household Head & Total Population, Selected Townships, 1842

Township	Household Head	Land held	Family Size	Total Population
Biddulph	93	14,399 acres	383	383
Fullarton	12	1,700 acres	45	45
Hay	17	2,300 acres	71	71
McGillivray	44	11,077	169	169
Usborne	32	3400 acres	163	163

Source: Huron County Museum & Archives, Assessment Rolls, Huron District, 1842.

Table 5.6: Settlement & Religion in the Huron Tract, Selected Townships, 1847

Township	Church of England	Church of Scotland	Roman Catholic	Methodist Wesleyan	Other Presbyterian	Baptist	Lutheran	Other	Total
Biddulph	751	—	400	—	6	29	—		1217
Fullarton	226	265	17	96	—	—	138		778
Hay	51	44	48	7	23	—	—	12	190
Hibbert	53	8	183	6	—	—	—		247
McGillivray	373	52	85	19	—	33	—		594
Usborne	197	37	21	83	21	—	—		399

Source: Huron County Museum & Archives, Assessment Rolls, Huron District, 1847.

The most impressive clustering of the Mahon migrants, however, appeared on the Niagara Peninsula. Thomas Brennan and his wife Bridget and their two children who came from the Kilmackenny townland, had connections in the Niagara region. After her arrival in August 1847, Bridget, at the age of 37, died at Grosse Île and the surviving members of the family sojourned at Quebec for the rest of the year and then moved further inland.[52] By 1848, it appears that only Thomas and his teenage daughter were still alive and living near Queenston, in between Niagara-on-the-Lake and Niagara Falls, where they reunited with fellow migrants from the Mahon estate. While there is no Patrick O'Connor listed on the original ledger of the 271 assisted families, the O'Connors and Brennans seemed to have known one another and the re-union of these families from Lissonuffy would have tragic consequences.

The Niagara Peninsula was well known to migrants from Roscommon. Local parish records from St. Vincent de Paul Catholic Church in Niagara indicate that there had been many Irish soldiers, some from Roscommon, attached to British regiments at Fort George in the town. The Royal Canadian Rifles, for example, contained men with Roscommon surnames, most of whom made appearances at Father John Carroll's Church for baptisms, marriages, and the burial of family members.[53] The Irish would find themselves well served in terms of their Faith. The Catholic Church was well established in the area with parishes in both St. Catharine's and Niagara-on-the-Lake, each served by Irish-born priests.[54] The area was also attractive to workers, particularly from Connaught and Munster, who were employed by the hundreds on the Welland Canal, a new waterway that helped commercial and military vessels circumvent the famous falls on the Niagara River that separated the Upper Canada from the United States.[55] The canal workers were noted for their violent behaviour and not necessarily motivated for sectarian reasons. More prevalent was the rivalry between Irish Catholics from Connaught and Munster, who resented any advantage taken by their countrymen on the canal works.[56] In fact, it was not until 1848 that riots between Irish Catholic canal workers and local Orangemen, erupted with a devasting loss of life for Catholics in the melee. With an Irish flavour well-established in the area, the free exercise of their Faith, and employment, it is not surprising that Brennan and the O'Connors would find themselves among fellow Rossies, including perhaps Thady Kennedy, from Gortoose McGuire townland, the widow of Michael Hopkins and her family from Culliagh, and Patrick Dalton from the Mullivetron townland. Also living in the area were the Glancy family, likely migrants from Roscommon who left prior to the Famine.[57]

In late May 1848, the Roscommon migrants received unwanted attention. The lifeless bodies of Patrick and Mary O'Connor were found, in varying states of decomposition on the banks of the Niagara River.[58] They had been dead for several weeks. Thomas Brennan and Mary O'Connor had often been seen in the company of one another. They were noted for their drinking and quarrelling while witnesses observed, in contrast, that Patrick O'Connor was a "character of industriousness and [a] quiet person."[59] Brennan's 16-year-old daughter was reported to have been travelling with her father and Mrs. O'Connor from Queenston to Chippewa on the morning of 4 May 1848, but she departed from them when she stopped into a road-side tavern for a drink. What happened next is a matter of great dispute, but the scenario may have developed as follows. The daughter returned to Queenston in the evening to the O'Connor's rented house, near the old Church, where the Brennans had lodged. In the morning she awakened, and all the residents were gone. If the Solicitor-General's account is correct, Brennan strangled Mary to death that night and returned to Queenston, whereupon he dragged Patrick out of bed by the hair, pulled him outside and bludgeoned him with his own hammer. He then returned for the boy, John, whom he tossed over the embankment overlooking the Niagara River. Brennan was later arrested in Toronto carrying $18- or $19-dollars cash and trying to hawk Mary O'Connor's plaid dress. In court, he testified to his innocence and that he and Mary were travelling to Mr. Kennedy's, perhaps Roscommon native Thady Kennedy, and that she, in fact, had murdered her own husband, who had amassed close to $20 in savings to be used as remittances to secure the passage of several of his daughters left behind with his brother William in Ireland.[60]

What is even more curious about this case is that aside from Brennan himself, who spoke in his own defence at the trial in September 1848, and his daughter who remained nameless within the trial transcript, all the key witnesses were potentially from the Mahon estate. Young John O'Connor, described as being "in great distress of mind," survived the fall and hobbled bruised and with broken arm to the house of Margaret Hopkins, herself, potentially a native of the Mahon estate. When Brennan's daughter arrived to collect the boy, he refused to leave, terrified of her, and making incredible the alibi that the O'Connors had gone to Lockport, New York, coincidentally another point of settlement for some of Mahon's migrants.[61] Later, while on the stand, Patrick Dalton, another Roscommon native, was lured into a heated exchange with Brennan. In the midst of the verbal melee, Dalton alluded to the murder of Brennan's mother back in Ireland, an act perpetrated by Brennan's own brother and sister. The evidence mounted: witnesses claimed they saw Brennan overlooking the precipice where the bodies were found; there were remnants of blood found on the defendant's hammer; and the strange circumstances of his arrest in Toronto, in which he had on his possession incriminating evidence. The jury found Brennan guilty in a matter of minutes and the court sentenced him to be hanged in October 1848. Later he confessed to the murder of Mary but stuck by his story that she had murdered her husband and he had never harmed the boy.

The Judge awarded care of John O'Connor to a local Mennonite farmer, John Fritz, and by 1851 young John O'Connor, now 9-years-old, was listed as being a Quaker.[62] Thomas Brennan was found guilty and executed on 4 October 1848; he was buried by Father John Carroll, in the St. Vincent de Paul Parish cemetery.[63] By the time of the 1851–1852 census, most of the Mahon migrants, except Dalton, had moved on, likely to the United States, given the proximity of Niagara to the American border. True to form, like most migrants of the era in Upper Canada, the Mahon migrants were on the move. The Brennan-O'Connor murder case reveals much about the agency of Mahon's migrants and their ability to rekindle old friendships and rivalries as they built a new life for themselves in Canada.[64]

It should be noted that for many Irish migrants in 1847, British North America was merely a way station, a temporary place to sojourn before entering the United States. In 1847, American authorities limited the number of Irish immigrants able to land in ports such as Boston, New York, Charleston, Philadelphia, or New Orleans, with heavy fines placed on ships that landed sick or indigent passengers. This meant that as few as 119,000 Irish were able to land in the United States.[65] The alternative for less than scrupulous ship's captains and their financiers was to redirect their cargoes to British colonial ports—Halifax, Saint John, and Quebec—where health standards were less rigorous, emigrant agents appeared less perspicacious than their American counterparts, and fares for passengers were cheaper. For many Irish who intended to join friends and family in the growing Irish enclaves in American cities, cheaper fares and lower standards required them to undertake a more circuitous route through British North America. The ports of Halifax and Saint John, which had direct shipping routes to Boston and New York, offered the Irish a quick transition from a transatlantic crossing, to passage of a regular cargo ship or steamer to the "Boston States." From Quebec, the Irish would proceed inland by boat to Montreal, from where New York was accessible by road, or by the Lake Champlain-Hudson River waterway. Farther inland, Kingston and Toronto provided access to American ports across Lake Ontario, and the Niagara peninsula, which was a major place of departure for migrants heading to upper New York State, Pennsylvania, Ohio, and the mid-West.

Mahon's migrants were no different from their fellow travellers from Ireland. Preliminary analysis of the United States Census of 1850 reveals that perhaps as many as 29 families from the Mahon Estate made their way south to the United States. Most prospective matches were discovered in New York, with at least three families settling in Pennsylvania, four in Ohio, and two in Illinois. The expansion of the agricultural frontier beyond the Appalachian Mountains, and the growth of new service centres, in the mid west and across the Mississippi, attracted many immigrants, including the Irish. Some families from the 1,490 may have set down roots in more remote places such as St. Louis, Missouri, or New Orleans, Louisiana, which already had large Irish communities, who might provide a comfortable cultural and religious environment for Mahon's migrants. In fact, St. Patrick's Roman Catholic Church, just off Canal Street in New Orleans, was served by Father Patrick Plunkett, himself a native of Roscommon.[66] As was the case in the British colonies to the north, Irish migrants found themselves employed in industrial cities as labourers and as farm workers on the frontier. Fourteen heads were listed as labourers, nine did not have employment, and three worked at other unskilled jobs. With three-quarters of this American data set listed among the lowest of those in the occupational spectrum, the

Strokestown "matches" appear to confirm stereotypes of the Irish navvy in American labour history.[67] The tracing of the Mahon migrants in the United States is still a work in progress but the preliminary results are a testament to the agility and determination of the migrants and the possibility of pre-existing migration chains between the United States and Roscommon.

The search for Mahon's migrants is ongoing, as more records come to light and new clues are revealed. What is important to be gleaned from the research thus far is that however harrowing the crossing and early weeks of their days in Canada may have been, the estimated deaths of Mahon's migrants were greatly inflated. One could point to the fragmentary evidence or hearsay testimony provided to the Canadian and Irish press, or perhaps the more cynical might see such exaggerations to vilify Mahon and his entire class. What is clear is that one in five household heads died on route to Canada, and perhaps as many as one in three of all the 1,490 succumbed to typhus and other diseases before they were able to land at Quebec. While this is horrific, in and of itself in terms of the loss of life, it does tend to deflect attention away from those families that survived the experience, moved on, and reset their lives on the Canadian and American cities and rural frontiers. As Table 5.7 demonstrates, one in every three households was able to start anew as part of the burgeoning underclass of labourers and farm workers in North America. It is also true that even some orphans, Daniel Tighe included, were able to live the dreams that their parents had for them. Yet, with at least 40 per cent of families still unaccounted for, there is much detective work yet to do.

Table 5.7: Status of Mahon's Migrants After Leaving Ireland, 1847-48

Status of Household Head	Number	Percentage
Died at Sea or In Quarantine	58	21.2
Confirmed Not Travelling	3	1.2
Location in Canada	71	25.9
Location in United States	29	10.6
Location/Status Unknown	113	41.2
Total Identified	161	58.8
Total Households from the Estate	274	100.00

Source: *Census of Canada*, 1851-1852; Registers of Catholic Parishes in Canada East and Canada West (online Familysearch.com); Library and Archives Canada; RG 19 D-5, v.2532, Department of Finance, Travel Vouchers and Expenses, 1843-1854; André Charbonneau and Doris Drule-Dubé, *A Register of Deceased Persons at Sea and on Grosse Île in 1847* (Ottawa: Canadian Heritage, Parks Canada, 1997).

NOTES

1. The departure of the four ships that carried the Mahon Passengers varied according to their time of arrival at Grosse Île and the length of their quarantine. *Erin's Queen*, the first ship to arrive, on 11 July, departed for Quebec on 23 July, leaving 71 dead at Grosse Île and 20 dead on board ship during the wait. The *John Munn* left on 12 August after ten days in quarantine. The *Virginius* left the same day, after having spent 13 days in quarantine and leaving 90 dead on the island and unloading 19 more victims who had died on board ship. The *Naomi* departed Grosse Île on 10 August, after 11 days in quarantine. Eighty-seven of her passengers were buried at Grosse Il while 31 more, who had died on board ship during the quarantine, were transferred to the island for interment. Andre Charbonneau and Andre Sevigny, *1847—Grosse Île: A Record of Daily Events* (Ottawa: Canadian Heritage and Parks Canada, 1997), pp. 156, p. 184, p. 196, and p. 199.
2. The mobility of migrants to the Canadas is evidenced in David Gagan, *Hopeful Travelers: Families Land and Social Change in Mid-Victorian Peel County, Canada West* (Toronto: University of Toronto Press, 1981) and Michael Katz, *The People of Hamilton, Canada West: family and Class in a Mid-Nineteenth-Century City* (Cambridge: Harvard University Press, 1975).
3. Marie-Claude Belley, "Un exemple de prise en charge de l'enfance dépendante au milieu de XIXe siècle: les orphelins irlandais à Québec en 1847 et 1848," (Thèse [M.A.] – Université Laval, 2003), p. 62.
4. Marianna O'Gallagher, "The Orphans of Grosse Île: Canada and the adoption of Irish Famine Orphans, 1847–48," in Patrick O'Sullivan, ed., *The Irish World Wide: The Meaning of the Famine* (5 vols, London and Washington, 1997), pp. iv, 104–105.
5. This process is mythologized by Historica Canada, "Irish Orphans," Heritage Minute #16, DVD, 1991, re-launched 2012. See Jason King, "Remembering Famine Orphans: The Transmission of Famine Memory between Ireland and Quebec," in Christian Noack, Lindsay Janssen & Vincent Comerford, eds., *Holodomor and Gorta Mor: Histories, Memories, and Representations of Famine in Ukraine and Ireland* (London: Anthem Press, 2012), pp. 115–140.
6. John Francis McGuire, *The Irish in America* (New York: D. & J. Sadlier, 1880), p. 138.
7. Hughes, "Adoption in Canada". 104; Dominique Goubau et Claire O'Neill, "L'Adoption, L'Eglise et l'Etat : les origines tumultueuses d'une institution légale," *Les Cahiers de Droit*, 38, no. 4 (decembre 1997), p. 771.
8. Margaret E. Hughes, "Adoption in Canada," in D. Mendes da Costa, QC, ed., *Studies in Canadian Family Law*, vol.1 (Toronto: Butterworth, 1972), p. 105.
9. Veronica Strong-Boag, *Finding Families, Finding Ourselves: English Canada Encounters Adoption from the Nineteenth Century to the 1990s* (Toronto: Oxford University Press, 2006), p. 18.
10. Bettina Bradbury, "The Fragmented Family: Family Strategies in the Face of Death, Illness, and Poverty, Montreal, 1860–1885," in Joy Parr ed., *Childhood and Family in Canadian History* (Toronto: McClelland and Stewart, 1982), pp. 109–111.
11. Marianna O'Gallagher, "Children of the Famine," *The Beaver* (February-March, 2008), pp. 50–56.
12. Jean Larrivée, "Une Ville en Pline nature," Jeannot Bourdages, et al. *Rimouski Depuis Ses Origines* (Rimouski: Société d'histoire du Bas Saint-Laurent, 2006), pp. 3–4.

13. Sylvain Gosselin, "Les terretoires et ses premiers occupants," in Bourdages, pp. 21–22.
14. Census of 1851–52 indicated that 3,653 were in the district, most of whom were rural dwellers. See also, Paul Larocque, "Un Region de Peuplement (1790–1855)," in Bourdages, 95–112.
15. Larocque, pp. 114–117.
16. Ibid., 100. The parish was erected in the 1820s and named after St. Germain d'Auxerre, the patron of Paris. Coincidentally, the father of the first seigneur was Germain Lepage. Gabriel Langlois, *Dossier Sur La Paroisse de Saont-Germain de Rimouski (histoire religieuse) 1701–1987* (Rimouski: Centre Pastorale, 1988), p. 12 and pp. 55–56.
17. Marianna O'Gallagher and Rose Masson Dompierre, *Eyewitness: Grosse Isle, 1847* (Ste-Foy: Carraig Books, 1995), p. 253 and pp. 262–264.
18. Lebel to Cazeau, 18 April 1848 as cited in Larocque, pp. 116–117.
19. Ibid., p. 117. For more on Father Destroismaisons see Langlois, p. 151.
20. Jacques Watts, "L'emigration britannique de 1847–1848," *L'Estuaire*, 21 (juin 1998), pp. 21–23.
21. *Berean*, 18 November 1847.
22. Census of Canada, 1851, Canada East, St-Gregoire, Famille Brassard.
23. See Jason King, "Remembering Famine Orphans," pp.115–40.
24. The translated and transcribed eye-witness testimonies of several of these mainly French speaking female religious communities who cared for Famine Irish emigrants in Montreal's fever sheds can be found at https://faminearchive.nuigalway.ie/
25. *Armagh Guardian*, 12 October 1847.
26. *Ancien Journal*, vol. 1 (1847), 9 June 1847, p. 500.
27. Marianna O'Gallagher, "The Orphans of Grosse Île," p. 102.
28. Ibid.
29. Carol McCuaig, *The Kerry Chain, The Limerick Link* (Renfrew: Juniper Books, 2003) and Carol Bennett McCuaig, *The People of St. Patrick's: Mount St. Patrick Parish, 1843–1993* (Renfrew: Juniper Books, 1993).
30. For a detailed account of the Famine migrants in Bytown see: Michael McBane, *Bytown 1847: Elisabeth Bruyère & Irish Famine Refugees* (Ottawa: Michael McBane, 2022). Also see https://irishfaminestories.ca/en/compassion_and_struggle.
31. City of Ottawa Archives, Sisters of Charity (Grey Nuns), General Hospital Ledger, Bytown, 1847.
32. *Names of Emigrants: From the 1845–1847 Records of James Allison, Emigrant Agent of Montreal*, Publication No. 94–2 (Ottawa: Ottawa Branch, Ontario Genealogical Society, 1994).
33. Mary Lee Dunn, *Ballykilcline Rising: From Famine Ireland to Immigrant America* (Amherst: University of Massachusetts Press, 2008).
34. *Elmira Star-Gazette*, 27 June 1939.
35. Nancy McMahon, "Les Religieuses Hospitalieres de St-Joseph and the Typhus Epidemic, Kingston, 1847–1848," in Canadian Catholic Historical Association, *Historical Studies*, p. 58 (1991), pp. 41–55. Also see https://irishfaminestories.ca/en/kingstons_famine_orphans.
36. Family Search, *Register of St. Mary's Cathedral, Baptisms, Marriages & Burials, 1843–1849*.
37. Queen's University Archives (Kingston), Register of the House of Industry, Entry for December 1, 1847.

38. *Census of Canada, 1851–1852*, Canada West, Durham County, Hope Township, Michael Duffy.
39. For a detailed account of the Famine migration to Toronto see: Mark G. McGowan, *Death or Canada: The Irish Famine Migration to Toronto, 1847* (Toronto: Novalis, 2009).
40. Ibid., pp. 95–96.
41. Library and Archives Canada [hereafter LAC], RG 19 Department of Finance, Emigration Service Fund, D–5, vol. 2532, voucher, Toronto to Gore, 30 August 1847, #7320.
42. LAC, RG19, D–5, volume 2532, vouchers #3246, #2753, and #750
43. See fn. 36.
44. *Hamilton Gazette*, 27 September 1847.
45. *Census of Canada, 1851–1852*, Canada West, Hamilton, St. George's Ward, Queen Street.
46. Robert C Lee, *The Canada Company and the Huron Tract, 1826–1853: Personalities, Profit and Politics* (Toronto: Natural Heritage Books, 2004), pp. 5–7.
47. Ibid. pp. 173–175.
48. Between 1849 and 1865 the Huron tract townships were incorporated into the new county of Huron and the counties of Middlesex and Perth.
49. Derek Nile Tucker, "Successful Pioneers: Irish Catholic Settlers in the Township of Hibbert, Ontario, 1845–47" (MA Thesis, McMaster University, 2002), pp. 34–35. Irish farmers formed the majority of these with about, 40 per cent having arrived before the Famine. My thanks to a team of senior undergraduate students in my Irish Famine seminar at St. Michael's College, who in 2018, assisted me in researching several selected townships in the Huron Tract. I am deeply grateful to Olivia Brasch, Chiara Fallone, Britany Powell, Rachel McLeod, and Gabriela Escribano.
50. Archives of Ontario (AO), Canada Company Fonds, CC, B3, 033–384. Census of 1851, Canada West, Grey County, Bentick Township.
51. AO, Canada Company Fonds, CC, B3, 033–394.
52. André Charbonneau and Doris Drôlet-Dubé, *A Register of Deceased Persons at Sea and on Grosse Île in 1847* (Ottawa: Ministry of Heritage, Parks Canada, 1991), p. 66.
53. Ontario Roman Catholic Church Records, 1760–1923, images, Family Search (https://familysearch.org/palMM9.3.1/TH–1951–24494–13796–40?cc=1927566). Lincoln, Niagara-on-the-Lake, St. Vincent de Paul, Baptisms, marriages, burials, 1827–1849.
54. Ibid., p. 17. Edward Jackman, op, *A Brief History of the Roman Catholic Diocese of St. Catharines* (NP: Diocese of St. Catharine's, nd), pp. 13–14.
55. Paul Hutchison & Michael Power, *Goaded to Madness: The Battle of Slabtown* (St. Catharine's: Slabtown Press, 1999), pp. 11–16.
56. Ruth Bleasdale, "Class Conflict on the Canals of Upper Canada in the 1840s," *Labour / Le Travail*, vol. 7 (Spring, 1981), pp. 19–21.
57. All derived from *Census of Canada*, Canada West, Lincoln County, Niagara, 1851–1852.
58. *Globe* (Toronto), 27 September 1848.
59. Ibid., 27 September 1848.
60. Ibid., and *The Irish American*, "Irish Relatives and Friends (reprint of USA origin dated February 1871).
61. *Globe*, 27 September 1848.

62. *Census of Canada, 1851–52*, Bertie Township, Welland County, John Fritz, Farmer, aged 50, "Mennonist."
63. Ontario Roman Catholic Church Records, 1760–1923, images, Family Search (https://familysearch.org/palMM9.3.1/TH-1951-24494-13796-40?cc=1927566). Lincoln, Niagara-on-the-Lake, St. Vincent de Paul, Baptisms, marriages, burials, 1827–1849. Thomas Brennan, 4 October 1848.
64. Joy Parr, "The Welcome and the Wake: Attitudes in Canada West Toward Irish Famine Migration," *Ontario History* 66 (1974) uses the Brennan-O'Connor case as an instance of migrant trauma in the wake of the Famine. There is some truth in this, but she does not make the link with the much larger story of the Mahon Estate and the assisted migration. This is not her fault; she was not looking for such a connection since her article was primarily focused on Upper Canadian responses to the Famine migration.
65. Akenson, *The Irish in Ontario*, p. 32.
66. *Mélanges Religieux*, 7 August 1846, p. 404.
67. Malcolm Campbell, *Ireland's New Worlds: Immigrants, Politics, and Society in the United States and Australia, 1815–1922* (Madison: University of Wisconsin Press, 2008), pp. 37–42 and pp. 50–6.

CHAPTER SIX

"REMEMBER YOUR SOUL AND YOUR LIBERTY"

Childhood Memories of the Tighe and the Quinn Famine Orphans[1]

Jason King

"Remember your soul and your liberty," enjoined James Quinn, a 45-year-old Irish emigrant from Lissonuffy, part of the Mahon estate in County Roscommon, to his two young sons Patrick (aged 11) and Thomas (aged 5), as he lay dying in the quarantine station on Grosse Île, Quebec, in late August 1847.[2] Sixty-four years later, his son, the Abbé Thomas Quinn, stood before the First Congress of the French Language in Canada, on 25 June 1912, to express his gratitude to the people of French Canada for their "untiring charity", which afforded "my unfortunate parents ... the ineffable consolation of leaving their children in the care of French-Canadian priests." The adoption of Irish orphans like Patrick and Thomas Quinn, and Catherine and Daniel Tighe, into French-Canadian families and communities in 1847 has long been remembered in Ireland and Quebec as a tragic historical event that, nevertheless, brought the French and Irish closer together.[3] The return of the descendants of emigrant orphan Daniel Tighe from Quebec to Strokestown, in July 2013, provided an occasion for remembrance of the Famine exodus as a flagship event of "The Gathering."[4] The departure of the 1,490 assisted emigrants from Strokestown in May of 1847 was further commemorated by a glass wall memorial that was unveiled in 2014. It marks the beginning of the National Famine Way walking trail that follows in their footsteps along the Royal Canal to Custom House Quay in Dublin, a journey that is also fictionally recreated in renowned author Marita Conlon-McKenna's *Shoe Stories* from the perspective of Daniel Tighe.[5] At the beginning and end of the trail, actors recount Thomas Quinn's pledge to fulfill his father's dying utterance in the National Famine Museum, Strokestown Park and EPIC—The Irish Emigration Museum. Yet the meaning of his injunction to "remember your soul and your liberty" had changed considerably from his father's deathbed in 1847 to Thomas Quinn's reiteration of it decades later.

More broadly, these memorials help mark the symbolic reconnection between Famine emigrants and their Irish homeland as well as the generosity and hospitality they received in the Canadian host society. The Tighe and Quinn children were at once emblematic and highly atypical of Irish Famine orphans in Quebec. They were placed in French-Canadian households that endeavored to keep orphaned siblings together and made them beneficiaries of heritable property and a seminary education. As recipients of a priestly vocation and the family farm, they came to embody and transmit the familial legacies of their adoptive parents. And yet, as Mark G. McGowan has persuasively argued, the cultural memory and myth of Irish Famine orphan adoptions obfuscates a more prosaic social reality (see chapter 5). According to McGowan:

> the children were essentially in a semi-indentured service to the families in which they were placed ... siblings were separated from one another and sometimes at great distances; and ... many orphans were keen on leaving their placements as soon as possible in order to secure independence or reunite with extended family members elsewhere in British North America or the United States.

He adds that "the most famous of the Famine orphan stories, that of Daniel Tighe of Lisonuffy, Roscommon, and later of Lotbinière, Quebec, was atypical of the orphan experience. Few orphans were embraced by their placement families and few appear to have inherited property."[6] In short, the vast majority of Irish Famine orphans were regarded as child labourers rather than cherished as members of the family.

The Tighe and Quinn siblings were exceptional because they passed on personal and family memories and—in Thomas Quinn's case—written recollections of the Irish Famine migration to subsequent generations. Very few assisted emigrants from Strokestown left any personal account or material trace of their existence. This chapter examines the childhood memories of Catherine and Daniel Tighe and Patrick and Thomas Quinn as recounted in oral histories and the written testimonies of the latter. As the only survivor of Strokestown's Famine emigrants to document his experience (albeit decades later), Thomas Quinn's "Une Voix d'Irlande" (June 1912) and "Childhood Memories: (Arrival in Canada)" (June 1914) provide invaluable eyewitness accounts of the Irish Famine migration and reception of orphans in Quebec. In his groundbreaking study *The Coffin Ship: Life and Death at Sea during the Great Irish Famine* (2021), Cian

T. McMahon argues that interpretations of the Famine exodus should focus on the first-hand perspectives and "lived experiences of the migrants themselves." Academic research that eschews their testimonies strips "them of their liveliness, creativity, and agency," he contends. He offers an innovative methodology based on the recovery and amplification "of the long-lost voices of the emigrants themselves."[7]

Thomas Quinn's "Une Voix d'Irlande" and "Childhood Memories" provide one such "long-lost voice" from the Strokestown Famine migration. His oratory and reminiscences were, of course, compressed, distilled, refined, and shaped over decades into a set of core motifs that culminated with his father's dying utterance. His remembrance of his paternal injunction defined his impressions of the past and sense of his own life story. But in finding his voice, he also attests to the collective "lived experiences" of the emigrants who accompanied him yet left no records behind. The recovery of migrant testimonies like Thomas Quinn's provides a reminder that his fellow travelers had distinct impressions, memories, and life stories of their own. Yet Quinn's reminiscences are also shaped by the concerns of an aging priest serving a mixed French-Canadian and Irish Catholic congregation during a particularly fraught historical moment for his flock, a form of selective remembrance rather than vivid recollections of what transpired in Strokestown and at sea over six decades earlier. Indeed, when Thomas Quinn delivered his "Une Voix d'Irlande" address to the French Language Congress, he acknowledged a growing rift in "the relationship between my original and my adopted race."[8] In particular, the Irish clergy's support for Regulation 17 in Ontario, which was issued in July 1912, to restrict French language teaching in the province's Catholic separate schools, had incensed French-Canadians and aggravated ethno-linguistic and religious tensions between them and the Irish. "Why, in changing countries, do the noble, patient, chivalrous Irish people who have suffered oppression want to be oppressive in turn?" Quinn asked.[9]

Thomas Quinn recalled his childhood memories to recast Irish Famine orphans like himself as figures of ethno-religious conciliation and models of integration to help resolve tensions within his congregation. More specifically, he endeavored to alleviate potential conflict between his French-Canadian and Irish Catholic parishioners through personal reminiscences of past benevolence. As Irish Famine orphans who had travelled from Roscommon to Quebec and started new lives within the clergy, Thomas and his brother Patrick sought both to embody and reconcile the differences between the French and Irish sides of their congregations, which struggled for control of the Church and its medium of instruction. As child migrants they became intermediaries between their divided communities. Their story provides a case study of contested acculturation and changing affinities between their home and host societies. In honoring their father's pledge to "remember your soul and your liberty," they were confronted with their parishioners' split loyalties. More broadly, the Quinn brothers' struggle to reconcile the French and Irish sides of their congregations attested to shifting cultural fault lines and the gradual realignment of their ethno-religious into linguistic identities in the latter nineteenth and early twentieth centuries. Ultimately, their protestations of fidelity to their French-Canadian brethren were held in tension with their Irish ancestry.

Patrick and Thomas Quinn were born in Aughadangan or Curraghroe townland in the parish of Lisonuffy[10] on the Mahon estate to James Quinn and Margaret Lyons and were baptized on 26 February 1836,[11] and 11 January 1841.[12] They had three siblings who did not survive the transatlantic voyage. Daniel and Catherine Tighe were also born in Aughadangan townland to Bernard and Mary Tighe who had them Christened on 29 January 1836[13] and possibly 22 June 1840, though the record entry is incomplete.[14] Mary Tighe was widowed and accompanied her brother William Kelly as Head of Household with her children, including an elder son Thomas aged 14, when they were assisted to emigrate from the estate in 1847.

The Quinn and Tighe families joined hundreds of others from the estate as they made the long walk along the Royal Canal to Custom House Quay in Dublin where they embarked on steamers for Liverpool. They set sail on the *Naomi* on 15 June and endured one of the most harrowing transatlantic crossings in the steerage of an emigrant vessel (see chapter 4). According to A.C. Buchanan's "Return of Passenger Ships arrived at the Port of Quebec" recorded in the *British Parliamentary Papers*, the *Naomi* arrived in Quebec on 10 August 1847 after carrying 421 steerage passengers from Liverpool on a journey to Grosse Île that lasted 45 days, of whom 196 or slightly under 50 per cent perished, including 78 at sea, 31 on board ship at quarantine, and a further 87 in the lazarettos on the island.[15] Two days later, the *Virginius*, which also carried assisted emigrants from the Mahon estate, arrived at Grosse Île with an even higher mortality rate of over 50 per cent or 267 of the 467 steerage passengers on board. Even by the standards of 1847, the conditions on board the *Naomi* and *Virginius* were horrific and only obliquely recalled by the Quinn and Tighe children and their descendants in their subsequent recollections. In the words of Daniel's grandson Léo Tye, who was interviewed by Marianna O'Gallagher and met with Jim Callery, founder of the National Famine Museum at Strokestown:

> In 1847, Mary, widow of Bernard Tighe, left Ireland with her five children and her younger brother ... The voyage was a long nightmare of eight weeks. Drinking water ran low and food was reduced to one meal a day. Comfort and hygiene were non-existent. Typhus broke out on board, and the ship was ordered to stop at Grosse Île.

> Of Mary Tighe's family, only two children survived: Daniel (12), and Catherine (9). When the children left the ship, they never saw the other family members again, nor did they have any word about them.[16]

Likewise, Thomas Quinn's recollection of his Famine voyage decades later was equally sketchy: "In the designs of Providence, we were cast upon the shores of Grosse-Ile after a stormy passage of two months at sea. A malady ...– the famine fever – came to add its untold terrors to so much other suffering and misery," he declared at the French Language Congress in 1912.[17] The voyage of the Quinn family was also recalled in the *Roscommon Herald* in 1931:

> During the Famine of Black '47, a family named Quinn were driven out of their home near Strokestown by the cruel and wicked Major Mahon, whose infamous boast was that he would make Strokestown a Cattle Walk, and Elphin a Sheep Pen. He had the peasantry of a large district driven out and deported on the Coffin Ships [whose]... victims were flung out on the banks of the St. Lawrence, near Montreal ... There were, however, some survivors, and two have been traced.[18]

In fact, both the Quinn and Tighe children were evacuated from the quarantine station at Grosse Île in August and September of 1847 into the care of the Catholic Orphanage run by the "Charitable Ladies of Quebec" (and, after 1849, the Grey Nuns), who placed them into French-Canadian and Irish Catholic families. As grandson Léo Tye recounts:

> On 8 August 1847, Daniel and Catherine along with several other immigrants left Grosse Île on a sail boat which brought them to... the General Hospital [in Quebec] where they were very well treated. Then one morning, the pastor of Lotbinière, Fr. Edouard Faucher, came to get Daniel and Catherine and eleven other Irish children. He loaded them into his horse drawn "express wagon" [and] during the long trek, held one of the smaller children on his knees.[19]

Léo Tye also recalled how his grandfather Daniel and his sister Catherine were adopted by the French-Canadian Coulombe family who decided to keep the children together after they "cried so hard at the idea of being separated that they were inconsolable ... The Coulombes proved to be good parents to these two orphans", Léo Tye added. "Upon the parents' death, Daniel inherited their good farm, which since then, has been handed on from father to son."

Like the Tighe orphans, Patrick and Thomas Quinn were also escorted by clergy from Grosse Île to Quebec and then placed with a French-Canadian family. Marianna O'Gallagher contends that "Father Luc Trahan brought the [Quinn] children to Quebec and entered them in the orphanage on September 7, whence they were adopted by Georges Bourke of Nicolet on September 17,"[20] although Thomas Quinn himself recalls that they had travelled separately. According to the *Annals of Richmond County* in Quebec's Eastern Townships:

> Previous to his appointment at Richmond Fr. [Luc] Trahan had worked at Grosse Isle Quarantine Station in 1847... [He] took under his protection two orphaned boys, Patrick and Thomas Quinn whose father James Quinn and mother, Margaret Lyons, of Strakestown, [sic] Co. Roscommon, Ireland, had died of the fever. Through his efforts, the two boys were adopted by a French-Canadian family named Bourque, at Nicolet. They completed their education at the Seminary at Nicolet and both entered the priesthood. Fr. Patrick Quinn succeeded his benefactor Fr. Trahan as Pastor at... Richmond.[21]

The adoption of the Quinn and Tighe Famine orphan siblings into French-Canadian families thus symbolizes a wider story of social acceptance and the upward mobility of model immigrants who became thoroughly integrated into the agrarian and ecclesiastical institutions of Quebec's host society. Patrick Quinn was ordained in 1862 and went to Richmond in 1864, "where he served a full fifty years as parish priest, finally taking his retirement at the age of seventy-eight"[22] in 1914 (he died on 11 March 1915). Thomas Quinn was ordained in 1864 and "became the parish priest in St. Fulgence in South Durham—less than a 20 minute train ride from his brother's parish."[23] He subsequently served nearby in Quebec Eastern Township communities such as Saint-Félix-de-Kingsey (1876–1884), Pierreville (1884–1893), and Drummondville (1893–1902) before he retired (1902–1923) to live with the Grey Nuns in the Hôtel Dieu in Nicolet, and then on his own in an attractive Quebec cottage style house with a high sloping roof at 533 rue Saint-Jean-Baptiste that still stands.[24] He died on 6 October 1923. As parish priests and proprietors of the family farm, the Quinn and Tighe siblings left behind the Famine-afflicted Mahon estate and typhus-infested *Naomi's* steerage and Grosse Île fever sheds to start new lives ascending social ladders they could never have gained a foothold on in Ireland.

The most detailed eyewitness accounts of their Famine voyage from Roscommon and arrival in Quebec can be found in the testimonials of Thomas Quinn. His "Childhood Memories (Arrival in Canada)" is recorded in the annals of the Sisters of Charity, or Grey Nuns, in Nicolet whom he visited in June 1914 on his return from St. Anne de Beaupré and "talked movingly about his emigration to Canada."[25] As he recounted:

> My parents ... were part of this huge flock of people fleeing Ireland in those frightening days of 1847, doing so in order to escape from English oppression as well as from the Famine which was devastating the whole country due to the failure of the

> crop. My parents came to Canada where they only found death at Grosse-Île. They died of this infamous Typhus and their bodies still rest on that Island. Loaded onto a ship, or rather confined in its hold, emigrants fell ill since Typhus which affected so many of them would easily erupt in those filthy conditions; about 5 500 people died during that 2 1/2-month long journey. Up to 50 or even 60 poor bodies a day would be thrown into the sea.
>
> If this was not enough, another calamity affected us as drinkable water and food were lacking; daily rations were cut although already scarce; everything concurred in causing more deaths. Although we were born in a family of 5 children, only my brother and I, respectively aged of 10 and 5 years old, escaped from death.[26]

Thomas Quinn's memories of the transatlantic voyage are generic and stylized, distant recollections lacking in detail about his voyage in the *Naomi*. Even so, he does reminisce that "drinkable water and food were lacking; daily rations were cut although already scarce," as Léo Tye similarly attests from his grandfather Daniel. Their recall of the harrowing conditions on board an emigrant vessel is distilled into the increasing scarcity of food and water below deck.

Thomas Quinn's recollections of his departure from Grosse Île are much more vivid. In his own words:

> Divided in groups, we were then sent to many different towns of the country. I was among 25 others who arrived in Nicolet where Parish Priest Mr. [Louis Théophile] Fortier gave us his help. We were then sent to Mr. Georges Bourque. I was so weakened by the misery and deprivation, and of such a delicate temperament, that people hardly believed I was 5 years old. When I got there, I was put to bed, and fell into a deep sleep. When I woke up, all my compatriots were gone. They had been adopted by Christian families. Since I was the last of them staying in Nicolet, I was adopted by Mr. Georges Bourque who always treated me well and with tenderness. Suffering from Typhus, my elder brother Patrick had been quarantined on Grosse-Île; but he finally joined me in Nicolet where he was adopted by the Geoffroy family. He came to see me a few days after his arrival, but I did not recognize him at first; but then I loudly expressed my fear, thinking that he was coming to find me to share again the dark days that we had just gone through. In fact, my elder brother was a bit jealous of me since I was treated very well as "a little gentleman" and him not so well as "a little peasant". My adoptive father could not resist Patrick's legitimate desire to come and live with us, and he agreed to keeping us both: what a joy it was for the two brothers to live together again.[27]

Thomas Quinn's memories of leaving Grosse Île have a dream like quality tinged with a sense of delirium. They are the recollections of a desperately ill child "so weakened by the misery and deprivation" that he was separated from his orphan cohort before they were placed with French-Canadian families in Nicolet and St Grégoire.

His childhood memories are suffused with anxiety about this moment of separation when he fell into a deep sleep and awoke to discover that his compatriots were gone.

Yet Thomas Quinn was fortunate to have been left behind in the care of Georges Bourque, a caretaker in the Nicolet seminary.[28] Indeed, it would prove the formative experience in making possible his vocation and that of his brother Patrick. Shortly thereafter, Thomas received a visit from his brother in the home of his adoptive father but recoiled in terror: "I did not recognize him at first," he recalled, "but then I loudly expressed my fear, thinking that he was coming back to find me to share again the dark days that we had just gone through."[29] Yet his brother was no revenant reliving the horrors of the ocean voyage. Rather, Patrick had come to express a "legitimate desire" to be adopted into the same household. More to the point, he had left his orphan placement in the home of the Geoffroy family where he was treated as "a little peasant" to join his brother in becoming "a little gentleman." It is important to emphasize that the Quinn siblings had not been placed in the same household and that Patrick had fled his host when he expressed a "legitimate desire... for the two brothers to live together."[30] Ultimately, their good fortune belied "the fate of most of the 'adopted' Irish orphans in the Quebec cohort" as the exception that proved the rule.[31]

Thomas Quinn concludes his "Childhood Memories" in paying tribute to his adoptive father and the seminary in which he found a home. "We were both educated at the Nicolet Seminary and we both became Priests," he writes:

> being forever grateful to our adoptive father Georges Bourque. The latter spent his last 25 years with Priest Patrick Quinn in Richmond and never missed the chance to repeat that "these had been the nicest years of his life." The two proud Priests have always been friends of the French-Canadian race in loyally defending their religious and national interests.[32]

Thomas Quinn's loyalty and gratitude to the "French-Canadian race" became a repeated refrain in his oratory and guiding principle of his ecclesiastical career. Indeed, he "was ever grateful to the French Canadian people and it was an honor ... to proclaim it publicly when the occasion arose."[33] According to the unpublished Hayes papers held by the Richmond County Historical Society:

> Fr. Thomas Quinn, often related with emotion how, before leaving Grosse Isle, the admirable ecclesiastic who cared for his parents led him to the bedside of his father, who, when he recognized them exclaimed with his dying breath the old Irish slogan: "Remember your Soul and Liberty." The incident remained deeply graven in his memory.[34]

Indeed, Quinn equated his paternal injunction of remembrance with a pledge to preserve not only his French-Canadian parishioners' Catholic faith, but also their cultural identity.

As Famine orphans who were not only raised in a French-Canadians household but became priests themselves, the Quinn brothers provide a case study of Irish integration into Quebec's French speaking host communities. Thomas Quinn's childhood memories of separation from his orphan cohort and reunification with his brother in Nicolet are corroborated by the Hayes papers:

> Fr. Patrick Quinn was born February 20, 1836 at Strakestown [sic], County Roscommon, Ireland. He was the son of [James] Quinn and Mary Lyons, his wife. In common with countless others, his parents emigrated from Ireland in the dark days of 1847, hoping to better their fortunes in Canada, only to find a grave at Grosse Isle, where under the shadow of the recently erected Celtic Cross [in 1909], they lie buried, victims of the dread typhus which carried off the parents and three small children of a family of five. In the annals of the Irish Migration with its harrowing record of sorrow and death, there is no more pathetic incident than that of the Quinn family. The survivors, Thomas and Patrick, aged six and eleven respectively, were adopted by generous French-Canadian families at the insistence of Rev. Mr. Trahan and Robson, then in charge of the unfortunate orphans. Under the friendly guidance of Rev. Fr. Fortier ... at Nicolet, whither he was sent with twenty others, Thomas Quinn fell into the charitable hands of Mr. George Bourque, where he slowly recovered from the effects of the illness which had brought him nigh death while yet at sea. Meanwhile Patrick Quinn at Grosse Isle was slowly convalescing only to find himself bereft of his parents: death had claimed both of them and the two little girls. Patrick was later sent to Nicolet and adopted by the family of Mr. Joseph Geoffroy. Separated and amongst strangers at six and eleven years of age, respectively! Such was their plight when the generosity of Mr. Bourque prompted him to adopt Patrick and thus bring the disconsolate boys together. Both were placed at Nicolet Seminary where they received the full collegiate education of that institution.[35]

Like Catherine and Daniel Tighe, the Quinn brothers were initially placed in different households and only reunited because of the compassion of their French-Canadian benefactors who took in more children than they had originally intended. The "disconsolate boys" escaped the fate of many Famine orphans who "were often separated from one another and sometimes at great distances."[36] Instead, they were placed at the seminary that employed their adoptive father where they received a "full collegiate education" rather than put in a situation of semi-indentured service.

In pursuing their vocation, the Quinn brothers became community leaders and emblematic figures of French-Canadian piety and patriotism. They also helped rehabilitate their adoptive father in the eyes of the church after his own enthusiasm for the rebellion of 1837 in Quebec. In his eulogy delivered in 1923, Elzéar Bellemere recalled that:

> Fr. Thomas Quinn had the ... benefit of being raised by a sincere patriot. Georges Bourque had in good faith taken part in the disturbances of 1837, and he was even forced to emigrate to save his life and spend some time in the United States. This good man was like George-Etienne Cartier and others mistaken in the impulses of his patriotism. But he deeply loved his country and he even shed blood for it; he thought well of his countrymen. This noble patriotic sentiment ... he transmitted into the souls and hearts of his adopted children. These orphans clung tightly to their protectors in particular, and in general to the people of French Canada whom they have always regarded as fellow countrymen sharing their own nationality, without, however, setting aside the affection they owed to their mother country.[37]

Bellemere made clear that the Quinn brothers inherited their benefactor's sense of patriotism but repudiated his youthful impulse to political violence. Indeed, he emphasized that:

> Fr. Thomas Quinn had the feelings of a strong and enlightened patriot. Although he was a native of Ireland, no one could say with more conviction and truth those words expressed from the heart of a famous patriot! "O Canada, my country, my love." He vigorously condemned the Fenian invasion in 1866, which he considered unfair to Canada and unnecessary for the cause of Ireland. He condemned with the same energy the campaign organized by a number of his countrymen against the existence and rights of the French language.[38]

Thus, Thomas Quinn channeled his patriotism into his pastoral role as a defender not only of the Catholic faith but also French-Canadian culture. His rejection of Fenianism was less remarkable than his renunciation of "his countrymen" opposed to the "rights of the French language." Indeed, his affection for his "mother country" did not extend to many of his compatriots.

Nevertheless, as they rose through the ranks of the clergy, the Quinn brothers endeavored to create institutions that would bring together their French and Irish parishioners. The most important of these was the St. Patrick's Society of Richmond, Quebec, founded by Patrick Quinn in 1877. Peter Southam notes in *Irish Settlement and National Identity in the Lower St. Francis Valley* (2012) that "the experience of the Richmond Irish Catholic community's future pastors, the brothers Patrick and Thomas Quinn, became a legendary part of the Richmond area's collective consciousness ... Through their teaching, both brothers ensured that their parishioners in the Lower Saint Francis Valley did not forget the lessons of the Famine."[39] Perhaps the most vital lesson was the need to create institutions that would safeguard not only the spiritual but also the material wellbeing of their parishioners. Indeed, "three years later, Father Quinn, whose congregation in the 1870s was already slightly more *Canadien* than Irish, was similarly instrumental in founding the Société St-Jean-Baptiste."[40] He played a pivotal role in mobilizing French-Canadian and Irish Catholic support through his creation of similar fraternal associations from both sides of his congregation. According to Southam:

> From Quinn's perspective, the organizing of a local St. Patrick's Society had more than patriotic value. Its establishment, along with that of a local Société Saint-Jean-Baptiste three years later, promised to strengthen parish ties and, through Quinn's office of chaplain of both societies, reinforce his pastoral oversight. He no doubt understood that such organizations could serve the parish in material ways.[41]

Indeed, through these offices Patrick Quinn raised sufficient funds to establish and refurbish all of the town's Catholic ecclesiastical and social institutions which "came into existence under his administration and fostering care."[42] Even today, "Richmond's two most inspiring buildings—Sainte-Bibiane Church and what was once *le couvent Mont Saint-Patrice*—pay silent tribute to the man whose energy and vision led to their construction more than a century ago."[43]

Patrick Quinn's legacy of institution building was inspired by his father's injunction to safeguard the souls and the liberty of his French-Canadian and Irish parishioners. More broadly, the remembrance of Irish Famine orphans in Quebec tended to be evoked in a spirit of French and Irish fraternal association, especially to alleviate tension when relations between them became increasingly fraught in the latter nineteenth century. The popular memory of the Famine orphans took shape a generation after their migration in the 1860s, during a moment of heightened ethno-religious conflict and social friction between Quebec's French-Canadian and Irish Catholic communities.[44] Even in 1847, the Canadian Irish *Pilot* newspaper acknowledged "the humane and Christian dispositions of our [French-] Canadian brethren" who took in "these poor destitute little orphans" in spite "of the calumny which imputes to them hostility to the Irish race."[45] A letter published in Montreal's *True Witness* from an "English Catholic" in the Eastern Townships in 1859 similarly recalled those "French-Canadian protectors" who took in Famine orphans to question received wisdom about their ostensible "aversion and antipathy towards the Irish."[46] The letter alluded in particular to an "Irish boy, an orphan" who became a notary as proof that "he must have received a good education, and have been well cared for by his French Canadian benefactor. Is this, too, an example of aversion, hostility, and antipathy on the part of French Canadians towards Europeans and Irishmen?" the author asked. Apprehensions of French-Canadian aversion, hostility, and antipathy towards the Irish were assuaged by the orphans' conspicuous success under the auspices of French-Canadian protectors, even if they were the exception.

The ordained Famine orphan, Father Thomas Quinn, made it his life's mission to reconcile tensions between the French-Canadian and Irish sides of his congregation. This was his principal theme when he delivered his "Une Voix d'Irlande" address at the First Congress of the French Language in Quebec City on 25 June 1912. The Congress was held to defend the rights of French speakers not only in Quebec but across Canada which were perceived to be increasingly under threat since the controversy surrounding the Manitoba Schools Question had emerged a decade earlier. Its speakers, including former Canadian Prime Minister, Wilfrid Laurier, and Quebec intellectual and founding editor of *Le Devoir*, Henri Bourassa, were particularly incensed by the role that Irish Catholic clergy had played in clamouring to restrict the teaching of French in Ontario schools, which led to the issuing of Regulation 17 in July 1912. "To the disappointment of French Canadians, the Catholics bishops of Ontario, most of whom were of Irish ancestry, supported" it, notes Garth Stevenson.[47] In *Language and Religion: a History of English-French Conflict in Ontario* (1975), Robert Choquette claims that Irish-Canadian Bishop Michael Fallon, in particular, "was an extremist and the foremost agitator in the conflicts" that ensued from the implementation of Regulation 17.[48] Mark G. McGowan offers a more nuanced interpretation that "although Bishop Fallon has frequently been singled out as the 'bête noir' in the assault against the French," he was actually espousing views that were widespread amongst Ontario's English-speaking Catholic clergy, for whom he was initially "acting as the spokesperson, or perhaps 'fall guy.'"[49] In fact, Fallon was hardly alone in contending that French should not feature any more prominently in the curriculum than other languages, such as "Italian or Polish or Irish... for, I assure you", he claimed in January 1912, "that I can organize in very short order a province-wide demand for the teaching of Gaelic in the schools."[50] Indeed, one of the strongest defenders of Regulation 17 was Robert Sellar, author of *Ulster and Home Rule: A Canadian Parallel* (1912), *The Tragedy of Quebec: The Expulsion of its Protestant Farmers* (1907, 1916), and his fictionalized account of Irish Famine refugee Gerald Keegan *The Summer of Sorrow* (1895) which provided the source text for Ireland's fraudulent best-seller *Famine Diary* (1991).[51] In *The Tragedy of Quebec*, Sellar noted approvingly that "a considerable number of French-Canadians saddle the blame on Bishop Fallon and the Irish Catholics," whom he regarded as fellow travellers in resisting the predations of Quebec's French clergy.[52]

Throughout the Regulation 17 controversy, "the only English-speaking clerical support of the French Canadians seems to have come from an obscure priest Fr.

Thomas Quinn," observes Choquette.[53] As an Irish Famine orphan who was no less a member of Quebec's French-speaking clergy, Quinn struggled to reconcile his Irish ancestry with his pastoral duties as he addressed the First Congress of the French Language in 1912. "I do not belong by birth to the French family," he began.[54] "The language of my childhood is a foreign language, and if I am afforded the great honour to speak before this patriotic gathering, then it is as an adopted child and son of Ireland." "But, ladies and gentlemen", he continued, "the adoption was a complete success and I claim my place at the paternal table. The French language, it is mine as it is yours ... It is still the tongue of old, and it is in this language that I am here today to recognize the people of French Canada who adopted and took in an Irish son." Fr. Quinn then took it upon himself to denounce the "cruel irony" and "deplorable contradiction" that put him in a position of seemingly having to choose between the land of his birth and that of his adoption.[55] However, he left his audience in no doubt about where his loyalty belonged. Of his Irish compatriots in Canada, he contended that they were susceptible to the "blackest and most revolting ingratitude."[56] In the face of such ingratitude, Fr. Quinn sought to placate his audience by paying tribute to the generosity of the French-Canadian clergy and family that cared for him six decades earlier. As he recalled:

> It was in 1847. A famine ... threatened the Irish people with total extinction. The most astonishing part of the awful spectacle was, not to see the people die, but to see them live through such great distress ... Like walking skeletons they went, in tears, seeking hospitality from more favoured lands.[57]

After recounting the hardships his family, like the Tighes, had experienced for weeks on end during their voyage on the *Naomi* and in quarantine at Grosse Île, Fr. Quinn recalled how the French-Canadian priests were "stirred with compassion" and in "braving the epidemic contended for glory in rushing to their relief." "Sixty-six years have passed since then," he avowed, "but my soul belongs to the French-Canadian people, and my spirit jealously guards their rights and freedoms."[58]

In paying tribute to his clerical predecessors on behalf of his parents, Fr. Quinn was not simply expressing a personal debt of gratitude. He was also implicitly contrasting their generosity and open mindedness with the bigotry of his fellow English-speaking clergy in Ontario. To underscore this point, Quinn noted that his adoptive parents had

> enrolled me in an English school, run by two old women, who were imbued with a sense of narrow bigotry. One day when the procession of the Blessed Sacrament passed in the street, led by a priest, I wanted to kneel, following the Catholic

> custom. My mistress reacted violently with an expression I will not repeat. I was forced to obey her, but never returned to the school. My education in English was over. It was not the language of my soul or my freedom![59]

Nobody listening to Fr. Quinn could have been in any doubt that his personal experience of linguistic and religious suppression was being imposed on a much larger scale on French children in Ontario. Not only did Fr. Quinn proclaim his solidarity with his French-speaking brethren, however, he also likened their condition to his own. "The people of French Canada, too, were once abandoned by their mother country, and so they became an orphan," he declared, alluding to the British Conquest of Quebec in 1759. "They had imposed on them a foreign language, unknown, and said: 'It is not the language of our soul or our freedom.'"[60] In his remembrance of his father's dying utterance, Quinn identified his French parishioners' vulnerability with his own. Just as he was taken in as a helpless orphan by the French-Canadian people, he would now champion their linguistic and religious freedom in turn. "Dear descendants, God thank you," he avowed, "for your fathers cared for those starving and shivering with fever, and you are now seeking the right to speak your language, in the name and under the guise of religion, not to have imposed on you a foreign idiom! ... These attacks will succeed only in strengthening your national feeling and love of your mother tongue."[61] Finally, just as his adoptive father had taught him "to preserve his heritage and freedom," Fr. Quinn implored his audience to "struggle without fear, like O'Connell and Redmond, because your cause is right and just and like theirs cannot perish."[62] He thus equated Ireland's demand for Home Rule with the French-Canadian struggle for "la survivance." His reclamation of Irish ancestry was inspired by feelings of solidarity with his French-Canadian more than Irish parishioners.

In conclusion, with Fr Quinn's address to the French Language Congress in 1912, the myth of the Famine orphans had come full circle. His struggle to reconcile his Irish ancestry with his parochial duties epitomized a larger conflict between the memory of French-Canadian generosity in taking in Famine orphans and the more recent tensions that had arisen between French-Canadian and Irish Catholics as a result of Regulation 17 in Ontario, which divided the loyalties of Quinn. As a Famine orphan and French-Canadian priest, he was forced to choose between his Irish compatriots and his French congregation, the land of his nativity and his adoption. In reality, the memory of Famine orphan adoptions was based on a misnomer that Irish children were cherished in the homes where they had been taken in. As McGowan notes, "in most of the cases of 'adoption' there was no intention by the families concerned—French-Canadian or Irish—to adopt the children in their care.

The 1851–1852 census is clear that most were registered as non-family members."[63] Indeed, the vast majority were destined to become "little peasants" rather than "little gentlemen" like the Tighes and Quinns and left their placements as soon as possible. By contrast, Fr. Thomas Quinn appropriated the memory of Famine orphan adoptions as a metaphor for his pastoral care and mission to safeguard his French-Canadian parishioners in recompense for their compassion for Irish children. He endeavoured to alleviate the growing tension between French and Irish Catholics by alluding to his own life story as a parable of conciliation in which his acceptance by a French-Canadian congregation led him to become their paterfamilias in turn. His story thus helped give shape to the myth of the Famine orphans that emphasized French and Irish affinity to alleviate their deepening sense of rivalry.

The myth was formed in Thomas Quinn's childhood memory when he was summoned to his father's deathbed on Grosse Île and then separated from his orphan cohort and left semi-conscious in the care of the custodian in Nicolet seminary. It also took shape and fixated on the apparition of his brother who appeared not as a revenant from the "dark days" of the ocean voyage, but as a convalescent and disgruntled child seeking to be reunited in the same household after fleeing his original placement. Yet their joyful reunion from being separated amongst strangers also belied the misfortune of most of their fellow orphans.

The glass wall memorial at the National Famine Museum in Strokestown not only commemorates the 1,490 people like the Quinns and Tighes who were assisted to emigrate from the Mahon estate in 1847; it also marks a campaign to trace them and their descendants. There can be little doubt that the Quinn brothers, who left extensive archival records, oral histories and written testimonies, and created much of the cultural and built-up physical heritage in towns like Nicolet and Richmond, Quebec, should feature prominently in the public memory and help put a face on the "1,490." So did the return of the descendant Richard Tye of Famine orphan Daniel Tighe during "the Gathering" festivities in Strokestown in 2013, when he was reunited with his distant cousins and given "a hero's welcome" in his "ancestral home" 166 years after the Famine exodus.[64] Richard Tye, however, was not the first member of the 1,490 Famine cohort to make an emotional return journey to his homeland. Indeed, in 1887, Fr. Patrick Quinn himself "was able to realize the cherished dream of his life and to see once again his native land of Ireland, whence he had gone many years before under such trying conditions."[65] According to the Hayes papers, "in Ireland it was his good fortune to find members of his family still living, in the persons of several nieces and nephews. One of them, Mary Quinn accompanied him on his return to Canada and remained with him until his death".[66] The *Roscommon Herald* contended that the

Quinn brothers actually travelled together: "About 1889, they returned to Ireland and stayed at Duffy's Hotel, Strokestown, from which they visited the track of their birthplace in Kilmacnanny, parish of Curraghroe, Co. Roscommon."[67]

Although the Quinn brothers, unlike Daniel Tighe, did not leave any offspring themselves, their parishioners regarded themselves as their "spiritual children" within "an Irish and French-Canadian family" that is a cultural and institutional legacy of the Famine emigrants. Indeed, the St. Patrick's Society in Richmond, Quebec, is no less an institutional descendant of the Strokestown Famine cohort of 1847 than the progeny of the Tighe family. Likewise, one of the most poignant cultural artifacts from the Strokestown Famine exodus is the little, light brown jacket worn by five year-old Thomas Quinn when he arrived in Nicolet from Grosse Île, which is now housed in the town's Archives du Séminaire.[68] As a material cultural artifact, its miniature size confronts viewers with a palpable reminder of the absolute vulnerability of the Irish orphaned children like the Tighe and Quinn siblings who arrived in Quebec, and the great distance they traveled not only geographically but also socially to start new lives overseas. Together these artifacts, oral histories, and written testimonies comprise much of the legacy of the Tighe and Quinn orphaned siblings who emigrated from Strokestown to Quebec in 1847. It stands in stark contrast with the vast majority of their fellow migrants who left little trace of their existence beyond brief entries in estate papers, orphan ledgers, burial registers, and census records as painstakingly recovered by the contributors to this volume. Yet their childhood memories and voices also help attest and give shape to the life stories left unwritten by those who accompanied them only to perish or survive and create new legacies of their own.

NOTES

1. An earlier version of this chapter was published as "Une Voix d'Irlande' Integration, migration, and travelling nationalism between Famine Ireland and Quebec," in Ciarán Reilly ed., *The Famine Irish: Emigration and the Great Hunger* (Dublin: The History Press Ireland, 2016), pp. 193–208. Translations by Simon Jolivet.
2. Thomas Quinn, "Une Voix d'Irlande", in *Premier Congrès de La Langue Français au Canada. Québec 24–30 June 1912* (Québec: Imprimerie de l'Action Sociale Limitée, 1913), pp 227–232, pp. 229–230. James Quinn's death is recorded having occurred between 22–28 August 1847, in the "Weekly returns of deaths in the quarantine hospital at Grosse Isle", *The Morning Chronicle* (Quebec City), 16 September 1847.
3. Jason King, "Remembering Famine Orphans: The Transmission of Famine Memory Between Ireland and Quebec" in Christian Noack, Lindsay Jannsen, and Vincent Comerford, eds.,

Holodomor and Gorta Mór: Histories, Memories and Representations of Famine in Ukraine and Ireland (London: Anthem Press, 2012), pp. 115–144.

4. *Irish Independent*, 22 July 2013.
5. Marita Conlon-McKenna, *Shoe Stories*, https://nationalfamineway.ie/shoe-stories/.
6. Mark G. McGowan, "Rethinking Irish Famine Orphans in Quebec, 1847–1848," in Christine Kinealy, Jason King, Gerard Moran, eds., *Children and the Great Hunger in Ireland* (Hamden, Connecticut: Quinnipiac University Press, 2016), pp. 96–97.
7. Cian T. McMahon, *The Coffin Ship: Life and Death at Sea during the Great Irish Famine* (New York: New York University Press, 2021), pp. 2 and 248.
8. Quinn, "Une Voix d'Irlande", p. 228.
9. Ibid., p. 229.
10. *Roscommon Herald*, 23 May 1931. I am grateful to Mike Lennon for this reference.
11. National Library of Ireland, "Catholic Parish Registers at the NLI", digital images, National Library of Ireland (https://registers.nli.ie/registers/vtls000633935#page/8/mode/1up).
12. Ibid., (https://registers.nli.ie/registers/vtls000633935#page/30/mode/1up).
13. Ibid., (https://registers.nli.ie/pages/vtls000633935_007).
14. Ibid., (https://registers.nli.ie/registers/vtls000633935#page/27/mode/1up).
15. *Emigration vessels to Quebec, 1847,* No. 8, "*Return of passenger ships arrived at the Port of Quebec in the season of 1847", British Parliamentary Papers,* vol. 17, Sessions 1847–1848, pp. 471–477.
16. Marianna O'Gallagher, "The Orphans of Grosse Île: Canada and the adoption of Irish Famine Orphans, 1847–48," in Patrick O'Sullivan (ed), *The Irish World Wide: The Meaning of the Famine* (5 vols, London and Washington: Leicester University Press, 1997) iv, p. 90. Extracts from Marianna O'Gallagher's interview with Léo Tye and Jim Callery can be viewed at https://nationalfamineway.ie/about-the-1490/the-story-of-the-1490/
17. Thomas Quinn, "Une Voix d'Irlande," p. 229.
18. *Roscommon Herald*, 23 May 1931.
19. Marianna O'Gallagher, "The Orphans of Grosse Île," p. 91.
20. Marianna O'Gallagher, "Irish Priests in the Diocese of Quebec in the Nineteenth Century", Canadian Catholic Historical Association, *Study Sessions*, 50 (1983), pp. 403–413, p. 412.
21. Richmond County Historical Society, *The Tread of Pioneers: Annals of Richmond County and Vicinity* (2 vols, Richmond, Quebec: Richmond County Historical Society, 1968), ii, p. 39.
22. Nick Fonda, *Richmond, Then and Now: An Anecdotal History* (Montreal: Baraka Books, 2017), p. 128.
23. Ibid., p. 121.
24. Centre d'Archives Régionales Séminaire de Nicolet, Fonds Thomas Quinn, F083 "Notice Bibliographique," (https://archivesseminairenicolet.files.wordpress.com/2019/04/fonds-thomas-quinn.pdf).
25. "Monsieur l'abbé Thomas Quinn, 1841–1923. Souvenirs D'Enfance (Arrivée au Canada)," in *Metáire St-Joseph, Nicolet (Chronique). 1895–1935*, vol. 1, pp. 58–60, p. 58. Soeurs Grises de Montréal, Prov. Nicolet, Québec, Archives, Archives du Séminaire de Nicolet. Fonds Thomas Quinn Annexe.
26. Ibid.

27. Ibid., p. 59.
28. Centre d'Archives Régionales Séminaire de Nicolet, Fonds Thomas Quinn, F083 "Notice Bibliographique," (https://archivesseminairenicolet.files.wordpress.com/2019/04/fonds-thomas-quinn.pdf).
29. "Monsieur l'abbé Thomas Quinn, 1841–1923," p. 59.
30. Ibid.
31. McGowan, p. 117.
32. Monsieur l'abbé Thomas Quinn, 1841–1923," p. 60.
33. "Second Parish Priest of Richmond 1864–1914", n.d., (Richmond County Historical Society, Melbourne, Quebec, Hayes Papers, 03-G-F- 26.62).
34. Ibid.
35. Ibid.
36. McGowan, p. 96.
37. "Abbe Thomas Quinn, Oraison Funebre prononcée par M. Elzéar Bellemare [Octobre 1923]", Soeurs Grises de Montréal, Prov. Nicolet, Québec, Archives, *Métairie St. Joseph*, Nicolet (Chroniques), 1895–1923 , vol. 2, pp. 54–61, p. 57.
38. Ibid., p. 58.
39. Peter Southam, *Irish settlement and National identity in the Lower St. Francis Valley* (Quebec, 2012), pp. 94–95.
40. Fonda, *Richmond,* p. 126.
41. Southam, *Irish Settlement*, p. 151.
42. *Richmond Times*, 12 March 1915.
43. Nick Fonda, *Roads to Richmond* (Montreal: Baraka Books, 2010), ebook location 2278.
44. King, 'Remembering Famine Orphans', pp. 128–140.
45. *The Pilot,* 22 July 1847.
46. *True Witness and Catholic Chronicle*, 5 August 1859.
47. Garth Stevenson, *Parallel Paths*, p. 196.
48. Robert Choquette, *Language and religion: a history of English-French conflict in Ontario* (Ottawa: University of Ottawa Press, 1975), p. 254.
49. Mark G. McGowan, *The Waning of the Green: Catholics, the Irish, and Identity in Toronto, 1887–1922* (Montreal and Kingston: McGill-Queens University Press, 1999), p. 244.
50. Cited in Robert Choquette, *Language and Religion*, p. 164.
51. Jason King, "The Genealogy of *Famine Diary* in Ireland and Quebec: Ireland's Famine Migration in Historical Fiction, Historiography, and Memory," Éire-Ireland, vol. 47 (Spring/Summer 2012); Mark G. McGowan, "Famine, Facts, and Fabrication: An Examination of Diaries from the Irish Famine Migration to Canada," *Canadian Journal of Irish Studies* (Spring 2009).
52. Robert Sellar, *The Tragedy of Quebec: The Expulsion of its Protestant Farmers*, 4th edition (Toronto: University of Toronto Press, 1974 [1916]), p. 304.
53. Choquette, *Language and Religion*, p. 219.
54. Quinn, "Une Voix d'Irlande", pp. 227–228.
55. Ibid., p. 228.

56. Ibid., p. 229.
57. Ibid.
58. Ibid., p. 230.
59. Ibid.
60. Ibid.
61. Ibid.
62. Ibid., p. 232.
63. McGowan, "Rethinking Irish Famine Orphans in Quebec, 1847–1848," p. 117.
64. *Irish Independent*, 22 July 2013.
65. 'Second Parish Priest of Richmond 1864–1914', n.d., (Richmond County Historical Society, Melbourne, Quebec, Hayes Papers, 03-G-F- 26.62).
66. Ibid.
67. *Roscommon Herald*, 23 May 1931.
68. "Jacket once belonging to [Thomas] Quinn, a six year old Irish Famine orphan", 1847, Textile, Archives du Séminaire de Nicolet, 1990.21.226.1–32. It was put on display for the "Being Irish O'Quebec" exhibit at Montreal's McCord Museum in 2009 (http://www.mccord-museum.qc.ca/pdf/exhibits/Texte_Irish_EN.pdf).

CHAPTER SEVEN

THE MURDER OF MAJOR MAHON

Christine Kinealy

On 14 July 1847, the *Dublin Evening Mail* noted in its section on "Fashion and Varieties" that "Major Mahon has arrived at Strokestown House."[1] Four months later, he would be dead by an assassin's bullet. The murder of a relatively obscure Irish landlord in November 1847 ensured that the fate of the 1,490 emigrants from Strokestown, who had already achieved a grim notoriety over summer, would again feature on both sides of the Atlantic. More international outrage was expressed, however, over the death of one man than over the untimely loss of approximately 400 Irish lives. Major Denis Mahon's murder was the most sensational and debated assassination of a landowner in the nineteenth century, dividing public opinion at the time, and continuing to intrigue historians since then.

Major Mahon had inherited Strokestown Estate in 1845. Like numerous other Irish properties, it was in debt—in this case, to the tune of £30,000.[2] His hiring of a new agent at the end of the year, John Ross Mahon, proved to be a fateful decision. The Major needed little convincing that there were too many poor people on the estate and that the path to economic recovery lay in removing them—permanently. The appearance of potato blight in 1845, and even more destructively in 1846, provided a further compelling reason to clear the estate, with fewer rents than usual being paid, at a time when local poor rates were rising. Regardless of his desire to empty the estate, Major Mahon's early response to the food shortages was conscientious. As chairperson of the Strokestown Relief Committee he took his duties seriously, including protesting to relief officials in Dublin Castle about the closure of the public works schemes in August 1846.[3] He even chastised his fellow landlord and agent, Thomas Conry, for withdrawing a subscription to the relief committee when Conry learned that his tenants were outside the committee's jurisdiction.[4] During the transition from one relief system to another, Mahon provided a number of financial donations to alleviate the local suffering.[5] His interventions were praised in the Dublin press:

> PARISH KILGEFFIN. (From our Correspondent.) I feel happy in being able to inform you, as I know you will be [happy] to hear, that Major Mahon, of Strokestown-house, has signified his intention of contributing to the fund for relief of the poor of the parish of Kilgeffin, in proportion to the number of families upon his estate in that locality, as soon as a return shall be made to him by the active and humane secretary of the committee, the Reverend Mr. Beeche, whose exertions, we are sorry to say, have not been attended with that success which they deserve.
>
> The gallant major has contributed the munificent sum of £200 for the promotion of public works to employ the poor of Strokestown and its vicinity, in addition to £50 placed by him at the disposal of the relief committee of that district.[6]

In his relief work, Mahon was supported by Father Michael McDermott who, like Mahon, had arrived in the parish in 1845. From the first appearance of the potato blight, however, it was evident that Mahon's sympathies had boundaries. He did not believe that anybody should be allowed on to the relief works if they had not paid their rent "but could afford to pay it."[7] A similar logic would be applied when Mahon sought to clear his estate in 1847.[8]

Following the second appearance of blight, Mahon, along with Thomas Conry, Daniel Hughes, John Hague, Michael O'Beirne and Bartholomew Mahon were appointed to a reconstituted relief committee to oversee the implementation of the newly introduced Poor Employment Act.[9] Towards the end of 1846, Mahon left Ireland and spent the following eight months in England. During Mahon's absence, Ireland was undergoing some of the most intense suffering of the famine years as the public works proved to be an inadequate, inappropriate— and ultimately, deadly— means of providing relief. The potato failure in Roscommon in 1846 had been absolute, leading to a high dependence on the public works. Despite food prices being high, the average wage on the works was only 8*d* per day, which was lower than in many other distressed areas.[10] In March, the public works were closed and government soup kitchens were opened throughout the country. The Roscommon Poor Law Union, of which Strokestown was a part, was one of the last ones to make this type of relief available. In early June 1847, the despairing Poor Law official responsible for

Roscommon informed his superiors that he was feeding the most distressed poor in the union out of his own pocket.[11]

From different sides of the Irish Sea, Major Mahon and Father McDermott were also despairing about the situation in Strokestown. In early January, McDermott suggested that, under the superintendence of Mrs. Fallon, a private soup kitchen be established. The priest wrote to Mahon asking for a subscription, which he granted, in addition to "Miss Mahon" (the Major's daughter) contributing £1 to the fund.[12] In the first three months of the year, £558 was raised for this purpose, donations including ones from the Quakers and the British Relief Association. Yet, by early March no soup kitchen had been opened, leaving a frustrated Mahon to ask Ross Mahon, "who is the chairman of the relief committee?" In a separate letter, he opined, "Surely the committee should not allow such a waste of time, when people around are dying of want. A temporary kitchen even for the present moment would be desirable."[13] On 7 March, Mahon was continuing to lament the fact that no soup kitchen had been opened.[14] McDermott, who appeared to be the person leading the local relief committee during the Major's absence, was also despairing, but about the lack of funds.[15] In a letter dated 14 March, which was published in the *Tablet*, an English Catholic newspaper, McDermott made a direct appeal to Bishop John Briggs of Yorkshire on the grounds of "the many liberal donations lent by you to different parts of Ireland towards the relief of the suffering poor."[16] He explained:

> On this day we are only able to distribute a small quantity of bread and soup to about seven thousand applicants for relief, and when we had done, we could not promise the poor starved wretches any further assistance. This announcement was received with yells of despair such as would rend the hardest heart.[17]

McDermott described Strokestown as being "inhabited by the poorest peasantry on the face of the earth" and stated that, "It is not a matter of surprise to see on a morning twenty dead bodies thrown across the backs of asses." Moreover, in a phrase that may have offended Mahon, he added: "There is no resident landlord to employ or protect them."[18] This incident suggested that even before the two men would have their notorious war of words in September, the battle lines had been drawn.

Mahon's correspondence from England demonstrated that, despite his debts, he led a privileged lifestyle as he stayed in some of the most reputable clubs and hotels in the country. From the comfort of these places, Mahon would oversee the clearance and emigration of hundreds of families from his estate.[19] On 11 March 1847, he attended the marriage of his only daughter, Grace Catherine, at the prestigious St George's Anglican Church in Hanover Square in London.[20] It was a judicious marriage from a business point of view as the groom, Henry Sandford Pakenham, the eldest son of the Dean of St. Patrick's, was heir to the vast Pakenham and Sandford estates in counties Longford, Westmeath and Roscommon. It is unlikely that Henry, who on marriage added Mahon to his surname, imagined that, within the year, he would inherit his father-in-law's estate in Strokestown.

Mahon's desire to clear his estate was not unique although the scale of it was unusual. By early 1847, mass evictions and assisted emigrations were becoming commonplace in Ireland. The cruel way in which many evictions were carried out was criticized in sections of the Irish and British press. Ejectments on the Gerrard estate in Galway, for example, gave rise to the term "Gerrardism" and to accusations of "extermination."[21] Despite his ambitious plan to remove over 3,000 tenants from 28 townlands (out of a total of 10,000 tenants) and send them to Canada, Major Mahon appeared determined to avoid these pitfalls. Working closely with his agent, Ross Mahon, he paid for the passage to Quebec and provided the emigrants with accommodation and food stores for the long journey. An obscure source recently unearthed by Mark G. McGowan suggested a level of comfort was attached to the assisted emigration of the first wave of 1,490 tenants in the spring of 1847, a paper describing them as displaying "marks of comfort."[22]

Mahon's well-timed absence from Strokestown meant that the messy day-to-day business of getting thousands of his tenants to leave their homes for ever was handled at a discrete distance. His actions even won praise from some of the provincial press in both Britain and Ireland where he was commended for financing such an ambitious programme of emigration, with one newspaper avowing that the 300 to 400 families involved were "enabled to do by the wise liberality of Colonel Mahon, who has supplied them with the means of emigrating, and defrays the entire expense of their passage and maintenance during the voyage."[23] As the Major made his plans to return to Ireland in the summer of 1847, he may have allowed himself to bask in this praise and to congratulate himself on the fact that, despite the outlay of almost £6,000, he had turned a national disaster into something that would be of long term benefit to the Strokestown estate.

Major Mahon's return to his estate in the summer of 1847 was a leisurely affair. He arrived in Dublin on the last day of June and visited his sister in County Louth before travelling to Strokestown in mid-July.[24] Mahon's homecoming coincided with a period of unprecedented social unrest and dislocation throughout Roscommon.[25] On 15 May, Daniel O'Connell had died in Genoa in Italy, leaving Catholics and nationalists without the man who had led them for over 20 years. In June, the clergy of Strokestown and adjoining parishes, led by Bishop George Joseph Plunket

Browne of Elphin, contacted the Repeal Association in Dublin to express sympathy to O'Connell's remains. When the remains arrived in Ireland, the clergymen in the diocese intended to hold special masses at each church in the area. Browne apologized for not being able to pay their full subscription in repeal rent, explaining it was because of "the present awful and deplorable state of our starving flocks."[26]

For some months, Strokestown had been attracting some less than salubrious attention in both the local and national press. As early as January 1846, George Knox of Strokestown, a relative of Major Mahon and Crown agent on nearby Ballykillcline Estate, was escorted by "a strong military and police force" as he performed his duties, because he had "earned the displeasure of the Molly Maguires."[27] Around the same time, following an attack on 20 policemen in nearby Rooskey, local magistrates debated whether a new police station should be established in Strokestown, but they concluded that it would be better to send reinforcements to the existing ones.[28] Only weeks later, a Dublin newspaper carried the story that:

> Our Strokestown correspondent reports that Strokestown House, county of Roscommon, the residence of Major Mahon, was plundered of fire-arms on Thursday last; and that Mr. Saul, steward of the Major, was also robbed of his arms on the same day.[29]

A month following the robbery, Rev. Thomas Lloyd of Strokestown was threatened with a death notice being posted on the vestry door, allegedly from local Rockites.[30] The notoriety of Strokestown was evident from the attention in both the local and national press:

> Every day brings intelligence from Strokestown of fresh outrages. Shooting horses, taking up arms, turning land at night, and beating persons who are obnoxious to the Mollys. Age or station is no security against the ferocity of these worse than savages. On Friday evening, Mr. Hedian, nearly 80 years of age, whilst coming up the street, near his own house, was struck on the head, and severely hurt. Last week four men entered Major Mahon's steward's house, in the demesne, in the open day, broke in the doors and took away a large pistol and two powder flasks. A few days before, they shot a horse of Miss Stuart's, of Fairview, whilst ploughing in a field about 3 miles from that. On Monday night last, a farm belonging to Mr. Daniel Hughes of Lisheen was turned up.[31]

Major Mahon's decision to relocate to England in late 1846 would have brought a respite from the unrelenting negative reports on the so called "state of the country," but also begs the questions, why did he choose to return in July 1847, at the height of the Famine crisis?

In July 1847, a special report for a London newspaper on the condition of Ireland held up Strokestown as an example of social unrest as evidenced by the "fierce litigation now going on at the quarter sessions."[32] The readers were told that "at Strokestown, one of the divisions of the county of Roscommon, there were 1,900 civil bills, and 200 ejectments for non-payment rent."[33] Such singling out suggested something unusual was happening in the locality. This was confirmed by the Assistant Barrister having to postpone his attendance at the Roscommon Quarter Sessions and proceed to Strokestown instead, to hear over 200 cases.[34] The story was taken up by a number of leading newspapers, including the nationalist *Freeman's Journal*, which did not mention Major Mahon by name, but made its disgust clear in an article entitled "famine, fever, and extermination" averring:

> The landlords are acting their part in this tragic scene. Shylock-like they must have their "pound of flesh." Only think of two hundred ejectments having been entered for hearing at Strokestown, and nineteen hundred civil bill processes, principally brought against the starving tenantry. About five times the number that we ever recollect to be brought into court at any time within the last twenty years.[35]

Into this maelstrom of discontent and friction, Major Mahon returned to his estate, determined to oversee more clearances.

Major Mahon may not have been resident in Strokestown for the best part of a year, but he immediately threw himself into the role of gentry and landlord. Only a few days after his return, he attended the Roscommon Assizes having been sworn into the Grand Jury. His former agent, Thomas Conry, sat on the same Jury.[36] The workload of the jurors was described as "exceptionally heavy," with reference made to the unusually high number of murders:

> The different offences with which the several parties stand charged are thus classed: murder 5, manslaughter 6, burglary 8, robbery 13, cow stealing 6, appearing armed and assaulting dwelling houses 22, highway robbery 6, violent assault 1, robbery of arms/ larceny 7, sheep stealing 1, killing sheep 1, cutting and maiming with intent to kill 1, forcible possession 1, total 71.[37]

Major Mahon did not immediately become involved in local relief measures. He did not attend the monthly meeting of the Strokestown Relief Committee on 24 July, first appearing on 28 August. The timing of the meeting was not auspicious as the country was transitioning from relief provided—for the most part, for free—by the soup kitchens, to all relief being channeled through the unpopular Poor Law. Although the latter had been extended to include outdoor relief, the ethos remained that those claiming it were "undeserving."[38] At the relief meeting, disagreement arose between Mahon and Father McDermott. Their previous encounter would have been well in advance of the emigration of the Strokestown families. At the time of this meeting, however, news was coming from Canada describing the terrible condition in which the Irish were arriving there. On 9 June, approximately three weeks after the arrival of the first immigrants, Archbishop Signay of Quebec had issued a circular letter to the Catholic Archbishops and Bishops of Ireland, which opened with a warning about "the dismal fate that awaits thousands of the unfortunate children of Ireland who come to seek in Canada an asylum from the countless evils afflicting them in their native land."[39] Shortly after, news reached Ireland of the terrible fate of the Strokestown families.[40] The *Erin's Queen*, the first of the four vessels to arrive in Grosse Île, was named in a report that appeared in the *Cork Examiner*, on 18 July. When referring to the disease and mortality of the emigrants it added, "it is afflicting to read such a report."[41] Variations of this report appeared in other Irish newspapers.[42] The delayed arrival of the *Virginius*, with its high loss of passengers, proved particularly shocking to readers in both Ireland and Britain. Again, it was singled out in newspaper reports, with one paper stating, "The mortality among the Irish emigrants to Canada has filled their poor relations at home with dismay, and every account is devoured with the most intense anxiety."[43] When the story was picked up the London *Times* on 17 September, it was clear that the death of the Strokestown migrants had become a matter of national interest.

Not surprisingly perhaps, the reunion between Major Mahon and Father McDermott was terse. According to some reports, Mahon questioned McDermott on his actions in the intervening period, especially in regard to the names on relief lists and, allegedly, on the misuse of funds. The disagreement quickly descended into a vitriolic and *ad hominem* argument, which spilled into the public arena.[44] Moreover, the priest did not back down but, according to Mahon, repeated his accusations in even more forceful language during his sermon the next day, which happened to be a Sunday.[45] McDermott's words would be parsed over in the months following Mahon's murder. Letters between the two men followed, with each believing the other to be guilty of a personal attack. Both men, figures of authority for different reasons, would have lost face by backing down, especially knowing that the eyes of Strokestown were watching.

In August 1847, the Poor Law—financed by local taxation—became responsible for providing all relief in Ireland. The Roscommon Poor Law Union and those adjoining it were officially recognized as being "distressed" by the British government. Only 22 of the 130 unions in Ireland were so designated.[46] The hardship caused by the closure of the local soup kitchens and transfer to Poor Law relief would have been compounded by Mahon's continuation of his policy of clearances. Neither the suffering of the local poor nor the grim news from Canada gave pause to the determination of Mahon to remove a large portion of tenants, with clearances and emigration schemes continuing into October.[47] An indication that Mahon was concerned with the turbulence in the area was his request to Ross Mahon about collecting his six-barrel pistol from Dublin one month after he had arrived home.[48]

Major Mahon was killed on the evening of 2 November, near the bridge of Doorty, four miles (6 kilometres) from his home. He was returning from a meeting of the Roscommon Poor Law Guardians. He was accompanied by Dr. Terence Shanley, who tried to save Mahon's life and would later provide crucial, but inconclusive, testimony on the assassination. Days after the murder, Shanley published an account of his final conversation with his "sincere, kind, and lamented friend," whose concern, he stated, had been for the local poor. Mahon was alleged to have said:

> Shanley, point out me what is best to be done, and we shall be able to keep them from destitution. They shall get plenty of bread, and think by getting on market days some cow heads and plain joints of mutton, with whatever Mrs. Mahon can send us from Strokestown-house, we shall be able to support the poor at a moderate expense. You will apply to Mr. M'Dermott for the boiler, and we will get it erected in one of the houses in Church-street, and then appoint some respectable person to superintend it according to our directions. By giving a little of our time we shall do much good.[49]

Was Shanley attempting to provide a *post hoc* view of the dead landlord as a man of compassion, whose final conversation was concerned with doing his duty towards his destitute tenantry? The conversation also suggested that Mahon was seeking to take control of relief provision away from McDermott, the implication being that the priest's handling of it was inefficient.

Mahon's dead body was brought back to Strokestown House. In his will, he had asked to be buried in the family vault.[50] On 4 November, Mahon was surreptitiously buried on the grounds of his demesne at night-time and without fanfare.[51] He could not have foreseen his ending would come so quickly or brutally. Nor could he have realized that the repercussions of his death would continue for decades. Within 24 hours of the murder, several persons had been detained and interrogated amidst fears that the real culprits were making their escape to America. One of the first people to be committed to the county prison was James Farrell. When arrested, he was suffering from typhus fever and died on 11 November, the autopsy recording he had suffered from an apoplexy.[52] It was a grim reminder that beyond the world of the Mahon investigations, a famine was continuing to rage. Despite hoping for speedy arrests, on 19 November, Thomas Redington, the Under-Secretary at Dublin Castle, informed the Home Secretary that, "every measure taken to arrest the perpetrators has been unsuccessful."[53] In desperation to have somebody to blame for the murder, tenants on the estate were threatened with eviction unless they gave evidence.[54] Henrietta, the Major's widow, even suggested that the witnesses should be assisted to go to America or Australia following the trial.[55] A number of tenants, however, preferred to take matters into their own hands—a collection being made to send prospective witnesses away before the trials took place.[56]

Mahon's murder polarized public opinion along pre-existing divisions. On the same day that he was buried, the *Freeman's Journal* carried a powerful account of the murder which they deemed to be "the latest stain upon Ireland."[57] For them, the assassination was "the result of the agrarian war which is still being waged in all its horrors between Irishmen for the soil of Ireland." They believed that the cruel system of land clearances would only be stopped by government intervention, appealing for "the necessity of legislative interference to put an end to such criminal mutual extinction."[58] Only a few days later, Ross Mahon wrote a detailed report describing his work during the previous year on behalf of Major Mahon. It presented a benign landlord who had acted kindly and fairly towards his tenants. When printing Ross Mahon's account, the *Belfast Protestant Journal* prefaced it by saying, "The following document is extremely satisfactory, proving that the charges against the murdered gentleman, of being a tyrannical landlord, are without a shadow of foundation."[59] The murder was swiftly condemned in the English press and in parliament, the London *Times* leading the way by describing it as an "Atrocious Assassination."[60] The patriotic *St James Gazette* designated the unfolding events as "terrorism in Ireland," and informed their readers, "There is a religious as well as agrarian warfare going on."[61] This assertion appeared to be true when the Rev. John Lloyd, also a landlord who ran a school near to Strokestown famous for proselytizing, was assassinated a month after Mahon.[62]

Major Mahon's murder was commented on by Queen Victoria. Despite having been on the throne for ten years in 1847, the queen had not visited Ireland. As her intermittent references to the country in her private journals reveal, she viewed Ireland as a problem and, despite the urgings of her ministers, she was in no hurry to go there. Over summer, as the British General Election approached, Victoria had approved of Lord Minto undertaking a special mission to Rome "to ask the Pope to use his influence with the Irish Clergy and to prevent their preaching repeal."[63] Some weeks later, again at the suggestion of her ministers, Victoria issued a second Queen's Letter asking Anglican churches for prayers and subscriptions for the victims of the

Irish Famine.[64] Her journal entry for 17 October reveals, "we took a short walk before Service at 11. There were additional Prayers and special Psalms & Lessons, it being the day appointed for Thanksgiving for the plentiful Harvest. There was a collection for the poor Irish—which I am afraid is a very unpopular measure."[65] Her response to Mahon's murder revealed her dislike of her Irish subjects:

> No fog & we found it fresh when we walked to the Gardens. — A shocking murder has again taken place in Ireland. An uncle, by marriage, of M[rs] Phipps, major Mahan [sic] who had entirely devoted himself to being of use to the distressed Irish, was shot when driving home in his carriage. Really they are a terrible people, & there is no civilised country anywhere, which is in such a dreadful state, & where such crimes are perpetrated! It is a constant source of anxiety & annoyance.[66]

A few weeks later, Victoria met with her Prime Minister, Lord John Russell, and they discussed the latest Irish bill concerning crime and outrage, which, for Victoria, arose out of the need "to try & arrest these horrible murderers."[67] Following its passage, she briefly noted in her journal that, "The Irish Protection Measure has passed through the H[se] of Commons & with great facility."[68] Victoria's journal in the final months of 1847 provided no sense of a country that was in the midst of a devasting famine, nor does it display any sympathy with the fact that thousands of her subjects were dying each day. The murder of one landlord, however, had caught the Queen's attention.

The Crime and Outrage Bill referred to by the Queen was rushed through parliament in the wake of the murder. As it made its progress through parliament, the members were repeatedly reminded of the "melancholy murder" of "this lamented gentleman."[69] Mahon was referred to as a landlord trying to make his estate solvent and in doing so, "no unnecessary harshness has been used, and very large sums have been expended in giving compensation and sending them [his tenants] to America ... in proof of the benevolence of his disposition." In contrast, the Strokestown tenants appeared to be rejoicing, "We have heard that bonfires, manifesting a very bad disposition among the peasantry of the neighbourhood, have been lighted since the murder, and that very considerable excitement prevails."[70] The celebratory bonfires were suggestive of a community that was complicit in the action, or approved of its outcome.

In the wake of Mahon's murder, a sermon by Father McDermott, in which he had allegedly attacked Major Mahon, was frequently repeated, with the suggestion that the priest had incited the assassination. Accusations against McDermott were most forcibly made by Lord Farnham, himself a landowner in County Cavan, who addressed the House of Lords at length on 6 December. In what became referred to as the "denunciation from the altar," Farnham claimed that, on 31 October, Father Michael McDermott had stated during Sunday mass, that "Major Mahon is worse that Cromwell and yet he lives."[71] The speaker who followed Farnham asked if the law, as it stood, would allow the government "to bring to trial those priests whose denunciations from the altar had been immediately followed by the death of the victims?" and if not, "whether the Ministry intended to strengthen the law in that respect, so as to enable them to deal with those who, by moral influence over their congregations, had incited and encouraged crime."[72] The ten words allegedly spoken by Father McDermott were to be cited frequently as proof of the priest's evil intentions, without any concrete evidence that these words had been uttered from the pulpit.[73] Moreover, they were being cited as a reason for a tightening up of the criminal law system in Ireland. Three days later, Farnham again spoke on this issue; this time he referred to "the delinquency of the Rev. Michael M'Dermott." Moreover, in the intervening period, there had been a further murder in the vicinity of Strokestown—that of the Rev. John Lloyd of the Aughrim Parish. Farnham was fulsome in his praise of the clergyman, describing him as "one of the very best of good men, charitable, kind, and humane to all persons, without any distinction, esteemed and loved by his parishioners and neighbours."[74] In a further twist, which gave an insight into the complex network of relationships between all parties involved, Pat Browne of Drumsna, a landlord and brother of Bishop Browne of Elphin, wrote to Pakenham Mahon to defend the honour of his family but also to verify that Major Mahon had treated his tenants with "the greatest kindness and forbearance," but that many owed at least two years' rent. More controversially, Browne claimed that the information presented by Farnham in the House of Lords had been written by him.[75]

The alarm of the authorities on both sides of the Irish Sea was encapsulated by the Earl of Clarendon, the Lord Lieutenant of Ireland. Only days after the murder, on 7 November, he explained that Mahon had died because he had "incurred the displeasure of the agitators."[76] He repeated the oft-quoted allegation that "two Sundays before Major Mahon was murdered, he was denounced by name from the altar, called *worse than a Cromwell*, and yet, says the priest, *this man lives"* (Clarendon's emphasis).[77] Clarendon also referred to Mahon's ongoing "kindness" to his tenants but that "he [M] last year discovered some irregularities in the management of the relief fund by the priest, who then vowed vengeance against him."[78] Without evidence, Clarendon sought to persuade other leading government officials of the priest's guilt, writing to the Home Secretary to that effect.[79] McDermott continued to insist that he never denounced Mahon at Sunday Mass, but Clarendon sought a solution in semantics: the Monday before the assassination had been All Saints' Day—so the denunciation could have taken place then. Clarendon was confident enough in his assertion to voice his opinion in a letter to the Prime Minister on

10 December.[80] With no evidence, the Lord Lieutenant of Ireland had identified both the villain—Father McDermott—and the motive. Only days later, however, in a private letter to Henry Reeve, a journalist with the *Times* of London, Clarendon admitted that while McDermott was "a vindictive ill-considered blackguard," there was insufficient evidence to put him in jail.[81] Clarendon's persistent insertion into the debate had another purpose. Convinced that civil society in Ireland was breaking down, he wanted more extensive powers of coercion. During a debate in parliament, the "monstrous" case of the murder of Major Mahon was cited as an example of the growing lawlessness of the country.[82] It was no surprise, therefore, that, on 20 December, the Crime and Outrage Bill (Ireland) was passed in parliament.

As 1848 commenced, the hunt for Mahon's assassins continued and Ireland seemed no closer to tranquility as the Famine entered its fourth year. Moreover, the anger and accusations continued even while the authorities desperately searched for the perpetrators. The year opened with news that, only two days earlier, John Mahon had received a threatening notice through the post that "promised a fate similar to that of his brother."[83] Only weeks later, the bailiff on the Strokestown estate who had accompanied the emigrants probably as far as Liverpool, John Robinson, received an anonymous warning that there was a conspiracy to have him shot.[84] Both the murder and the notorious altar denunciation continued to divide opinion. On 5 January, the editorial in the *Freeman's Journal*, entitled "Extermination of the Peasantry" deliberately linked the death of Mahon with the death of the tenants sent to Canada:

> The apologists of the clearances effected by the unfortunate Major Mahon on his estates in Roscommon have eulogized the mode of clearance adopted by him as the perfection of humanity and generosity, and boast of the thousands the unfortunate man expended in aiding his tenants to emigrate ... What precautions the "proprietors" took that the wretched, ignorant, helpless and friendless people should not perish on the coast of Canada with hunger and pestilence we know not, for we are not told. The records of the alm-houses and fever sheds of Canada tell the tale.[85]

The same issue included a letter from inhabitants of Strokestown who:

> ... unhesitatingly declare that we never heard the Very Rev. Michael McDermott on Sunday, or any holiday, or any other day, on which he ever addressed his flock from the altar to denounce Major Mahon, or express the words attributed to him in the reported speech of Lord Farnham, or any such words or any words of a similar import or meaning.

The paper hoped that the publication of this letter would "silence the Thugs of the English press and settle the Strokestown calumny for ever."[86] The letter was published in a number of English newspapers, ensuring that the murder remained in the public eye.[87]

Although British politicians were privately, if not publicly, acknowledging that the legal case against Father McDermott was not strong, the debate had served to reinvigorate a stereotype of a rebellious priesthood. Even their co-religionists in England were troubled by these reports and:

> Members of the Catholic English aristocracy appeared alarmed by the alleged actions of the Irish clergy in inciting hatred. The Earl of Arundel and Surrey wrote to Bishop MacHale of Tuam asking if such actions were true "and observing that not all the bigots of England could harm the Church as much as the crimes of its own children."[88]

The accusations against McDermott and his "denunciation" were kept in front of the public by the intervention of the Earl of Shrewsbury, the most prominent Catholic lay person in England. In a series of letters that were published both in the press and as a pamphlet, he called on Bishop Brown of Elphin to undertake "a most searching investigation' into the priest's behavior. When Browne did not immediately respond to this request, Shrewsbury contacted Archbishop McHale of Tuam.[89] Almost four weeks after Shrewsbury had written to Browne, the latter responded and politely, but unequivocally, defended Father McDermott. He commenced his letter by saying, "If I had been written to by any other peer in England, I might take exception to some portion of the letter." He went on to say that, based on his own investigation, Father McDermott "has not on Sunday, Monday, ferial, or holiday, nor at any time, not in any place, directly or indirectly, denounced Major Mahon, or encouraged any species of harm or injury to him."[90] Not only did Browne exonerate his priest, but he pointed out that Mahon had publicly insulted McDermott at a meeting of the relief committee. He also took the opportunity to criticize the large clearances that had taken place on the estate.[91] At this stage, John O'Connell, whose father Daniel had often been attacked by Shrewsbury, decided to make his opinions public:

> I have just read with feelings of the utmost astonishment, and with the indignation that I think it must give rise to in every Irish mind, the insulting dictatorial and disgraceful letter which Lord Shrewsbury has presumed to address to the Lord Archbishop of Tuam. I do heartily trust that his Lordship will not condescend to answer it ...
>
> How strongly the unbecoming, most reprehensible, and insulting tone of the letter of an *English layman* to an *Irish Archbishop* reminds us once again, that the old hostility against us is not that of Protestant against Catholic, but of *Englishman against Irishman*.[92]

Shrewsbury's publication of his correspondence with Browne and McHale resulted in another round of letters and retributions and counter-retributions, Browne stating that his letters had "created vast astonishment in the minds of the Irish people, and that it gave excessive pain to think that a nobleman who should be the hereditary champion of the Catholic faith should give the sanction of his name to the base and false calumnies that were uttered against us by our deadliest enemies."[93] Clearly, Mahon's murder had unleashed anti-Irish and anti-Catholic feelings that went far beyond the murder of one landlord.

While these exchanges were taking place in full public view, privately those associated with the Strokestown estate were watching with dismay. In April, John Ross Mahon wrote to Pakenham Mahon to refute claims made by Browne, especially in regard to evictions and surrendering of property. He reassured him that he had "sufficient evidence to meet the charge about the Relief Committee" and that Dr. Shanley was also willing to contradict any claims made by the Bishop.[94] Major Mahon's murder and its aftermath meant that, at a time when many priests in Ireland were risking their lives to keep their parishioners alive, anti-Catholic and anti-Irish sentiments were re-emerging as a force in politics. The British conservative press was reassured when, in early February, a Papal Rescript was issued that appeared to condemn the Catholic Church in Ireland, which according to the London *Times* was "decided in its rebuke, specific in its allegations, and searching in its inquiry." The Rescript noted the "political factiousness of the clergy" and "their allusive denunciations from the altar."[95] Even though there was no legal case against Father McDermott, he and his fellow clerics had been judged guilty. In spring 1848, a number of high-ranking Catholic clergy travelled to Rome where they presented a memorial to the Pope criticizing the Earl of Minto, the British representative to the Papal State,[96] and father-in-law of the Prime Minister, Lord John Russell:

> [W]e most ... solemnly declare to Your Holiness that British Diplomacy has everywhere been exerted to the injury of our Holy Religion. We read in the public papers that Lord Minto is friendly received ... by Your Holiness. Another cause of our serious alarm is the very general hostile and calumnious outcry now made in both houses of our Parliament and throughout Protestant England against the Catholic Priests of Ireland, falsely charging them with being the abettors of the horrible crime of murder whilst as true Pastors they are striving to ... console their ... perishing people and like good shepherds are in the midst of pestilence giving their lives for their flocks.[97]

In spring and summer, political unrest intensified throughout the country. A radical group of men and women who had formerly been supporters of Daniel O'Connell agitated for a nation-wide revolt against British rule. Their activities would lead to arrests, deportations and the suspension of *habeas corpus*, culminating in a short-lived and unsuccessful rising in Tipperary at the end of July 1848.[98] In the context of revolutions taking place throughout Europe, their calls for rebellion alarmed the British government in London and the gentry in Ireland. Making an example of the murderers of Major Mahon, therefore, took on a new urgency and fresh symbolism.

By the time of the trial in July 1848, many of the suspects had spent months in prison. Following multiple enquiries and arrests, the individuals suspected of the crime were James Cummins (also rendered Commons and Commins), Patrick Hasty, Patt Doyle and Michael Gardiner. Some had been imprisoned with their families, some were suffering from fever. The man thought to be the main conspirator, Andrew Connor, was notable by his absence, the authorities having failed to find him.[99] Ross Mahon informed Major Mahon's widow, Henrietta, that witnesses on both sides were "such bad characters."[100] Although many witnesses were unreliable and provided contradictory evidence, and some had been bribed, there was a determination to have an outcome. Ross also told Henrietta that the conviction of Patrick Hasty and James Cummins had only taken ten minutes' deliberation by the jury.[101] Hasty was found guilty, but the jury disagreed about Cummins. Owen Beirne was found guilty of the murder of the Rev. Lloyd. Henrietta Mahon, who was holidaying with her daughter Grace in Beaumaris in Wales, received news of the conviction from her brother-in-law that, "the Villain Patt Hastie [Patrick Hasty] has been found Guilty of the conspiracy," and that one of the "conspirators against poor Lloyd was found guilty."[102] The ruling of the court was:

> Owen Beirne, Michael Beirne, John Regan, Pat Regan, Luke Walsh, John Walsh, Pat Walsh, John Harrington, Luke Harrington, John Nocton, Michael Flanagan, and Martin Beirne, conspiring to murder the Rev. John Lloyd—Owen Beirne to hanged on 8th of August, and the remainder postponed.
>
> Pat Hasty, James Commons, Michael Gardiner, and Martin Brennan, conspiring to murder Major Mahon— Pat Hasty, to hanged on the 8th of August, and the remainder postponed.[103]

On 8 August 1848, Patrick Hasty and Owen Beirne were hanged in public in front of Roscommon Gaol. Hasty had been found guilty of the murder of Major Mahon, and Beirne of the murder of Rev. Lloyd. Beirne was described as a young unmarried man, who was not more than 27-years-old and "a comfortable country farmer." Hasty was aged about 47 and married with a family. He kept a *shebeen* (unlicensed establishment selling alcohol) at which the plot had, allegedly, been hatched.[104] The "dying declarations" of the two men, signed just before they were hanged, were made widely available.[105] Hasty, while admitting to the justice of his sentence, had attributed his "wretched end" to "a knowledge and participation in the accursed system of Molly Maguireism."[106] A large crowd was present at the hangings including several priests led by the Rev. John Madden, who were there to offer prayers. After the bodies had been hanging "for the usual time," they were lowered into coffins and given into the care of friends.[107]

In early 1849, Major Mahon's murder remained in the public eye as arrests and trials continued. It appeared that no expense was being spared in the hunt for the perpetrators. In February, Thomas Brennan of Carroward was arrested in Peterborough in England and taken into custody.[108] The trial of Patrick Cummins took place on 1 March 1849. According to one report, "the prisoner showed the greatest indifference throughout the entire proceedings."[109] He was found guilty of conspiring with others in the murder of Major Mahon and executed on 21 March 1849, also in front of the Roscommon County Gaol. He, too, made a dying declaration acknowledging his guilt although, as one paper pointed out, when about to receive his sentence, he had insisted on his innocence.[110] Public examples had been made of Hasty and Cummins, allowing more leniency to be shown to the other conspirators, Michael Gardiner and Michael Brennan. In early April, Gardiner was taken from Strokestown to Roscommon Court House under "a strong military escort." He was described as the treasurer of the fund to execute Major Mahon.[111] At this stage, it emerged that Gardiner had given evidence that had allowed the earlier convictions to take place. He was described as "a man much esteemed by the unfortunate deceased, for whom he, in return, professed the greatest good feeling."[112] Gardiner and Brennan were allowed to withdraw their plea of not guilty to the charge of conspiracy to murder and, on the Crown consenting not to press for capital punishment, they pleaded "Guilty."[113] Their sentence was transportation to Australia, but it appears that after languishing in prison for some time they were quietly released. Public interest in the murder of Major Mahon had dissipated and the two executions had satiated the demand for retribution. Behind the scenes, however, the hunt for Andrew Connor continued. He was last sighted working with his brothers and other Strokestown emigrants on the Welland Canal in Canada West.[114]

The murder of Major Mahon did not alleviate the suffering of the poor in Strokestown and may even have worsened it as the new owner carried out evictions with far more ruthlessness than Mahon had shown.[115] Rent arrears were also rigorously demanded.[116] Pakenham Mahon may have been motivated by a personal sense of revenge, especially as a "strong example" was to be made in the townland of Doorty—the scene of the murder—in terms of evicting tenants.[117] Throughout

Ireland, evictions increased after 1847 as a result of a particularly cruel provision in the amended poor law—the Gregory Clause.[118] At the end of January 1848, a member of the Society of Friends reported on the situation in Roscommon:

> The few landed proprietors who resided on their properties here have left us. I apprehend their means are very limited, from their not being able to get their rents; and I fear the cause of their leaving would prevent that sympathy and assistance we should otherwise expect from them for our starving poor ... I fear little if any subscriptions could be had to forward a soup-kitchen.[119]

The local people were not simply in need of food. Of all the counties in Ireland, only Galway received more grants of clothing from the Quakers than Roscommon.[120] The much-hated clearances also continued into 1848, still overseen by Ross Mahon. In April, from his business premises in Dublin, he informed Pakenham Mahon, then residing in London, that he would not be travelling to Strokestown in person as the local people were "much exasperated" with him. His colleague, Mr. Guinness, was travelling in his place.[121] Clearly, agrarian agitation did not end with Mahon's murder. In September 1852, a land steward from Clonfinla was murdered near Strokestown, his skull being smashed in. This "brutal occurrence" demonstrated to the outside world that lawlessness was continuing in the area.[122]

To conclude, Major Mahon was murdered as Ireland was entering its third year of food shortages, yet the British lawmakers had made it clear that the country would have to depend on its own resources. In this context, it is possible to see Mahon as a scapegoat for the British government's mishandling of the Famine crisis, which followed centuries of misrule and estate mismanagement. Following the advice of his estate agent, John Ross Mahon, Mahon undertook a vigorous policy of clearances and removals. The timing was inauspicious given the lack of regulation regarding emigration and the choice of Liverpool as the port of departure and the choice of the Robinson brothers as the agents who handled the journey. Retrospectively, it is clear that Mahon was badly advised, leading to the deaths of hundreds of Strokestown emigrants. Moreover, Mahon's clearances occurred at a time when the Catholic Church was emerging as a force in public debate and flexing its muscles in defence of its congregation. In the post-famine decades, their influence would become even further enhanced. In the late 1840s, the murder of a landlord in Strokestown revealed the multiple tensions within Irish society at all levels, and not simply just between landlords and tenants. It also highlighted the priorities of the British elite when it came to governing Ireland, and their perception of the Irish poor as being undeserving and ungrateful.

If Major Mahon had not returned to Strokestown in the summer of 1847, he would have been remembered as yet another absentee landowner who had ruthlessly cleared his estate during the Famine, but with especially lethal consequences. However, Mahon did return. Moreover, he continued with his policy of clearances. He also re-engaged with the thorny problem of providing relief through the inadequate mechanism of the Poor Law. Mahon's high-profile death reduced even further what little sympathy there was in England for the Irish poor. Yet, he was not the only victim. Two men who were convicted, possibly incorrectly, also lost their lives. Dozens of others spent long periods of time in prison. Meanwhile, it appeared, the real perpetrator of the assassination had escaped. His story would unfold 3,000 miles (5,000 kilometres) away, in Canada.

NOTES

1. "Fashions and varieties," *Dublin Evening Mail*, 14 July 1847.
2. The Encumbered Estates Acts of 1848 and 1849 were intended to facilitate the sale of estates that were greatly indebted.
3. The Strokestown Park Archive (SPA) records that Mahon contacted Colonel Jones on 22 August 1846, STR/1A/106 Letters from [John Walker], Secretary, Office of Public Works, to Denis Mahon [Chairman of the Local Relief Committee], Strokestown Park Archive, "Correspondence and General Docs" Series, 1800–1899. In regard to Major Mahon's philanthropy, he was a regular and generous donor to the Roscommon Protestant Orphan society, see, *Roscommon & Leitrim Gazette*, 23 May 1846.
4. SPA, STR/1A/111, Letter from Denis Mahon, Strokestown House and US Club [United Services Club], to "My Dear Tom" [Thomas Conry], 10 July 1847.
5. "Appalling Distress," *Westmeath Independent*, 15 August 1846.
6. "Parish of Killgeffin," *Dublin Evening Packet and Correspondent*, 7 July 1846.
7. SPA, STR/1A/84, list of 12 tenants recommended for relief work c. 1845.
8. SPA, STR/1A/132, photocopy of letter from Major Denis Mahon, US Club, to John Ross Mahon, 14 April 1847.
9. 10 Vic. cap. 107 [Poor Employment (Ireland) Act 1846]; SPA, STR/1A/103, list of seven individuals recommended to constitute a new Relief Committee, 12 September 1846.
10. Report from Joseph Crosfield, 3 December 1846, *Transactions of the Central Relief Committee of the Society of Friends* (Dublin: Hodges and Figgis, 1852), p. 145.
11. Poor Law Commissioners, London to Lord Lieutenant, Dublin, 12 June 1847, Public Record Office of England, Home Office Papers, HO 45 1942. For more on the soup kitchens see Christine Kinealy, *This Great Calamity. The Great Famine in Ireland, 1845–1852* (Dublin: Gill and Macmillan, 2007), pp. 140–157.
12. SPA, STR/1A/126, photocopy of letter from Denis Mahon, Hakes Hotel, Manchester Square, to John Ross Mahon, 23 January 1847.
13. Mahon's correspondence on this topic is quoted in Peter Duffy, *The Killing of Major Denis Mahon* (New York: Harper Collins, 2007), pp. 97–98.

14. Ibid.
15. His official title was Secretary and Treasurer of the Strokestown Relief Committee.
16. "State of the Country. Roscommon," *Tablet*, 27 March 1847.
17. Ibid.
18. Ibid.
19. The extensive correspondence between Major Mahon and John Ross Mahon in both the National Library of Ireland and the Strokestown Park Archive testifies to the careful planning involved in the emigration schemes.
20. "Marriages," *Oxford Journal*, 20 March 1847; "Marriages," *Annual Register for 1847* (London: F. and J. Rivington, 1848), p. 182. The marriage was also reported in the *Freeman's Journal*, 17 March 1847.
21. "Awful Extermination of the Tenantry," *Roscommon Journal and Western Reporter,* 14 March 1846, 22 March 1846.
22. Mark G. McGowan quoting *The Berean*, 24 June 1847, in Christine Kinealy and Gerard Moran, eds., *Irish Famines before and after the Great Hunger* (Hamden, Connecticut and Cork: Quinnipiac and Cork University Press, 2020), pp. 101–118.
23. From *Dublin Evening Herald* reprinted in "Emigration," *Westmeath Guardian and Longford News-Letter,* 27 May 1847; *Warder and Dublin Weekly Mail*, 29 May 1847; *North Wales Chronicle,* 1 June 1847, "News Summary," *Armagh Guardian*, 8 June 1847; *Manchester Courier and Lancashire General Advertiser*, 29 May 1847.
24. Duffy, *Murder*, pp. 136–137.
25. Rent strikes, secret societies and intra-community violence had been commonplace even before the social crisis triggered by the Famine, see, Ann Coleman, *Riotous Roscommon: Social Unrest in the 1840s*, Raymond Gillespie, ed., Maynooth Studies in Local History (Dublin: Irish Academic Press, 1997).
26. Letter from George J.P. Browne, Athlone, 25 June 1847, to Conciliation Hall, *The Pilot*, 28 June 1847.
27. "State of the Country: Leitrim and Roscommon," *Coleraine Chronicle*, 31 January 1846.
28. "State of Roscommon ... twenty Police Attacked," *Kings County Chronicle*, 21 January 1846. A party of constables were stationed in Strokestown Estate from 1847 to 1852, SPA, STR/1A/195.
29. "Robbery of Fire-Arms," *Dublin Evening Packet and Correspondent*, 28 February 1846.
30. "Arrest of a Molly Maguire," *Clare Journal, and Ennis Advertiser*, 26 March 1846.
31. No title, *Ballyshannon Herald,* 13 March 1846.
32. "Ireland," *London Daily News*, 10 July 1847.
33. Ibid.
34. "Roscommon Quarter Sessions," *Westmeath Independent*, 26 June 1847.
35. "State of the country" (from the *Roscommon Journal*), *Freeman's Journal*, 9 July 1847.
36. "Roscommon Assizes," *Westmeath Independent*, 17 July 1847.
37. "Roscommon," *Freeman's Journal*, 16 July 1847.
38. The Poor Law used the terminology of deserving and undeserving poor.
39. *Circular letter to the Catholic Archbishops and Bishops of Ireland, dated 9 June 1847* [S.l.:

s.n.]. Available online at: https://babel.hathitrust.org/cgi/pt?id=aeu.ark:/13960/t1xd1rn8f&view=1up&seq=5

40. See Jason King, "In the Footsteps of Strokestown's Famine Emigrant to Niagara: Transatlantic Press Coverage and Retribution for Major Denis Mahon's Coffin Ships," in Christine Kinealy and Gerard Moran, eds., *Irish Famines before and after the Great Hunger* (Hamden, Connecticut and Cork: Quinnipiac and Cork University Press, 2020), pp. 119–134.
41. "Immigrants in Canada," *Cork Examiner*, 18 August 1847.
42. "Immigrations to Canada" (from *Freeman's Journal* Correspondent), *Tipperary Free Press,* 21 August 1847.
43. The *John Munn* was also mentioned in this report, "The Ship Fever in Canada," *The Atlas,* 4 September 1847.
44. Duffy, *Murder*, pp. 139–141.
45. Ibid., p. 142.
46. Kinealy, *Calamity*, pp. 175–177.
47. SPA, STR/1A/124, account entitled "Major Mahon. Entries in Rental Acc[oun]t which may belong to Emigration Acc[oun]t for the period April to October 1847," 8 October 1847.
48. Duffy, *Murder*, p. 137.
49. "Extracts of Letter from Dr. Shanley, dated 10 November 1847," reprinted in *Belfast Protestant Journal*, 22 January 1848.
50. "Will of Denis Mahon of Strokestown House, Roscommon," National Archive of England (NAE), Wills, vol. 19, no. 3108309, PROB 11/2066/324.
51. "Assassination of Major Mahon," *Cardiff and Merthyr Guardian, Glamorgan, Monmouth, and Brecon Gazette*, 13 November 1847.
52. *Roscommon Globe*, 15 November 1847.
53. Thomas Redington, Dublin Castle, to Sir George Grey, Home Office, London, NAE, HO 45/2041. The lack of success extended to a number of other assassinations and attempted murders in Ireland.
54. SPA, STR/1A/171, Letter from John Ross Mahon, 26 Frederick Street, Dublin, to Henry Sandford Pakenham Mahon, concerning attempts to extract information on the assassination of Major Mahon from the tenantry, 19 February 1848.
55. SPA, STR/1A/211, File of letters, mainly to Henry Sandford Pakenham Mahon, from Henrietta Mahon, various addresses in England, mainly concerning business matters arising from her husband's death, 17 January 1848 to March 1849.
56. SPA, STR/1A/213, File of letters to Henry Sandford Pakenham Mahon, from Messrs Guinness Mahon, Dublin, 4 March 1848.
57. "Murder of Major Mahon," *Freeman's Journal*, 4 November 1847.
58. Ibid.
59. "Management of the Late Major Mahon's Estate," *Belfast Protestant Journal*, 22 January 1848.
60. *Times* (London), 5 November 1847.
61. "Terrorism in Ireland," *Saint James's Chronicle*, 21 December 1847.
62. "Frightful Murder of a Clergyman," *Liverpool Standard and General Commercial Advertiser*, December 1847.

63. Journals of Queen Victoria, 3 September 1847. Queen Victoria's journals have been digitized through a collaboration between the Bodleian Library and the Royal Archives and are available to UK visitors at: www.queenvictoriasjournals.org
64. See Christine Kinealy, *Charity and the Great Hunger in Ireland. The Kindness of Strangers* (London: Bloomsbury, 2013), pp. 107–115.
65. Victoria's Journals, 17 October 1847.
66. Ibid., 5 November 1847.
67. Ibid., 22 November 1847.
68. Ibid., 16 December 1847.
69. "Crime and Outrage (Ireland)," House of Commons Debates, *Hansard*, 29 November 1847, vol. 95, cc. 270–366, c. 284.
70. Ibid.
71. Ibid., 6 December 1847, cc. 676–681.
72. Ibid., cc. 700–701 These questions were asked by Captain Edward Harris, an English Naval Officer. John O'Connell challenged the speakers for their accusations, on the grounds that they were based on an "unproved charge."
73. Bishop Browne had carried out his own investigations in Strokestown.
74. "Crime in Ireland," House of Lords Debates, *Hansard*, 9 December 1847, vol. 95, cc. 856–858, c. 857.
75. SPA, STR/1A/201, Letter from Pat Browne, Clonfad, Drumsna, to Henry S. Pakenham Mahon, refuting an insinuation made against the Browne family in the aftermath of the death of Major Mahon, 1 March 1848.
76. Mrs Thomson, *Life and Letters of George Villiers. Duke of Buckingham*, in three vols (London: Hurst and Blackett, 1860), p. 208.
77. Ibid., p. 283.
78. Ibid., p. 284.
79. SPA, STR/1A/128, Transcript of letter from Lord Clarendon, Lord Lieutenant, to Sir George Grey, Home Secretary, 27 November 1847.
80. Bodleian Library, Oxford, Clarendon Letter Books, Clarendon to Lord John Russell, 10 December 1847.
81. Earl of Clarendon to Henry Reeve, 20 December 1847, quoted in Duffy, *Murder*, p. 182.
82. Crime and Outrage (Ireland) bill, House of Lords Debates, *Hansard*, 16 December 1847, vol. 95, cc. 1182–230.
83. *The Bucks Herald,* 1 January 1848.
84. SPA, STR/1A/159, 5 February 1848. Letter to John Robinson, from anonymous sender, warning him of a conspiracy to have him shot.
85. Editorial on "Extermination of the Peasantry,' *Freeman's Journal*, 5 January 1848.
86. Ibid., "The Rev. Dr. M'Dermott, of Strokestown." The letter was dated 31 December 1847.
87. "Father M'Dermott. Alleged denunciation of Major Mahon," *York Herald*, 22 January 1848.
88. James P. Flint, *Great Britain and the Holy See: The Diplomatic Relations Question, 1846–1852* (Washington, DC: Catholic University of America Press, 2003), p. 80.
89. "Earl of Shrewsbury, Alton Towers, to Archbishop McHale, 9 December 1847," reprinted in "Denunciations from the Altar," *Tipperary Vindicator,* 12 January 1848.

90. Ibid., George J. P. Browne, Athlone, to Shrewsbury, 3 January 1848.
91. SPA, STR/1A/151. The press cuttings include annotations that dispute some of Browne's claims, "Annotated copy of '*The Freeman's Journal*' including published letter from Bishop George Browne, defending the actions of Rev. McDermott," 29 April 1848. The digitized press cuttings can be viewed at https://nationalfamineway.ie/about-the-1490/what-happened-to-the-1490/
92. "John O'Connell to the editor of the *Freeman*, 5 January 1848," *Tipperary Vindicator*, 12 January 1848.
93. "The Earl of Shrewsbury," the *Pilot*, 14 February 1848.
94. SPA, STR/1A/169, Letter from John Ross Mahon, 26 South Frederick Street, to Henry Sandford Pakenham Mahon, Harcourt Street, refuting claims made by Bishop Browne, 29 April 1848; Ibid., STR/1A/202, Letter from John Ross Mahon, Strokestown, to Henry Sandford Pakenham Mahon, 26 February 1848.
95. "The Pope and the Irish Clergy,' first appeared in the *Times*, reprinted in *Fife Herald*, 17 February 1848.
96. Minto's position was an unofficial one which was the subject of a debate in the House of Lords led by Lord Stanley, "The Court of Rome—the Earl of Minto," House of Lords Debates, *Hansard*, 14 December 1847, vol. 95, cc. 1052–1062.
97. This incident has been explored by Donal Kerr in "England, Ireland, and Rome, 1847–1848," *Studies in Church History*, 25 (1989): 259–277.
98. See, Christine Kinealy, *Repeal and Revolution. 1848 in Ireland* (Manchester University Press, 2013).
99. For what became of the elusive Andrew O'Connor see King, "In the footsteps of Strokestown famine emigrants to Niagara," pp. 119–134.
100. SPA, STR/1A/184, Letters from John Ross Mahon, Roscommon Court House, to Mrs. Mahon [Henrietta Mahon, widow of the late Major Denis Mahon], 12 July 1848.
101. Ibid.
102. SPA, STR/1A/182, Letter from John Mahon, Thornfield, Mount Talbot, to [his sister-in-law] Henrietta [Henrietta Mahon, widow of Major Denis Mahon], 15 July 1848.
103. "The Crown Court," *Roscommon Messenger*, 19 July 1848.
104. "Execution of Hasty and Beirne," *Newry Telegraph*, 12 August 1848. This report pointed out that, as a result of his marriage settlement, Hasty had received £200 or £300.
105. Copies of the confessions and an account of their execution are in the Strokestown Park Archive, SPA, STR/1A/154, Printed confessions of Patrick Hasty and Owen Beirne, found guilty of conspiring to murder Major Denis Mahon and Rev. John Lloyd, 8 August 1848.
106. "Executions," *Liverpool Standard and General Commercial Advertiser*, 15 August 1848.
107. "Execution of Hasty and Beirne," *Kilkenny Journal, and Leinster Commercial and Literary Advertiser*, 12 August 1848.
108. "The Murder of Major Mahon," *Newry Telegraph*, 24 February 1849.
109. *Roscommon Clonmel Chronicle*, 6 March 1849.
110. *King's County Chronicle*, 28 March 1849.
111. "The Murder of the Late Major Mahon," *Clare Journal, and Ennis Advertiser*, 13 April 1848.

112. "Murder of Major Mahon," *Armagh Guardian*, 2 April 1849.
113. "The Murderers of Major Mahon," *Inverness* Courier, 15 March 1849.
114. See, King, "In the footsteps of Strokestown famine emigrants," in Kinealy and Moran, *Famines*, pp. 119–134.
115. Ciarán Reilly, *Strokestown and the Great Irish Famine* (Dublin: Four Courts Press, 2014), pp. 111–114.
116. The Strokestown Park Archive contains many examples of legal actions taken against tenants by the new landlord—crops being seized, cattle distrained, etc. See, for example, SPA, STR/1A/156, Warrants or Orders to Distrain against Thomas Morton of Castlenode, for arrears of rent, 1 December 1848; STR/1A/158, Copy of legal opinion of Richard Pennefather Lloyd, to Henry Sandford Pakenham Mahon, offering advice on distraining, 10 October 1849.
117. SPA, STR/1A/218, File of letters to John Ross Mahon, from Henry Sandford Pakenham Mahon, various addresses, including 83 Gloucester Place and Devonshire Place, London, 11 January 1848.
118. The provisions stipulated that anybody occupying more than a quarter of an acre of land could not receive poor law relief.
119. Roscommon, 31 January 1848, *Transactions of Society of Friends*, p. 372.
120. Ibid., p. 383.
121. SPA, STR/1A/212, File of letters to Henry Sandford Pakenham Mahon, London, from John Ross Mahon, various addresses including 26 South Frederick Street, Dublin and Strokestown, concerning the affairs of the Strokestown Estate.
122. "Strokestown," *Kerry Examiner*, 10 September 1852.

CHAPTER EIGHT

MAKING HISTORY VISIBLE

Strokestown and the Famine Story

Caroilin Callery

Introduction: Museum & Archive[1]

The greatest catastrophe of nineteenth-century Europe was so traumatic for Ireland, so painful for those involved and those who followed, that it was buried under a veil of silence for almost 130 years. In cases of such seismic traumas, it often passes to those several generations later, to historians, community activists, educators, and descendants to gently lift and peel away this veil, and to compile, retell, research, and contextualise the reality and truth of what actually happened. In the process, they break the silence and give voices back to those who were forgotten through pain. Commemoration and exploration allow the forgotten to be remembered, respected, and finally waked, to acknowledge and celebrate those who survived, and importantly to explore the lessons to be learned from their struggles.

Commemoration also often depends on fate and chance discoveries and for these to align with the right person in the right place at the right time—which happened in Strokestown 15 May 1979. First it is necessary, however, to examine the intervening period. Not long before his assassination, Denis Mahon's only surviving child, Grace Catherine Mahon, married Henry Sandford Pakenham Mahon, in March 1847. His only other child, Thomas, had died as a teenager, reputedly in school in England, where he was buried in Arborfield, on the estate of his godfather Sir John Conroy, one of the clan Conroy of Cloonahee. So important was Conroy that the Duke of Kent assigned him to take care of his wife and baby daughter Victoria, upon whose upbringing he had considerable influence. Grace Catherine's marriage was a merger that Denis Mahon hoped would save his estate from the ruin it was facing. This marriage saw the estate grow from c.11,000 acres to c. 30,000 acres. It also brought status as Henry Pakenham was related to the Duke of Wellington. The assassination of Major Denis Mahon occurred while Grace Catherine and Henry were reported to be on an extended honeymoon in the Isle of Wight, where the Mahons had a substantial house. Grace Catherine was Olive Pakenham-Mahon's grandmother, and she lived until 1913. After the assassination, Major Mahon's widow, Henrietta Bathurst Mahon, was immediately whisked away to London for her own safety. Grace Catherine swore she would never set foot in Strokestown again.[2]

Following the assassination and the departure of Henrietta and Grace Catherine, the Mahons became absentee landlords for the first time. Henry Sandford Pakenham Mahon slid into Denis Mahon's boots and managed the estate with John Ross Mahon and, by means foul or fair, in early 1848, initiated mass retaliatory evictions for the assassination, with no emigration assistance being provided. Thus, by the early 1850s they did bring the Strokestown Estate back to financial stability—unlike so many other estates that found themselves seized and sold under the Encumbered Estates Acts.[3]

In March 1893, Henry and Grace Catherine's son, Captain Henry Pakenham Mahon (Harry), inherited the Strokestown Estate.[4] Harry returned to live in Strokestown with his wife, May Burrard. They had one child, Olive Hales Pakenham Mahon, who was reared in Strokestown Park and inherited the estate in January 1922. In 1914, Olive married into the King Harmon Family of the Lough Key Estate in Boyle, a few months before the outbreak of the First World War. She was to become a wife, widow, and mother within 12 months, when her husband Edward went missing in action at the Second Battle of Ypres. She returned to Strokestown Park as she gave birth to a daughter, Lettice Stafford King Harmon. Lough Key was inherited by Edward's brother. In December 1921, Olive married for a second time, to Major Wilfred Stuart Atherstone Hales, who was leading a battalion of the East Yorkshire Regiment stationed in the house during the War of Independence. As a consequence, the family name changed to Hales Pakenham Mahon.[5] They had three children, Elizabeth in December 1923, and twins Nicholas and Denys Catherine on 3 February 1926. In 1933, tragedy struck the family once more when Denys Catherine died at 6-years-of-age.[6]

Nicholas Hales Pakenham Mahon, a Colonel in the Grenadier Guards, was the heir to the estate. But in the 1970s, particularly during "the Troubles" that had erupted in Northern Ireland, Ireland was not a place for British Army officers to retire and Nicholas chose to sell it instead.[7] For whatever reason, Olive actively encouraged a local businessman with whom she had a fractious yet cordial relationship to join the bidding. On 15 May 1979, the final bidding played out between three interested parties in London and Jim Callery, a local garage owner, eventually bested his competitors and purchased Strokestown Park from Olive Hales Pakenham Mahon. This transaction ended the family's nearly 320-year reign in the town and placed the house and demesne in the hands of a man whose family had been former tenants, occupying a 13-acre plot in the nineteenth century. Jim Callery's intention for his new property was clear—he needed some of the demesne lands which backed onto his business to expand. He intended to keep the land he required and sell on the house and remainder of the lands.

Jim Callery's plan did not work out as he initially intended. Jim asked Olive while she still resided in the house if he could go in and have a "rummage" around. That rummaging was to change the fate of Strokestown Park forever. On that fateful day, in the "Smoking Room," with a leaking roof, he discovered boxes full of papers. Serendipitously, upon opening one box, one of the first documents he put his hands on was the now famous Cloonahee Famine Petition, sent by starving tenants on the estate. He could not believe his eyes as he read it. The petition was dated 22 August 1846. It stated:

> ... our families are really and truly suffering in our presence and we cannot much longer withstand their cries for food. We have no food for them, our potatoes are rotten and we have no grain. We have been turned away from the relief works by the Board of Works supervisor ... We are not for joining in anything illegal or contrary to the laws of God or the land unless pressed to by HUNGER.[8]

This document was from the Townland of Cloonahee where Jim lived and had been raised, as had generations of his family for several hundred years. The names in the list of signatures were familiar to him: Caulfield, Kelly, Dockery, Mc Hugh, Tracey. These were his people—memories of the Famine stories his grandmother, Ann Flynn Callery, had told him came flooding back.

As Jim explored the room further, he discovered boxes of papers and, sadly, thousands of similar pleas and petitions in what would become the Strokestown Park Archive. The collection itself contains over 55,000 documents which offer a microhistory of the Famine and its effect on the people of Strokestown and the Irish Famine migration of 1847. For Jim, it was as if "voices" rose from those boxes asking, "Who will tell our story?" Upon finding the Cloonahee Petition, Jim Callery told Olive he would purchase the contents of the house if she would leave the archive, and she agreed. The seed for the National Famine Museum had been sown. In the words of Fintan O'Toole:

> Jim didn't really choose to do this, you know, he accepted a responsibility. I'm not sure if Jim knew when he took over the house what he was getting into quite! But having bought that house and having found that archive he did what very, very few people would do, which was accept the responsibility for it. Seems to me to have done so without question. And I think he has done so out of a deeply instinctive compassion for his own community, for his own history, for his own closure, for Strokestown, for Ireland, but also just for people.[9]

The *Irish Independent* would identify the project as the greatest act of philanthropy since the formation of the State.[10]

O'Toole's words are a fitting tribute to Jim's dedication, passion, and unceasing restoration of the National Famine Museum at Strokestown Park House in several states of arrested decay over a period of 40 years. In addition to the physical restoration of the property, Callery's group opened the National Irish Famine Museum in 1994. More recently, he has continued to show leadership in further developing its legacy for future generations. Since 2019, Callery and the Westward Group have worked with Fáilte Ireland and the Irish Heritage Trust to redevelop the National Famine Museum into a €5 million state-of-the-art facility that was unveiled in 2022. In 2021, at the age of 87, he walked 160 kilometres with his daughter, Caroilin, along the National Famine Way, an officially accredited walking trail from Strokestown to Dublin that follows in the footsteps of Strokestown Missing 1,490 Famine Emigrants who left the estate in 1847.[11] Their journey was filmed and broadcast over two episodes on the RTÉ programme *An tSlí.* But, perhaps, the final word should be left to Jim's solicitor (and later Judge) Peter Connellan, who remarked on their return from London in 1979 after the acquisition of Strokestown Park House from the aristocratic Pakenham Mahon family that "the wheel has turned full circle."[12]

The Canadian Connection

While many in Ireland were aware of Major Denis Mahon's assisted emigration scheme, recent scholarship based on records in the Strokestown Park Archive as exemplified in this book has traced the scheme's meticulous planning and scope. From early on, the curators of the museum knew of the four ships that had landed in Grosse Île, Quebec, in 1847, but they did not discover the ship lists in the archive until decades later. In the late 1990s, a number of connections began to develop between Strokestown and Canada. More specifically, the National Famine Museum in Strokestown Park was twinned in 1998 with Grosse Île and the Irish Memorial National Historic Site of Canada in the province of Quebec. Grosse Île had been the quarantine station during the Great Famine, where, in 1847 alone, over 5,000 Irish emigrants were buried—among them, many of Major Denis Mahon's assisted tenants. On 15 August 1909, members of the Canadian and American branches of the Ancient Order of Hibernians had erected a Celtic Cross on Grosse Île to honour the Irish immigrants who were quarantined and died there. Designed by Jeremiah Gallagher, the monument commemorated the 60th anniversary of the Great Famine and, even today, it is the largest memorial of its kind in North America. Jeremiah's granddaughter, Marianna O'Gallagher, continued his work and was perhaps the most important custodian of the Famine Irish legacy on the island and proved instrumental in forming its association with Strokestown. In 1998, Parks Canada erected a glass wall memorial adjacent to the cemetery on the island upon which were engraved the names of the Famine Irish immigrants who had perished there. It would also be the last gathering place of those of Strokestown's missing 1,490 assisted emigrants who survived the gruelling transatlantic voyage before they were scattered to the four winds and "lost."

In the late 1990s, Jim Callery and Marianna O'Gallagher met and formed a lasting friendship. After the formal twining of the Grosse Île and Strokestown Park in 1998, there were a number of exchange trips. On one such trip, in 2000, Jim donated a Celtic Cross made in Ireland on behalf of the National Irish Famine Museum to the people of Quebec City, where it was erected in Artillery Park. During his visit, O'Gallagher excitedly told Jim that she had become aware of a man called Léo Tye, whose story is explored in this volume.[13] She informed him that Léo—now in his 90s—was the grandson of one of the descendants of the Strokestown Famine emigrants. Léo's grandfather, Daniel Tighe, a Famine orphan, had survived to 89 years of age and had lived with Léo until his death in 1924, when Léo was 17 years old. Most important, Daniel had recounted the story of his famine journey to his grandson many times. Jim immediately undertook this unique opportunity to record a rare first-hand account of the Strokestown migration and met with Léo Tye; Marianna O'Gallagher served as a translator for the recorded interview.[14] The opportunity to complete the interview was serendipitous, because Léo died in 2001, at the age of 95.

In August 2009, the Irish in Quebec City prepared for the centenary celebrations of the erection of the Celtic Cross on Grosse Île, led by Marianna O'Gallagher, now in her 80th year but still full of energy. Jim Callery had been invited to the numerous celebrations organised around this centenary. Jim, his wife Adeline, and daughter Caroilin, travelled to Canada for this event. During their visit they planned with Marianne O'Gallagher to make the Strokestown Famine migration of 1847 to Grosse Île more visible as it had been largely forgotten in Roscommon. Marianna suggested a youth exchange project, which she sadly did not see come to fruition after she passed away in 2010. Jim Callery returned to Canada to say a final farewell to his dear friend and give a eulogy at Marianna's funeral.

Strokestown—the Quebec Connection Theatre Project

From the seed planted by Marianna O Gallagher grew the Strokestown-Quebec Connection Youth Project (2010–2013).[15] The lead facilitator was Maggie Gallagher Dagge. The project was designed to engage the Strokestown community's youth about what had happened to the hundreds of people, including their ancestors, who had been assisted to emigrate in 1847. It was a multi-faceted, multi-disciplinary project that was group led and focused, using the medium of arts, technology, and research-based workshops to explore and recover local stories and sources, especially that of the Tighe/Tye Family family. Participants were particularly taken by the story of little 9-year-old Catherine and 12-year-old Daniel Tighe which is recounted in chapter 6 of this volume. These children from the past were within touching distance of their own ages and they could not imagine having to make such a journey as the Tighes had. It was a story that captivated them and one of the main elements they chose to explore. They also viewed the Léo Tye/Jim Callery interview facilitated by Marianna O'Gallagher. As a result, the group expressed an interest in researching the Tighe family story on the ground in Strokestown. The neophyte historians asked numerous questions: Were there any traces of them in the church records? Could we work out if they were connected to any of the Tighe families living in Strokestown today? Was there any idea of where in the parish of Lisonuffy they had come from? And thus, the Tighe/Tye family story became one of the lynchpins of the project.

As the participants worked with local historians on the church records, they were delighted to discover Daniel Tighe's baptismal certificate along with that of his brother Thomas Tighe, as well as a pre-Famine grave in Lisonuffy that was believed to belong to the family. The group also learned that two local Tighe families were potentially distant cousins of the Quebec Tye's. By this time, the whole Strokestown community had begun to engage with the story and RTE 1, Ireland's national broadcaster, ran a feature on the Youth Project, focusing on the Tye story. The youth group compared how the cultural memories held by the Tye family formed part of their identity in Canada, which contrasted sharply with their lack of remembrance in Strokestown. During the project, they assessed previously unseen raw video interview footage, researched parish family records, interviewed local families, and engaged directly with the Tye family in Canada. They also travelled to Grosse Île in Quebec and visited Daniel's great-grandson Richard Tye on the farm that he had inherited in Lotbinière where they paid their respect at Daniel and Catherine's graves.

Memories of Leaving and the Language of Return

This research inspired the Youth Project to invite Richard Tye to return "home" to Strokestown from Quebec as part of "The Gathering" in 2013. Although he was in his 70s, spoke no English, had no passport, and had never left Canada before, he accepted the invitation to return to his family's ancestral home. On 18 July 2013, Richard Tye and his wife set foot on Irish soil for the first time, 166 years after little Daniel left, bringing full circle his great-grandfather's journey from Strokestown in 1847. During their visit, Strokestown community members and groups hosted events and opened their doors and their arms to welcome the Tyes back to their ancestral home. Richard did not speak English and so as he ambled around the town people often came up to him and simply touched his arm, smiled, and nodded. The story again caught national attention with news reports and a follow up *Nationwide* programme on RTE.

The first night of their return was particularly poignant. The Tyes from Quebec, their distant cousins the Tighes from Strokestown, Jim Callery and a full audience gathered in the Library at Strokestown Park House—a place where Daniel and Catherine would never have imagined being. At one point, Richard Tye, who had an interpreter, reached out to clutch the shoulders of Jim Callery and Philip Tighe to mark the occasion. His great grandfather Daniel, the sole survivor of his family, went on to have eight children, and thus there are hundreds of descendants living today.[16]

Strokestown Archive and the Missing 1,490 Famine Emigrants

There were other parallel developments in 2013. The importance of Strokestown's archival collection became obvious when Ciarán Reilly uncovered Denis Mahon's assisted emigration tenants lists of 271 families representing some 1,490 souls.[17] The lists were inscribed on 27 sheets of paper with one sheet per townland, recording the head of household and the number travelling with him. This was the first time that scholars had established a precise number of persons for the scheme and the first time that their names had seen the light of day since the 1840s.

The search for Strokestown's missing 1,490 assisted emigrants and their descendants is being led by Professor Mark G. McGowan, as discussed in this book. From 2015–2019, he has led a number of research teams of exceptional undergraduate students at St. Michael's College, in the University of Toronto, to engage in the search for the families who left the estate.[18] They were tasked with taking the tenant lists and tracking individual household heads, and other family members, through the quarantine station at Grosse Île, to where they may have sojourned and settled in British North America and the United States. Their painstaking research has provided a much clearer sense of what happened to the Strokestown 1,490: who died, who survived, and the creation of new lives by those who finally settled in Canada and the United States. The names many of the husbands, wives, and children, have been restored to the historical record, and new life trajectories of families have been plotted across several generations.

As the new research project in Canada was being planned, there was another development taking place in Ireland that would highlight the plight of 1,490. The success of the 2013 Gathering Celebration for the return of the Tighe Family led directly to Strokestown Park being named as the site of the official National Famine Day Commemoration on Sunday 11 May 2014. During the event, Taoiseach Enda Kenny unveiled a new Glass Wall Memorial inspired by its counterpart on Grosse Île, which named the families who emigrated from the Strokestown Park estate in 1847. It provides a fitting testimonial to the power of archival records to reclaim and recover the forgotten—to pay homage and retrieve dignity by simply naming and making visible. This event was extremely moving and might force one to think how Denis Mahon could never have conceived that, within 160 odd years, the names of those he cleared from his estate could ever take precedence over his own, only a stone's throw from his palatial home.

National Famine Way

The journey of Strokestown's 1,490 assisted emigrants commemorated on the Glass Wall Memorial also inspired the creation of the National Famine Way. In an effort to "Make History Visible," the Strokestown Park team decided to follow in their footsteps, taking their story out from behind the walls of the museum and across the country from west to east. In 2015, Caroilin Callery led a group of five walkers[19] re-enacting their journey in costume, behind a horse and cart, to the evocative sound of the secondary school children reading the 271 family names whose footsteps they traced. The 100 mile/160 kilometre trek of the 1,490 took them from Strokestown to Clondara, and then the entire length of the Royal Canal to Custom House Quay in Dublin where Rowan Gillespie's Famine statues called "The Departure" are now located. In a particularly poignant moment, Jim Callery, at 81 years of age, joined the Famine walkers for the first leg of their journey.

The story of the Strokestown 1,490 resonated across Ireland and abroad. Gut wrenchingly, as the group walked on the second day, prior to departing Ballinacarrigy, 600 people were reported to have drowned when a modern-day coffin ship capsized in the Mediterranean Sea, mirroring the fate of a similar number of the 1,490 who would not survive their voyage in 1847. "Our past was their present," reflected Caroilin Callery. Two further Famine walks followed in 2017 and 2019.[20] The National Famine Way was subsequently launched as a fully accredited walking trail supported by clear signage, a map (produced by Ordnance Survey Ireland), excellent digital interpretation, and a Passport/Guide that informs and supports walkers along each stage of the route.[21] It is waymarked by over thirty pairs of bronze sculptural children's shoes cast from nineteenth-century ones found in the attic of a derelict Strokestown cottage. Nothing was known of the child they belonged to, but local folklore holds that such offerings were made to invoke good luck. These evocative shoes symbolize the hopeful journey the Strokestown 1,490 embarked on and the fact that so many of the travellers were children under 14. The binding evokes the difficulties they encountered and the eternal bind to the place they were leaving. These bronze shoe sculptures also provided the thematic link for Marita Conlon-McKenna, the acclaimed author of the children's classic *Under the Hawthorn Tree*, to write her *Shoe Stories*, set in each location along the National Famine Way.[22] They are recounted in the voice of 12-year-old Daniel Tighe as he embarks with Strokestown's 1,490 fellow assisted emigrants from the estate to Dublin. Indeed, the National Famine Way App invites walkers to discover the route from the perspective of little Daniel Tighe's *Shoe Stories.* His family legacy is also explored in this volume.

The search for Strokestown's missing 1,490 emigrants further inspired the Great Famine Voices project that is funded by the Government of Ireland Emigrant Support Programme.[23] It brings together Irish emigrants, their descendants, and members of their communities to share family memories and stories. In doing so, it is creating a poignant record of those who came from Ireland to North America and Great Britain, especially during the period of the Great Hunger but also in the years that followed. Great Famine Voices is an ambitious project that is building a detailed picture of memories and stories about the Irish emigrant experience that are at risk of being lost. Strokestown Park no longer only holds the story locally but is now reaching out to connect with the descendants of Irish emigrants in Great Britain and North America whose ancestors survived and legacy lives on. The creation of the National Famine Way in 2015 coincided with the founding of the Famine Summer School.[24] For many years, Strokestown Park had welcomed the renowned Professor Christine Kinealy, who naturally became one of the keynote speakers at the first Summer School. The event brings together some of the world's leading famine scholars to share their ideas and research at Strokestown Park and Ireland's Great Hunger Institute at Quinnipiac University, which hosts it every second year.

Strokestown Park Archive

These outreach activities and endeavours to "make history visible" were inspired by discoveries in the Strokestown Park Archive.[25] The archive is the jewel in the crown of the Strokestown Park Estate, but it had remained uncatalogued until recently. In January 2019, Martin Fagan, an experienced archivist, set about this important task that will allow for future access to worldwide academics, historians and interested parties. It will also allow for the development of a number of new educational projects. The cataloguing and sharing of the Strokestown Park Archive is a remarkable achievement following from Jim Callery's chance discovery of the Cloonahee Petition in the dank boxes of papers decaying in Strokestown Park House. Strokestown has not only become a new hub of scholarly activity, but it has also been the catalyst of a new public history of the Great Famine. Ultimately, it was discoveries in the Strokestown Park Archive that led to the recovery of the records of the estate's missing 1,490 assisted emigrants. In telling their story and reclaiming their names, this book acknowledges their struggles and the struggles of other emigrants past and present.

NOTES

1. Parts of this section were previously published in Caroilin Callery, "Afterword—Jim Callery (1934–): A Modern Famine Hero" in *More Heroes of Ireland's Great Hunger*, eds Christine Kinealy, Jason King, Gerard Moran (Cork and Hamden CT: Cork University Press and Quinnipiac University Press, 2022), pp. 219–225.
2. See chapter by Christine Kinealy on the murder of Major Mahon.
3. Ciarán Reilly, *Strokestown and the Great Irish Famine* (Dublin: Four Courts Press, 2014), pp. 147–162.
4. "Death of Mr. H.S. Pakenham Mahon," *Isle of Wight Observer*, 1 April 1893.
5. "Court and Society," *Belfast News-Letter*, 18 January 1922.
6. "Denys Catherine Pakenham Mahon," *The Peerage*, at: http://www.thepeerage.com/p52577.htm
7. "Colonel Nicholas Hales Pakenham Mahon" Obituary, *Independent* (London),13 May 2012.
8. Strokestown Park Archive, STR/1A/105.
9. Fintan O'Toole, Launch of Inaugural Irish Famine Summer School, Percy French Hotel, Strokestown, 16 June 2015.
10. "Keeping the past alive can make hard work now," *Irish Independent,* 16 May 2014.
11. https://nationalfamineway.ie/
12. Interview Jim Callery, 7 February 2022, Cloonahee House, Elphin, Co. Roscommon.
13. See Marianna O'Gallagher, "The Orphans of Grosse Île: Canada and the adoption of Irish Famine Orphans, 1847–48", in Patrick O'Sullivan ed., *The Irish World Wide: The Meaning of the Famine*, 6 vols (London and Washington: Leicester University Press, 1997), vol. 5, p. 90.
14. Jim Callery and Marianna O'Gallagher's meeting with Léo Tye can be viewed at https://nationalfamineway.ie/about-the-1490/the-story-of-the-1490/
15. It was a three-year Roscommon Leader Partnership funded Arts Based Youth Project which ran in the Irish National Famine Museum from October 2010 to August 2013, with 15 participants aged between 12 and 14 years, at the start of the project.
16. The Tighe/Tye family tree is currently being reconstructed by Canadian genealogist Ronalda MacCarl.
17. See Ciarán Reilly, *Strokestown and the Great Irish Famine* (Dublin: Four Courts, 2014). The list of the 1,490 assisted emigrants from Strokestown can be viewed at https://nationalfamineway.ie/about-the-1490/what-happened-to-the-1490/
18. These undergraduate research teams were: Team 1--Elizabeth McDermott, Kiera O'Sullivan & Julie Maher; Team 2—Chiara Fallone, Pamela Smofsky, & Jessica Bush. Archaeologist Kathleen McGowan served as team supervisor in Ireland both years. Two additional teams researched the whereabouts of 1,700 Irish Famine orphans in Canada (1847–1848) Team 3: Conor Finan, Michaela Vukas, Britany Powell, & Megan Drasic-Gaudio; Team 4-Jaime McLaughlin, Bridget Hager, Emma McKean, & Sophia Romaschenko. Historian, Dr. Laura Smith served as on-site supervisor for Team 4's conference presentation at Quinnipiac University.

19. Cathal Póirtéir, Michael Blanche Jr, Ger Glennon, Patricia Rogers, and Bernie Kelly.
20. A particularly valued partnership grew with New Horizon Athlone Refugee Asylum Seeker and Support when a number of the group participated in the Canadian Wake 2019 launch night and then accompanied the walkers in Mullingar. It was heartrending to hear them say "this is our story." Another developing collaboration began in 2019 with Professor LeAnne Howe, member of the Choctaw Nation, who attended a musical adaptation of her poetry collection with Doireann Ní Ghríofa entitled *'Singing, Still' – A Libretto for the 1847 Choctaw Gift to the Irish for Famine Relief* (2017). The performance was recorded and subsequently made into a film in collaboration with LeAnne Howe entitled *The Story of the Choctaw Gift* (2020) that can be viewed at https://youtu.be/c14SiP49ezY. The obvious connections between the National Famine Way with the Trail of Tears, when President Andrew Jackson displaced thousands of Cherokee, Choctaw, Chickasaw, Creek and Seminole First Nations beginning in 1830, were explored both at the event and in the film.
21. The Guide is in the style of a Passport and is dedicated to little Daniel Tighe whose journey the reader can follow by listening to each instalment of Marita Conlon McKenna's *Shoe Stories* on the National Famine Way App at each pair of bronze shoes along the route. It also introduces the story of the shoes and the Tighe family story. It serves as a form of certification whereby walkers can collect a stamp along the route and upon completion of the National Famine Way at EPIC, The Irish Emigration Museum at Custom House Quay in Dublin. Finally, along with the Passport, all registered walkers will receive a ship ticket with details of one of the Strokestown Famine emigrant families in whose footsteps they will follow. See https://strokestownpark.ie/national-famine-way/
22. See https://nationalfamineway.ie/shoe-stories/
23. See https://strokestownpark.ie/great-famine-voices/.
24. See https://strokestownpark.ie/famine-summer-school/.
25. See https://strokestownpark.ie/treasures-of-the-strokestown-famine-archive/

ABOUT THE CONTRIBUTORS

CAROILÍN CALLERY has been involved with the National Famine Museum at Strokestown Park since its inception in the mid 1980s. She is a Director of the Westward Group which owns the property and is also a Director of the Irish Heritage Trust. She is a strong advocate of making history visible and was strongly involved in the development of the National Famine Way.

PROFESSOR CHRISTINE KINEALY is Director of Ireland's Great Hunger institute and professor of History at Quinnipiac University. She has published extensively on the Great Hunger and, more recently, on the abolition movement in Ireland. She has received many awards and accolades for her work both inside the Academy and as a public intellectual.

DR JASON KING is Academic Coordinator of the Irish Heritage Trust and National Famine Museum, Strokestown Park, and a member of the Government of Ireland National Famine Commemoration Committee. He has published extensively on Ireland's Great Hunger and the Irish Famine Migration to Canada.

PROFESSOR MARK G MCGOWAN is a Professor of History and Celtic Studies at the University of Toronto and Principal Emeritus at St. Michael's College (UofT). He is the author of many award-winning books and articles on the Catholic Church in Canada, Irish migration and settlement in Canada, the Great Famine, and religious education.

MIKE MURPHY MA FBCart.S. is head of Cartography in the Geography Department University College Cork. He has worked as Cartographer and joint editor on *Atlas of Cork City*, *Atlas of the Iveragh Peninsula*, *Atlas of the Great Irish Famine* and *Atlas of the Irish Revolution*. He also conceived and headed up *The Great Irish Famine Online Project*.

DR CIARÁN REILLY is a lecturer in the Department of History, Maynooth University and Assistant Director of the Centre for the Study of Historic Irish Houses & Estates. He is author of several books on the Great Famine including *The Irish Land Agent, 1830–1860: the case of King's County* (Dublin, 2014) and *Strokestown and the Great Irish Famine* (Dublin, 2014).

INDEX